BLACK PROFESSIONAL WOMEN
IN RECENT AMERICAN FICTION

For Rhonda:

This book celebrates beautiful
successful black professional women
like you. What a joy to
meet. Hope you will enjoy
the text.
　　　Carmen Marshall
　　　　(Way)

BLACK PROFESSIONAL WOMEN IN RECENT AMERICAN FICTION

Carmen Rose Marshall

McFarland & Company, Inc., Publishers
Jefferson, North Carolina, and London

LIBRARY OF CONGRESS CATALOGUING-IN-PUBLICATION DATA

Marshall, Carmen Rose, 1943–
 Black professional women in recent American fiction / Carmen
Rose Marshall.
  p.   cm.
 Includes bibliographical references and index.

 ISBN 0-7864-1712-9 (softcover : 50# alkaline paper)

 1. American Fiction—African American authors—History and
criticism. 2. Women and literature—United States—History—20th
century. 3. African American women in the professions—Books
and reading. 4. American fiction—Women authors—History and
criticism. 5. American fiction—20th century—History and criticism. 6. African American women—Books and reading. 7. African
American women in the professions. 8. African Americans in the
professions. 9. African American women in literature. 10. African
Americans in literature. 11. Professions in literature. I. Title.
PS374.N4M36   2004
813'.54093522—dc22

                                                    2003021841

British Library cataloguing data are available

Cover image ©2003 Comstock

Manufactured in the United States of America

*McFarland & Company, Inc., Publishers
 Box 611, Jefferson, North Carolina 28640
 www.mcfarlandpub.com*

For Florett Maude Martin Marshall
and
Nadia and Laura

Acknowledgments

I wish to express my thanks to Dr. Daryl Dance, Dr. Norma Manatu, Dr. Marty Brooks, Dr. John Burt Foster, Jr., and Mary Grace Paden. I appreciate the help of librarians and faculty members Peter McTague, Carol Estes, Helen McKann, and Christine Kush. I also thank Hadi and Jo for technical assistance who offered encouragement and assistance as I wrote the text. I am especially grateful to the many black professional women who completed questionnaires, met in small groups to discuss their responses to contemporary fiction by black women writers, and allowed for interviews. Because most remain anonymous and the list of those who identify themselves is so long, I am unable to add individual names. However, because this text is about the agency of black professional women, the absence of the names of my peers should not be misunderstood as denying them agency. I also recognize the help earlier offered by Dr. Marilyn Mobley McKenzie, Dr. Devon Hodges and Dr. Marilyn Broadus-Gay. My sincere appreciation goes to my family, Clive, Nadia, and Laura, who became even more graciously self-sufficient as I worked on this text. My special thanks to my mother, who told me at age six that I was a good writer.

Table Contents

Preface

The idea for this book began to germinate after I went to several bookstores to purchase realistic novels with black career women as protagonists for my daughters, who I knew intended to become professionals. I had hoped to find characters who were engaged in their jobs and who were exercising a high level of agency in the workplace and in their private lives. Surprisingly, hardly any existed. I wondered why the novels did not reflect the lived lives of the many black career women I knew.

This statement does not imply that my acquaintances did not encounter problems at work, in society at large, or at home. Rather, it means my colleagues were creating space for themselves to function as autonomous individuals despite the obstacles they faced. In early 1993, I read Gloria Naylor's *The Women of Brewster Place* (1982), Paule Marshall's *Brown Girl, Brownstones* (1959) and *Daughters* (1992), Toni Cade Bambara's *The Salt Eaters* (1980), Toni Morrison's *Song of Solomon* (1977) and *Tar Baby* (1981), and Alice Walker's *Meridian* (1976). As diverse and refreshing as these novels are, none of them reflect highly skilled professional protagonists as self-empowered. All the major characters are hampered from experiencing autonomy in both their professional and personal lives, with possibly three becoming self-directed at the very end of the novels.

My curiosity was piqued, for I knew and read of many black professional women who were quite successful in careers that were nontraditional for their race and gender. I also knew some black women writers on a professional level, and from what I perceived, their lives evidenced agency in the workplace. Some, in fact, had published several books and were well known in their fields. Why did the texts they write not reflect their own autonomy? I was puzzled by the discrepancy, and found it imperative to try to solve the enigma. This book is an attempt to answer the question why there is a paucity of novels representing the highly autonomous female

professional protagonist, despite the demand for novels with self-empowered primary characters.

This text is a study of why so few contemporary novels fail to affirm
the professionalism of black women protagonists by not having them
involved in their jobs, and by profiling them as having limited agency in the
workplace and their private lives. By contemporary, I mean novels written
from the 1980s, particularly beginning with Toni Cade Bambara's *The Salt
Eaters*. To provide a unique perspective, I merged two methodological
approaches by combining literary criticism with an ethnographic study. This
strategy allowed me to examine several novels from the 1980s to the present, while focusing primarily on the trailblazing text *The Salt Eaters* (1980),
and the international bestseller *Waiting to Exhale* (1994) by Terry McMillan.
Through a survey instrument, I sought to discover whether black professional women cultural consumers were satisfied with the novels they so
faithfully purchased, read, and critiqued, and what their responses were to
these realistic texts.

At present, minimal scholarship exists that interrogates the successes,
problems, and challenges black professional women in the workplace or
their fictive representations experience on a regular basis. One particularly
well-documented source is *Our Separate Ways: Black and White Women and
the Struggle for Professional Identity* (2001). Ella L.J. Edmondson Bell and Stella
Nkomo note that when they examined the literature written about women
of the managerial tiers of corporate America, black women were rendered
invisibible.[1] Their seminal text investigates the specific concerns of African
American professional women and how business practices and private concerns impact their upward mobility. My study differs in that it focuses on
the fictive representation of professional women's lives, and offers important insights into how gender, race, class, and the overextendedness of black
women professionals on behalf of the black community impede their success in the corporate arena. It also presents the characteristics that would
contribute to fulfilling the readerly desires of black women cultural consumers and a crossover readership, which seek accurate professional representation, particularly because the work underscores the important concept
of agency—that is, self-determination.

The text presents the varied voices of the survey respondents. It
acknowledges several internationally recognized African American women
who could serve as models for the protagonist within a new paradigm—
black professional women characters as self-empowered in the workplace
and in their private lives. This work verifies that although a large segment
of black women readers desire novels with autonomous black women protagonists, very few are available on the market. A large majority of the

survey respondents agree that this historical moment is auspicious for filling the dearth. Given this readership's demand, and given the explosion of books written by black women writers, the question that needs to be answered is how will future novels featuring black female professional protagonists, represent them as satisfying the desires of the next generation of readers.

Introduction:
The Dearth of Self-
Actualized Black Professional
Women Protagonists

Phillis…. It is not so much what you sang, as that you kept alive,
in so many of our ancestors, *the notion of song.*

Alice Walker

The last three decades of the twentieth century have seen the triumph
of many black professional women against almost insurmountable odds in
the marketplace. Over two million of these women have successfully
launched and maintained impressive careers both in corporate America[1] and
in their own enterprises. In spite of their successes in almost every field, few
novels celebrate the remarkable rise of the black woman. Many black middle-class professional women are clamoring for realistic fiction that portrays
black career women who, in addition to wanting stability in their personal
lives, are bent on accruing wealth, living elegantly though not consump-
tively, and having a high level of agency. Although there is no monolithic
"black woman," black women readers as a whole want to see their goals and
even a few of their dreams depicted as realizable. Since the publication of
Terry McMillan's *Waiting to Exhale* (1992), novels representing the middle-
class experience of black women have become increasingly more in demand.
Connie Briscoe, author of the best selling novel *Sisters and Lovers* (1994),
argues that black women readers prefer novels that do not portray poverty
and the problems associated with it.[2]

Close examination of these texts reveals that they do not represent black professional women protagonists performing their jobs in the work-place, nor doing so with a strong sense of autonomy. The most thorough portrayals of such work experience may be Connie Briscoe's *Big Girls Don't Cry* (1996) and Bebe Moore Campbell's *Brothers and Sisters* (1996). At the other end of the spectrum is Terry McMillan's *How Stella Got Her Groove Back* (1996). Here, Stella speaks of her job at home but is never seen in the workplace utilizing her skills as a broker. The screenplay producers recognized this gap and remedied the situation for the viewers, but the readers may ask, "How can we have professional women who hardly spend any time in the workplace?" Of course, a focus on women on the job does not imply that work is the only aspect of the protagonists' lives that is important, but it does validate their position as professionals.

It is instructive here to clarify two terms used in this text. The first, "black professional women," refers to persons, or characters, who are engaged in some activity which provides substantial economic remuneration and which requires academic or specialized training beyond the high school level. Such women have achieved a level of success because of their competence, productivity, and visibility in executive, managerial, administrative, academic, or technical positions. The second term, "agency," means that characters have a certain degree of power and control over their lives; that is, characters with agency have the means to independently design their goals, choose a strategy to successfully achieve them, and are confident and flexible enough to adjust the strategy if necessary, thereby gaining a sense of security and empowerment. These terms are meaningful in helping us to envision autonomous individuals.

Career women as a whole want their professionalism reflected in some of the literature they read. Millions of non–African American female readers also bought these novels about black professional women, which suggests that in addition to wanting a good read, they may identify with the black professional woman protagonist because they too are women and professional. The fact is, not many novels from any racial group portray the professional woman in high-profiled positions actually performing her job routinely in the texts. Her absence argues for a common pattern that regards professional women, in general, as not fully accepted by a culture in which highly skilled professions, such as neurosurgery, are understood to be careers for men. Black women writers representing the black career woman are, in a sense, writing not just for black women, but also for a larger audience of women. Millions of women of every race successfully compete in corporate America, yet they are not often realistically portrayed in novels.

The scarcity of portrayals of career women becomes even more noticeable with the proliferation of texts and scholarship by black women writers over the last three decades. This rise has changed the literary landscape in terms of the diversity and reading habits of the American public both inside and outside the black community. Earlier, the literary scene was dominated by white male canonical texts whose authors either rendered black women writers invisible, or relegated their work to a marginalized status. Black women writers and scholars addressed their exclusion from the canon by resurrecting texts that were considered inferior or that challenged the status quo. In this way, they attempted to regain their voices by critiquing the politics that determined which books were deemed worthy of scholarship and high esteem.

This resurrection of past texts and the increased voice of black women writers can be seen as a continuum that informs the current need by black women readers to see their concerns and lives reflected in novels. The ability to exercise power has always been a primary issue in black women's writing. From their emergence into American literary history, black women writers have consistently tried to give their protagonists some margin of self-directedness despite the limiting environment in which the protagonists were placed, or else to illustrate why their attempts at self-empowerment have failed. In other words, contemporary black women writers and readers can claim a writerly-readerly insignia—a coat of arms, if you will—that links them with a tradition of women exercising agency, albeit limited. For instance, *Incidents in the Life of a Slave Girl* (1861) by Harriett Jacobs is the most popular slave narrative written by an African American woman. This text is unique, for it demonstrates the sexual oppression black women endured during slavery. But far more important for this discussion is the fact that the black female protagonist, Linda Brent, despite social and economic constraints, has enough agency to escape slavery with her children and successfully tell her story of sexual abuse and resistance. Until its publication, black women were primarily portrayed as victims or unconscious partners complicit with their exploitation. *Incidents* made the reading public aware that black women resisted sexual domination.

Similarly, the first novel by an African American woman writer that attempts to introduce a semiprofessional is *Colored American, Contending Forces: A Romance Illustrative of Negro Life North and South* (1900) by Pauline E. Hopkins. The novel depicts the struggles of the newly emancipated slave woman. The protagonist, Dora, demonstrates some autonomy in both her public and private life as she helps her mother with a boardinghouse and rejects her unprincipled fiancé. When she marries, her relationship with her husband evidences equality in their discussions, and although she does not have a career independent of him, she intends to work with him in an industrial school for blacks. Indeed, the text may be regarded as propagandist in its attempt to improve the image of the race, but Hopkins denies the stereotypes of black women as being sexually promiscuous or intellectually deficient.

Another text, *Quicksand* (1928), written by Nella Larsen during the Harlem Renaissance, also shows black women seeking some autonomy even if they fail to maintain it throughout their lives. The protagonist, Helga, is biracial and given the historic moment has difficulty accepting her identity. She flees her unchallenging teaching career in the South and tries to become more independent in New York, but eventually gives up her profession as a teacher to marry a rural preacher. However, the quicksand of her marriage and repeated childbearing ruin her chances for self-empowerment. Here, Larsen uses her feminist character to suggest the possible ways marriage can sabotage a woman's career.

Depictions of the modern black professional woman began to appear in the 1980s and can be seen as a response to two complementary movements: black nationalism, and particularly for this discussion, the Black Arts Movement of the 1960s. Both movements had a revolutionary effect on the art that was produced, and they singularly influenced the creation of novels that reflected the black career woman. Larry Neale, one of the founding fathers of the Black Arts Movement, writes:

> The Black Arts Movement is radically opposed to any concept of the artist that alienates him from his community. This movement is the aesthetic and spiritual sister of the Black Power concept. As such, it envisions art that speaks to the needs and aspirations of black America. In order to perform this task, the Black Arts Movement proposes a radical reordering of the Western cultural aesthetic.... It proposes to separate symbolism, mythology, critique, and iconology.... A main tenet of the movement is the necessity for black people to define the world in their own terms.[3]

The practicality of art as rendered here is very African in origin. Zadia Ife agrees with Leopard Sengho, poet laureate of Senegal, that African art has three primary characteristics; it is "functional, collective, and committed." It is, therefore, understood to address our daily needs.[4] This aesthetic is radically different from the philosophy of art for art's sake. Although today the black community does acknowledge art as valuable whether or not it endorses a pragmatic purpose, the Black Arts Movement's aesthetic, foregrounded in African philosophy, became functional by raising the "collective" consciousness of the black community toward understanding and accepting that "black is beautiful." Hence, the artistic works coming shortly after the 1960s emphasized the positive values, characteristics, and potential found in the African American community. The Black Arts Movement's contribution to the creation of novels is that the literature of the 1960s and '70s allowed for a positive sense of selfhood for the first large wave of black women entering the mainstream work force as professionals. As a group, they gained a greater self-respect that was vital for success, and so provided a pool of professionals from whom the early women novelists could create potential career protagonists.

By the 1980s and early 1990s, when black women began entering the professional work force in larger numbers than in the 1970s, a corresponding shift occurred in the level of agency that writers gave to their female protagonists. Toni Cade Bambara, coming out of the Black Arts Movement, began to chart the professional woman's role in the corporate world. *The Salt Eaters* (1980) shows the difficulties these first generation career women experienced in the job market as well as in their own personal lives, which often hindered them from achieving a consistently high level of autonomy. This pioneer black woman writer and others soon to follow her were writing from their newly found experience as professional women.

The profile of these protagonists of the '80s and early '90s belong to a transitional period. While the women characters are not the victimized and often struggling professional women presented before the 1960s, they lack the level of power in the workplace that later protagonists enjoy. They no longer fit the old familiar stereotypes: the "mammy" figure frequently found in the mass media, the tragic mulatto who cannot negotiate her identity despite the privileges conferred because of her light skin color, the matriarch or Sapphire figure who is supposed to emasculate men, or the sexual deviant. Writers like Bambara often portray black women as professionals in nontraditional fields for black women. However, these portrayals reflect the professional who is not yet fully acculturated to the structure and behavior of corporate America in relation to black employees. Bombarded with different forms of oppression, the protagonists experience severe stress in the workplace.

This new protagonist represents an extension of a pattern that feminist scholar Mary Helen Washington identifies as the "emergent woman." Washington interprets Alice Walker's historical understanding of the progress made by black women in novels in this manner: "She sees the experiences of Black women as a series of movements from a woman totally victimized by society and by men to a growing developing woman whose consciousness allows her to have some control over her life." Washington presents three groups of black women. The first is the "suspended woman" who is completely victimized and therefore cannot achieve her goals. Washington associates the "suspended woman" with Zora Neale Hurston's comment (in *Their Eyes Were Watching God* [1937]) that black women are "the mules of the world." The second type is the "assimilated woman." Assimilated women escape the physical brutality that suspended women endure, but experience a "kind of psychic violence that alienates them from their roots and cuts them off from real contact with their own people, and also from themselves." Many of these women of the 1940s and 1950s became assimilated into the mainstream culture by "passing," and thereby prospered financially. The third group is the "emergent woman." Members of this category are politically astute regarding their economic and social rights, for they participated in the Civil Rights struggle. However, being the first to enter mainstream America, they experienced "a harsh initiation" before they became assimilated into the new work environment.[5] Clearly, the protagonists of *The Salt Eaters* and *Waiting to Exhale* have moved beyond this model because they entered the elite professions in corporate America, but lacked the autonomy that one would expect, considering their academic achievements and professional training.

Black women writers have historically risen to the challenge of representing black women and their achievements in every demographic shift of the group. Terry McMillan in the 1990s announced, "Times have changed."[6] Hence, she creates *Waiting to Exhale* (1992), whose four protagonists are black professional women. They are indeed hampered by factors in their public and private lives, but by representing all four women as college graduates with three employed in fields nontraditional for most black women in the 1980s, McMillan captures the demographic shift in the number of black women entering the professional ranks in the 1980s and 1990s. It seems the climate is opportune for black women writers to scale another level of their creative representation of the black professional woman. This shift is especially urgent since much of the black women readership is anticipating in the new millennium more novels that will further enhance their self-awareness.

The readership's demand alone cannot determine what the writer creates. Novelists have the privilege to choose characters or situations they find very compelling. No constraints from their readership should coerce them from being true to their craft. Jesse Hill Ford, when asked to respond to what it means to be a Southern writer, says he has no obligation to the South except to not misrepresent it, or not to support it when it is wrong.[7] Likewise, black women writers can only present black professional women as they envision them. Furthermore, because a large percentage of black women are still struggling to enter the professional ranks, it is imperative that these women, who have played and still play a significant role in the black community, be honored and sensitively represented in fiction. However, as the demographics change, there is a corresponding shift in black middle-class female desire for a varied kind of text. As the demand becomes more insistent, black writers of realistic fiction wishing to follow the pragmatic aesthetic promoted in the Black Arts Movement (which continues to have a strong impact on African Americans writers) may want to consider how best to meet the needs of this segment of the market.

Another reason to suggest why the time might be right for new representations of the black professional woman can be found by looking at the last thirty years through the lens of human psychology, particularly Abraham Maslow's theory of "self-actualization.[8] I recognize that Maslow's concept of the stable self as represented in the self-actualized individual conflicts with some post-structuralists' critiques in which subjectivity/identity is called into question. According to Denise Riley, theoretically, the concept woman—positive feminine gender—is a construct that lacks fixity since in different historical moments it has had diverse meanings. Furthermore, any type of self changes position depending on the several subjectivities society reads into it, especially in terms of race and class.[9] However, though it may be difficult to locate, it is necessary to use the term "woman," and here specifically the black professional woman as a vehicle to talk about how women are positioned in society and how they achieve agency. Furthermore, the respondents in my survey and those found in *Our Separate Ways: Black and White Women and the Struggle for Professional Identity* (2002) argue from this position. They express a certain level of agency in their professional lives not only by succeeding in their administrative positions, but also by being able to critique the unfair practices of their corporations.[10] They corroborate with Maslow's concept of self-actualization as an adequate designation of who they perceive themselves to be.

Abraham Maslow, in contrast to Western Judeo-Christian philosophy and Freudian theory, postulates that human beings are innately good, though they have a hierarchy of needs which, if not satisfied incrementally, does not allow for the actualization of the self. He presents two primary levels of needs—Deficiency needs, and Being needs—which themselves have tiers and are sequentially charted. Deficiency needs include basic physiological needs such as food, shelter, sleep, air, sex, and safety. The second tier of the Deficiency needs are psychological in nature, involving emotional security, love and self-esteem. The third primary level of need concerns self-actualization; that is, experiencing one's fullest potential and utilizing one's creative powers. At this plane, one experiences a "clearer perception of reality" and is better able to apprehend life and enjoy it. This degree of sophistication allows individuals to have frequent, longer, and more meaningful "peak" experiences than the average person who is still attempting to have his Deficiency needs met. A strong sense of "urgency, intensity, and priority"[11] accompanies these needs, the strongest found at the basic physiological level. A famished individual has no immediate interest in art or music. If the Deficiency needs are not met, then the inner Being needs are not "prepotent"—that is, urgent—and are persistently pushed to the side, so the human animal can survive. Once the more intense needs are satisfied, then the inner-self's experiences of "unfolding"[12] can begin to emerge. This process allows for the autonomous individual to experience "meta-motivation," and extended and frequent periods of illumination.

Two very important concepts arise from Maslow's theory. First, the self-actualization process is fluid; hence, environmental factors, inner emotional states and ill health, for example, can create an imbalance, and the Being needs must be re-actualized. Second, all human beings have an intrinsic "higher human nature/motive that manifests itself in diverse creative forms." The self-actualized person often has feelings of transcendence, which persist for some time.[13] Maslow acknowledges that even people who are not fully autonomous can have these wonderful, intensely liberating moments, but such moments are far less often realized and are possibly of shorter duration. The truly self-actualized individual seems to have certain characteristics that others do not, such as a greater acceptance of the self and of others, a love of the arts, and an appreciation for the beauty in her surroundings. She is efficient, a risk taker, and more self-reliant. Although actualized individuals experience high levels of self-development, health, and self-satisfaction, they do have faults, as do other human beings. Therefore, they must seek to maintain harmony between their Deficiency needs and thinking, and between their Being needs and cognition.

Maslow also proposes "value objectivism" as opposed to "value relativism." In the foreword to Maslow's text, Rodney Lowery summarizes Maslow's concept of Being (somewhat synonymous to a higher aesthetic such as beauty). Being/Beauty has often been thought of as different for each person. However, Maslow believes that Being/Beauty has its own intrinsic value, and so, since this potential is in all of us, it allows for *"Wonderful possibilities, inscrutable depths"* for all humanity. These "peak experiences" can be identified as epiphanies whereby intense illumination is realizable.[14] Maslow suggests that the best way to find empirical evidence that a higher moral principle exists is to study the lives of those individuals who are self-empowered—"their choices, and tastes and judgments"—and what their experiences are during those periods when they display those characteristics of self-actualization.[15]

How does Maslow's theory of self-actualization relate to the creation of novels with black professional women exercising agency in the work-place and in their personal lives? Until the 1970s, few black professional women were in the work force. At least 80 percent of black women were only allowed jobs as maids and factory employees, and were given the most difficult, dangerous, demeaning, and lowest paid jobs. Racism, sexism, and classism intersected to make self-actualization within the workplace virtually impossible but for a rare few, since the majority lived at subsistence levels, had minimum safety, had very little sense of belonging and love outside their communities, and received no respect from the majority of the mainstream population they encountered. If Maslow is correct, the entrance of black women into the professional ranks in conjunction with social improvements in the 1970s allowed Deficiency needs to be stabilized, and thus made it possible for the latent Being needs to become prepotent in larger numbers of these women. Maslow writes, "The gratification of one basic need opens consciousness to domination by another, 'higher' need."[16] Thus, for black professionals in larger numbers, the process of self-actualization within the context of work had begun.

Toni Cade Bambara's amazing feat in portraying the black career woman actually doing her work in *The Salt Eaters*, and having some margin of agency in her life, can justifiably be understood as the trailblazer for all other novels that seek the self-actualized protagonist. Writers such as Toni Morrison, Alice Walker, Paule Marshall, and Marita Golden in creating portrayals of black career women can be seen as reflecting this process and participating in it, even if the agency afforded the protagonists is limited.

But these writers anticipate and participate in the application of Maslow's theory. As engaged as the psychologist was in his theoretical formulations, he was particularly interested in the applicability of his findings. Maslow capitalizes on the "chicken experiment" in which some chicks consistently chose the foods that were more beneficial to their health and sustenance. When the poorer choosers were given the same diet as the wiser chickens, they, too, became healthier. Maslow's epiphany clarifies for him that, in human terms, the good chicken choosers were synonymous with the self-actualized human beings who see reality clearly. Therefore, to find empirical evidence that higher human values exist, we must study both these autonomous individuals and the transcendence the ordinary person experiences occasionally. Furthermore, if one wants to find "Being"—a healthy, productive, satisfying life that allows him to experience his full potential—he must study the lives of other self-actualized individuals.[17]

The genius of Toni Cade Bambara is that she intuited exactly what Maslow here proposes. Her novel represents the striving autonomous black woman of the 1980s, and makes it possible for other black women to have an expanded vision of the black career woman, albeit a limited one (considering the problems this first generation of career women encountered) as a fluctuating self-actualized individual of the professional ranks. Maslow's theory of how reading about self-actualized persons could help others become autonomous may reflect why 89 percent of the subjects in a survey I conducted said they needed the novels of self-empowered protagonists to act as models. Maslow's theory of self-actualization partly helps to explain the explosion of black women's texts since the 1980s.

These are the central questions this book raises: If black professional women are demanding more novels in which the protagonists are career women exercising agency in the workplace, what are the factors that contribute to the dearth of these texts? How is the concept of agency for black professional women treated in contemporary fiction of the 1980s and the early 1990s, and particularly in *The Salt Eaters* and *Waiting to Exhale*? What do the professional women respondents say about the desirability of the novels available? How do their theoretical construction of meaning and response to the novels reflect their lived lives?

A segment of this study that needs elaboration is the black community's characteristics that appear to undermine black professional women's agency. One of the possible problems in extending the representation of black women to figures whose success is primarily based on their work role is the definition of success within the black community. It must be acknowledged that communal enjoyment and responsibility are African traditions that slaves brought to America. However, black literary tradition is contested. Historically, some writers have represented success as a redefinition and even a rejection of some communal values. Feminist scholar Patricia Hill Collins enumerates the varied services black women have created and performed in nurturing power within the black community, such as helping the least able to become functional.[18] Both Bambara and McMillan value the black community, yet their artistic response to it is conflictive. In *The Salt Eaters* and *Waiting to Exhale*, service to the black community becomes problematic for professional women. The novelists acknowledge that the black community is very meaningful to its members, and traditionally has been regarded as the primary place for the black individual to find a strong sense of identity. However, when service to the community becomes detrimental to the giver, then the act requires careful scrutiny. Both novels demonstrate how the sexist practices of the black community become inimical to the reach for autonomy by the black protagonists. The position this text takes is that communal vision of success has sometimes been distorted and sometimes damages African American women's ability to be self-determined.

Patriarchal practices come in different forms. Theologian Jacquelyn

Grant, for instance, illustrates the exploitation of black female parishioners in black churches. She argues that although black women make up more than "seventy percent" of church congregations, they get no reward for being the "backbone" of the institution. Their backs become the ladder on which others climb to economic power and prestige. In fact, sexist practices penalize them for entering the pulpit.[19] She challenges the church to concentrate on eradicating both racism and sexism. A more recent study, *Black Women in the Academy* (1999), points out that women's subordination in the church is slowly evolving into more powerful leadership roles, and that some professional black women are returning to the church not for religion, but as a means of "extended network."[20] However, there seems to be a lack of extended critique in which black women theorists present as harmful the persistent demands of the black community on black professional women. Since community plays such a pivotal role in black people's lives, it is understandable that its members would be hesitant to question its practices. Critics outside the black community are more forthright in identifying the abuse of black women by black institutions.

According to historian Jacqueline Jones, black women have served in organizations such as the National Council of Negro Women, black sororities, "local welfare agencies, national groups like the Urban League, and the YWCA [which] relied on relatively well-educated black women volunteers." Their professionalism lent credibility to local organizations. She notes that during periods of violent confrontation, it was often they and their children who faced angry enemies, rather than self-serving men who refused to fight for equality.[21]

Arthur Ashe in his autobiography validates this critique. He candidly but regretfully discusses how he refused to become involved in civil rights activities. He writes, "While blood was running freely in the streets of Birmingham, Memphis, and Biloxi, I had been playing tennis. Dressed immaculately in white, I was elegantly stroking tennis balls on perfectly paved courts in California and New York and Europe." He notes that he had many opportunities to become involved, but he ignored them. It could be because tennis players then rarely were involved in politics. He adds that some friends told him he was participating in the movement by succeeding at tennis, but he knew differently. Sometimes he felt "a burning sense of shame," and the more successful and prosperous he became, the more "anguish" he experienced, for although some blacks were pleased with his spectacular performance, many young people his age who were fighting and dying for the cause of freedom looked with "disdain and contempt" on his awards. It took the assassinations of both Dr. Martin Luther King Jr. and Senator Robert F. Kennedy before "I spoke out for the first time in public about race and politics." Thus, when in 1985 he protested in front of the South African Embassy in Washington, D.C., against the apartheid regime that denied blacks playing tennis with whites, "No one knew better than I that a demonstration such as this one ... was mainly a staged or token affair, a piece of political choreography." Ashe profited immensely from his own individual efforts and the proceeds of the Civil Rights Movement. He received pecuniary gains and immortality, as his memorial stands on Monument Avenue in Richmond, Virginia. In retrospect, many will overlook Ashe's choice, for he later served the black community well. He became the first African American selected as captain of the Davis Cup team. Furthermore, he participated in humanitarian efforts such as the protection of Haitian refugees.[22]

Ashe is a reflection of the middle-class black males who refused to become involved in the Civil Rights protests. Lawrence Otis Graham, a lawyer and author of the controversial text *Inside America's Black Upper-Middle Class*, illustrates many instances of the same behavior among this group.[23] Black women, professional and otherwise, felt it incumbent on themselves during these very stressful times to overexert themselves, if necessary, on behalf of the black community's solidarity.

What are the consequences of this overextended labor? Jones, in assessing how the black women view their service, argues that black feminists in the 1970s found themselves in a contradictory position when they attempted to celebrate black women's strengths—"that championship tradition" with their "culturally shaped resilience, strategic coping and defense mechanisms." Jones postulates that it was with overworked bodies that they attempted to keep the black community afloat and keep different artistic forms flourishing. As a result, during the late 1970s, black feminists became aware that the generational stress had begun to manifest itself in hypertension, alcoholism, and the highest rates of diabetes, breast cancer, and obesity. Exhausted physically and emotionally by their dependents, many had difficulty fully re-energizing themselves.[24] Jones perceives black women's attempt to maintain a unified black community as harmful to them in many ways.

An important non–African-American writer who addresses black professional women's inordinate service to the community is Stephanie Golden. In discussing the "ethic of care," she notes that service is often related to victimhood, for those who continually sacrifice usually have the least power. Western society socializes men to be victimizers, women to be victims; hence, it is women who are expected to be the primary bearers of burdens. One of the most victimized groups in the United States is black women. Golden notes, "African American women have felt a duty to subordinate their desire for individual development to the needs of black people as a whole, putting their energy into holding families together and supporting men under assault." Many prioritize social uplift above their professional goals. Furthermore, they practice the generationally learned behavior of "not making waves ... swallowing down of feelings." Too many became the "punching bags for black men's displaced rage, but they quite often patiently bore the abuse as another of their duties to the family and race."[25] There were exceptions to the rule, such as the women who controlled their own sexuality, but black women have been the ones for generations to sacrifice the most for their children's education and for their race.

Not much in-depth investigation by black women to date critiques how service to the community becomes oppressive to the black professional woman. The problems these women experience are discussed by black feminist critics primarily in the light of the triad oppressions of race, gender, and class in anthologies such as *Words of Fire: An Anthology of African American Feminist Thought* (1995) and *All the Women Are White, All the Blacks Are Men, But Some of Us Are Brave* (1992). Both are pertinent to the discussion of black female oppression in general, and to the black professional woman in particular, but little focus is specifically on the career woman's role in the black community. Two books, however, are instructive.

Sheila T. Gregory's text, *Black Women in the Academy* (1999), mentions black professional women as being overextended, even though that focus was not central to her book. She concurs with other researchers such as Coleman-Burns that, historically, black girls are educated primarily to serve the black community, and service is the expectation from black girls and women. She finds that this "rich tradition" of supervising family, work, and community has been very costly to them since they alone are socialized to bear the burden. So ingrained is this behavior that some black professional women in her study accepted only those positions that did not conflict with their community service, and they continued to seek other positions that provided opportunities for even more effective sacrifice. In addition, some did not seek advanced degrees and career mobility "to eliminate the risks to marriage and family." In fact, when the professional women in her study were asked to choose which "discretionary activities" were most important to them, the first choice was religious activities, followed by social concerns, then family, and finally professional associations.[26]

What is the result of the black career women in Gregory's study placing professional activities as number *four* on their list of priorities? In academia where this study was centered, as of 1998, "African American women constitute only 2.2 percent of full-time faculty in higher education. Half of these are in the historically black colleges and only one percent are represented in predominantly white institutions, and of these, most are in the community colleges."[27] Furthermore, many must leave academia, for tenure is predicated on research and publication. Gregory finds black career women primarily engaged in teaching and service more than their peers, and thus have less credibility and visibility than their white counterparts. Racism and classism play a significant role in the women's work environment, but black women's socialization to serve rather than promote their own professional interests has misdirected their career activities, and consequently helped compromise their potential for tenure. Predictably, those who received tenure (more than one-half of all earned doctorates are in education) "typically had the lowest faculty progression and retention." Furthermore, most were concentrated in the instructorship position primarily in smaller colleges or community colleges, not large research institutions.[28]

The second text, *Sinners, Saints, and Saviors: Strong Black Women in African American Literature*, provides critique on the image of black women portrayed as excessively strong. Professor Trudier Harris discusses the negative effects of overextended black women who perpetually work long hours under difficult circumstances. They never seem to have the "'luxuries' of failure, nervous breakdown, *leisured existence*" (emphasis mine), but must continually endure (often silently) extreme hardship and pain.[29] When these characters first appeared, they worked for whites, but now they sacrifice for the black community.

Harris argues that hardly any writer addresses the damaging effects such perpetual grind must have on these "super women" in terms of ill health, disease, and dysfunctional families. She expresses concern that literature written by blacks, even black women, perpetuates this image of the excessively strong woman, even though they know the portrayal to be false.[30] Black women are not endowed with any more physical strength than white women are. They have been forced to do more than their share of work in the white and black worlds, but they have paid a terrible price. My focus in viewing black professional women as overextended on behalf of the black community as well as oppressed by racism, sexism, and classism is informed by a close reading of *The Salt Eaters* and *Waiting to Exhale*, and other critiques that see this area as problematic.

Both Toni Cade Bambara and Terry McMillan show characters in conflict over oppressive forces, but in McMillan's text, which is the more current of the two, these forces seem less isolated. Bambara makes serving the black community a top priority; paradoxically, even she seems to be saying that black career women will need to rethink what constitutes upward mobility and health. McMillan is more forthright in advising women against being overextended, and studies such as Gregory's offer a convincing argument. What is especially appealing is that McMillan breaks the cycle of the isolated black professional woman in the corporate world; her protagonists are friends and support each other. Hence, the four black career protagonists are portrayed as less conflicted and better able to control their circumstances.

How these two trailblazing novelists perceive their work is instructive. Toni Cade Bambara's response is all encompassing and captures the excitement of the new workplace phenomenon: "Given the range of experiences available to a soul having the human adventure in this time and place, given that we have just begun to tap the limitless reservoir of cultural, societal, global possibilities ... I come to the novel with a sense that everything is possible."[31] Bambara stretches the limits of the possible in *The Salt Eaters* in content, structure, and style. Terry McMillan belongs to a newer generation of writers than Bambara, and she writes from a more restrictive perspective: "We do not feel the need to create and justify our existence anymore. We are here. We are proud. And most of us no longer feel the need to prove anything to white folks. If anything, we're trying to make sense of ourselves to ourselves."[32] Thus, these writers are able to make readers inside and outside the black community aware of the change that is taking place in black women's consciousness and among black career women.

To illustrate how Bambara's and even McMillan's works differ from black female writers who came after them in the mid–1990s, such as Bebe Moore Campbell, a few lines from the beginning of the first chapter of each novel will suffice.

In *The Salt Eaters*, Bambara's protagonist, Velma Henry, is seated on a stool in the South West Infirmary, having recently attempted suicide. The local healer of nontraditional medicine says to her, "'Are you sure, sweetheart, that you want to be well?' Velma Henry turned stiffly on the stool.... So taut for so long, she could not swivel."[33] McMillan's *Waiting to Exhale* begins: "Right now I'm supposed to be all geeked up because I'm getting ready for a New Year's Eve party that some guy named Lionel invited me to."[34] McMillan's protagonist is concentrating her energies on finding yet another man. On the second page, however, she does say she is not the type to wait for things to happen; she effects the changes she wants. On page three, having heard of a job in Phoenix, she has applied, interviewed, and has gotten the position. There is chronological progressive delineation in how the writers introduce their protagonists to the reader: a movement from an almost catatonic state to active preparation for social life as primary with serious consideration of a job coming in a close second.

I see a new kind of black female novelist writing about the black professional woman emerging in the mid–to late 1990s. These novelists are more career conscious regarding their protagonists, and do not always relegate jobs to secondary status, thus providing them greater agency on the job site. To illustrate the contrast, Bebe Moore Campbell's novel *Brothers and Sisters* (1994) begins:

> When Esther Jackson looked up from the stack of slick new hun-
> dred-dollar bills she was counting inside the teller's cage of the
> downtown branch of Angel City National Bank and glanced out the
> plate glass window, the black woman inhales sharply. "You're out of
> balance," she said woodenly to Hector Bonilla. Her English was
> clipped, as precise and well enunciated as that of any news televi-
> sion anchor ... [she is] the regional operations manager.[35]

The reader feels Esther Jackson's presence as a woman in charge of her workspace. Jackson is represented as having a certain level of agency from the beginning of the novel that is absent from the texts of Bambara and McMillan. So within a fifteen year span, we have moved from a novel whose protagonist is near catatonic throughout the text to one that has four black middle-class women protagonists in nontraditional fields for black women (though personal problems overshadow their careers) to Campbell's novel that portrays the professional black woman on the first page of the novel doing her job. As we near the next ten-year mark from McMillan's publica-tion of *Waiting to Exhale*, we see significant changes in the delineation of how black women writers position their women protagonists in the novels.

The ability of the younger writers coming after McMillan—and even McMillan herself, as evidenced in *How Stella Got Her Groove Back* (1996)—to capture the black professional woman in the mid–1990s is partly due to the novelists of the 1980s and early 1990s paving the way. Now these more recent writers can underscore the autonomy of black professional women. Writ-ers like Connie Briscoe in *Big Girls Don't Cry* (1996) are able to represent the very successful black women, for they have the added advantage of been accustomed to many more professional women in the work force and in just about every conceivable position. For instance, today Oprah Winfrey wields such a powerful force in the national and international television broadcast industry that according to social critic Jeffrey Louis Decker, the newly coined term "the Oprahfication of television talk-show format" has come into vogue to reflect her technique.[36] This is a phenomenon that was impossible for Bambara to imagine when she wrote her text, and even for McMillan to sufficiently internalize in order to creatively incorporate it in *Waiting to Exhale*.

Others have recognized this new level of autonomy that recent black women writers give the black professional protagonist. Journalist Lynell George suggests that current writers have more "freedom to write without political or social constraints." He further adds that black female writers still appreciate the plight of blacks in the dominant capitalist culture, but he records Bebe Moore Campbell as saying, "What Terry's success gave us was permission.... I didn't always have to write about 'The Problem.'" Other young writers echo the same sentiment. George quotes Sheneska Jackson, who, after hearing Terry McMillan read at a local college promised herself, "I'm not going to write another slave book.... For a long time I thought the only way to be recognized was if you were writing about something on the cotton plantation." Jackson does "address urban realities—the scar of gangs and drugs—but at the same time reflect[s] the upscale lifestyle open to her characters by virtue of their social position: 'I wanted to put it in the '90s terms.... Bottom line. We wanted to see our own self on the beach.'" Hence, she wrote *Caught up in the Rapture* (1996).[37] The socioeconomic empowerment gleaned in the corporate marketplace by African American women, coupled with the centrality of black women in the feminist/black studies movement and the groundwork by the women writers of the 1980s and early 1990s made it possible for the most recent contemporary black female novelists to do greater justice to the autonomy of the black professional woman in works such as Connie Briscoe's *Sisters and Lovers* (1996).

Comments from Bambara, and to a lesser extent McMillan, suggest that they belong to a transitional group of writers representing the black professional woman. In an interview with Claudia Tate, Bambara identifies herself by saying: "I'm a nationalist; I'm a feminist."[38] These potentially conflictive positions are reflected in her professional protagonist. Bambara's *The Black Woman* (1970) is an anthology that reflects her concerns for both women's and civil rights issues, so it is to be expected that this stance will control, to a large extent, how her protagonist is represented. In discussing her craft, Bambara voices her primary purpose for writing *The Salt Eaters*:

> I gave myself an assignment based on an observation: there is a split between the spiritual, psychic, and political forces in my community. The novel grew out of my attempt to fuse the seemingly separate frames of references of the camps; it grew out of an interest in identifying bridges; it grew out of a compulsion to understand how the energies of this period will manifest themselves in the next decade.[39]

It seems plausible, then, to expect that her protagonist will manifest the "split" of consciousness that reflects the division in the community, as well as contain the "bridge" that could heal the lack of cohesiveness. Indeed, Bambara does say, "I am about the empowerment and the development of our sisters and our community,"[40] but again the concern for women is tied to the black community's well-being. As necessary as this dual concern may seem, it creates a "bicultural" tension in the character, who must deal with both the mainstream corporate world and the black community in which she lives. Writer Ella L. Bell's culturally specific meaning of "bicultural" is implied here: it is "the impact of a cultural double bind—the balancing act black people, in general, must manage as they move from one cultural context to the next."[41] In the United States, that often means negotiating the norms of the white and black communities. The bicultural issue impacts Bambara's character in *The Salt Eaters* since the interests of the black community often directly or indirectly affect the amount of agency the black professional woman can have in her job. So although Bambara does not directly say in her discussions that Velma Henry cannot maintain a high level of agency in her career, the text bespeaks a conflict that Bambara implicitly understands must detract from the protagonist's energies to perform at maximum level in the job market.

Terry McMillan's novel *Waiting to Exhale* (1992) presents a different kind of text and so requires more in-depth discussion of her philosophy of writing. McMillan identifies herself not as an academic writer as Bambara is, but as "pop fiction writer."[42] Theorist John Fiske defines popular culture as the culture of the socially inferior, the powerless, and so registers the conflict of a power struggle typical of a capitalistic society and our social experiences. But that power struggle is continuous and includes the interpretation of social experience, what is understood as one's connection to the social order, and the commodities and cultural artifacts the system produces: "Reading relations reproduce and re-enact social relations, so power, resistance, and evasions are necessarily structured in them." Therefore, popular culture evidences different patterns of resistance and subterfuge, between overt attack and guerrilla strategy.[43]

This definition may cause the reader to question why McMillan's novel is here discussed with academic texts and how earlier, while presented as a transitional writer, she now conforms to certain guidelines stipulated by Fiske. The answer is that my focus is not on types of literature or the aesthetic criteria of the novels, but rather on the use value of texts, that is, the way readers use texts to empower their lives. Even if McMillan's novel is not understood to be politically correct by some critics, and does not have a perfect vision of empowerment, it offers some liberatory moments that powerfully affect the readers, as so-called "high" literature does. Furthermore, McMillan's style and some of the content allow the text to be regarded as transitional.

Fiske's theoretical analysis of popular culture finds expression in McMillan's work. McMillan does not confront all the forces of oppression head-on as Bambara does, but like the guerrilla, takes potshots at the misrepresentation of black professional women's portrayals, and at least keeps the representation in constant agitation about the possibility of change. Interestingly enough, scholar Ada Guy Griffin understands "black culture [as] a product of an ongoing struggle between the extremes of defiance and assimilation, of resistance and complacency."[44] One can expect some significant divergence from how the black professional protagonist is represented in mainstream literature, especially by a black female popular writer. Consequently, McMillan's protagonists in *Waiting to Exhale* are involved in a struggle of a different kind, and do not have as much agency as one might expect. However, her black professional women could have more autonomy in areas that Bambara's protagonists could not.

McMillan explains her philosophy of writing as it reflects "The New Aesthetics of Trey Ellis." McMillan writes: "We are a new breed, free to write as we please, in part because of our predecessors, and because of the way life has changed."[45] That change is political, social, and literary. Hence, McMillan's text confronts the inequities in the American culture indirectly, which fits John Fiske's conception of popular culture as negotiating on an ongoing basis the everyday issues of life with family, work, or school conflicts.[46] *Waiting to Exhale* concerns itself primarily with the individual needs of her protagonists, not communal ones.

That female protagonists have the freedom to travel, explore their sexuality, and speak as many expletives as they please definitely marks a paradigm shift in literature. Culturally, women are not supposed to use "indecent" language though men may; educated women are expected to be sufficiently fluent to adequately deal with life's frustrations, including those that young black professional women encounter while struggling to maintain a place in the corporate world. But within the medium of popular fiction, the language used transgresses the Victorian morality that even the black middle-class community has embraced, primarily imposed to circumscribe the behavior of women. However, McMillan argues that recent writers "reflect a wide range of experiences that are indicative of the times we live in now. Our backgrounds as African-Americans are not all the same. Neither are our perceptions, values, and morals."[47] The varied landscape of writers and characters allows the protagonists of *Waiting to Exhale* to use expletives primarily to vent their frustrations, to speak as is customary, and occasionally as a means to find the inner resources to maintain meaning in their lives.

Furthermore, although the feminist movement in general and the black feminist movement in particular have created space for women to express their sexual desires as openly as men do, some sectors of both the black community and mainstream culture frown on the black woman writer expressing her characters' sexual pleasure in a public forum. The concern reflects the history of writers representing black women as overly sexualized beings. The excessive portrayal of the women's sexual behavior in *Waiting to Exhale* shocked many readers, but Fiske contends, "The struggle over meanings of the body and the validation of its pleasures is a power struggle in which class, gender, and race form complexly intersecting axes," for the higher class perceives the spirit as superior to the body.[48] Hence, so-called "undignified speech" and blatant sexuality seem to fall under the rubric of popular culture.

The women's consumptive behavior may also seem uncharacteristic of professional protagonists having a high level of agency. Robin, for example, goes on a shopping spree to assuage her pain after she is rejected by her lover. She lacks the sophistication necessary to critique her participation in the capitalist system that subordinates her. This lack of awareness may seem problematic since McMillan not only expresses appreciation for what her own parents' generation has provided for its children, but also interrogates the behavior of some of the older generation "having scraped their way to relative wealth and, too often, crass materialism."[49] McMillan might be using Robin to critique the behavior. However, it must be acknowledged that black professional women have desires other than professional ones, and McMillan privileges emotional needs. Additionally, until these women began to enter their professional fields, their lives were defined by lack of the very items they now crave.

Fiske helps us negotiate a final element of this contradictory terrain. Popular culture contains both aspects of domination and chance for the disempowered to oppose and evade those forces of control. Popular culture is created at the juncture where the production of commodities collides with people's lives; it is the product of the masses, the skill of craftily manipulating what the system furnishes.[50] American society is consumerist. McMillan's characters participate in consumerism, but their spendthrift behavior, especially Robin's, is aimed at providing pleasure, sexual and otherwise. Therefore, in one sense, the protagonists fall prey to capitalist principles; nevertheless, the focus on their own individual pleasure becomes transgressive of the patriarchal system that says women's pleasure is derived primarily from men. The behavior also disrupts the capitalist system whose only concern is profit, not how it may contribute to the well-being of the consumer. The levels of irony get more intriguing when one considers that McMillan's characters in *Waiting to Exhale* seek some or most of their pleasure through the men in their lives.

How much agency the protagonists of *Waiting to Exhale* have is debatable. Although they are all professional women, their obsession on getting a "man" is quite problematic for some readers. Jack E. White argues that all McMillan has done is to create new trashy stereotypes typical of romance novels, but they are now blacks. Her focus, according to the critic, is on financial success, not issues that concern male-female relationships. He feels it would be quite disturbing if blacks, so happy to be seen on the Hollywood screen, accept such poor quality filmic renditions such as that of *Waiting to Exhale*, and so have all blacks appear unsophisticated.[51] One can argue that his attempt to dub the film/book as mere "trash" when it resonates so significantly with many black professional women may need interrogating.

Critic Jacqueline Bobo admits being surprised at the fervor demonstrated by some fans she was informally interviewing at a McMillan reading. She observes that McMillan writes about the average black person who has been denied much attention. The women's emotional involvement with *Waiting to Exhale* becomes evident when one informant of her survey group reports:

> I'll tell you why she's selling. Because she is like one of us sitting right here talking about the stuff that we usually talk about. That's why we can identify. Anybody who's been single can definitely identify, because you've met some Michaels, and have been in some relationships with some Russells. And then she writes it just like we would say it.[52]

Of course, many black professional women do not respond favorably to *Waiting to Exhale*. One of the respondents to the questionnaire sent out for this book reports that she could not even finish reading the text, so repulsed was she at the language and sexual behavior of the protagonists. Nevertheless, millions did respond positively to some aspects of the text and that amount of engagement cannot be easily dismissed.

Other factors must be operating here and are worthy of study. The issue may be partly due to ideology. Cultural critic Edward Said refers to those "grand narratives of emancipation and enlightenment [which] mobilized people in the colonial world [African Americans, as a minority group, belonged to this category] to rise up and throw off imperial subjection."[53] The subjugation here takes the form of pervasive negative stereotypes along with the denial of access to money, power, and a resultant voice (until now), to refute on a large scale the false assumptions about black women and about black women as professionals. The novel, in one sense, then, creates a kind of transformation in the consciousness of the black women readers: they are important enough to be given fictive representation.

What may seem to some critics to be blind acceptance of everything *Waiting to Exhale* presents, including even the negative stereotypes, may be a cultural way of accepting the text that represents them. Bobo, in speaking about one group of women's response to the filmic version of *Waiting to Exhale,* remarks that although the women enthusiastically praised the film, a careful analysis of the viewers' responses reveals that "their seeming conflation of the film with the novel was due to a complex process of negotiation. Black women sifted through the incongruent parts of the film and reacted favorably to elements with which they could identify and that resonated with their experiences." The women were exuberant because they were now made visible, and that visibility was now accessible to large black audiences.[54]

Janice Radway finds a similar situation with white women readers of romance fiction. She critiques the facile attempt of scholars who underestimate the knowledge women glean from the romance they read, and the power that knowledge affords them to resist patriarchal dominance. Literary critics assumed that the women readers were simply sponges that absorbed without any resistance the patriarchal presuppositions forced upon naïve readers. However, Radway discovers that the same white women who normally accept the male-centered system do so in order to secure their economic well-being, but also use the reading of romance as a means of resisting that very social structure. Reading created space for them to disregard their incessant domestic duties.[55] Thus, Jack E. White's analysis is too facile in its evaluation of black women as cultural consumers of both the novel and the film. And even if McMillan does indeed create new stereotypes as White insists she does, McMillan represents all four protagonists as college educated, middle-class, and professional, and thus produces a "grand narrative of emancipation" from the "mammy" and "Sapphire" portrayals. She also fractures the elitism that some fair-skinned blacks proclaimed as their mark of distinction from the darker skinned African Americans using the insidious "brown bag" policy.

Because the few novels that represent the black professional women as protagonists are so valuable in the construction of black career women's identity, it is important to explain the delimitations of this work. I chose the two texts, *The Salt Eaters* and *Waiting to Exhale,* primarily because they give novelistic representation of the black professional woman protagonist positioned in the workplace, performing her daily responsibilities, and having some level of agency on the job. The texts also have a strategic position on the time line of these evolving novels, and the twelve-year span between their publication provides enough time for changes to develop in the representation of the protagonists. Bambara's *The Salt Eaters* is the text that birthed the black professional woman as a somewhat autonomous protagonist. Twelve years later, McMillan's text with its four middle-class protagonists, reflects black professional women as well represented in corporate America.

Other texts published during the 1980s to mid–1990s by black women writers represent the black professional woman, such as Toni Morrison's *Tar Baby* (1981), Gloria Naylor's *Mama Day* (1988), Paule Marshall's *Daughters* (1992), and McMillan's *How Stella Got Her Groove Back* (1996). In Morrison's text, the black career woman as protagonist is not situated in the job site. Jadine is an art historian, but nowhere in the text does Jadine actually perform in that capacity. The text focuses on socioeconomic issues, and on Jadine negotiating her role with her uneducated lover. Toni Morrison consistently creates characters who interrogate the self and the social and cultural milieu they participate in, but for a study that focuses on black professional women having agency, this novel could not be considered. Gloria Naylor's *Mama Day* has a protagonist who belongs to the clerical profession, but like Morrison's Jadine, Cocoa is never seen engaged meaningfully in her job.

Paule Marshall's *Daughters* evidences a distinctive shift in how the protagonist is envisioned. Ursa McKenzie is seen performing her job within the text (though toward the end of it) as she prepares for her new career. She exercises some autonomy when she leaves her first place of employment for ethical and personal reasons. The company exploits the poor and restricts her personhood by enforcing a dress code that denies her ethnicity. By the end of the text, she is independent of her father's and lover's control. Therefore, we find a noticeable change in the development of the professional representation of black career protagonists from the time Bambara published *The Salt Eaters*. McMillan's *How Stella Got Her Groove Back* does not actually have Stella working on the job so it was not selected; however, she is an enormously successful professional broker with a six-digit salary. In fact, when she loses her job, she feels relieved to get away from the stress of corporate America. Furthermore, she has plans to begin her own business. Most of the novel is centered on her love relationship with the young Jamaican, Winston Shakespeare, whom she meets while vacationing on the island. Stella's portrait as a successful black professional woman with some autonomy in her life has appealed to millions of a crossover readership. Stella's pleasurable absence from work and her youthful figure, beautiful enough to attract the love of a man twenty years her junior, have earned for Terry McMillan a built-in black readership and millions of dollars.

A few of the novels that come after the mid–1990s evidence a much more sophisticated representation of the black professional woman who has a high level of autonomy. Bebe Moore Campbell's *Brothers and Sisters* (1994), Sheneska Jackson's *Caught Up in the Rapture* (1996), and Connie Briscoe's *Big*

Girls Don't Cry (1996) are examples. Campbell's protagonist is self-empowered. She is efficient, and although a racist male partner tries to incriminate
her, she is exonerated. She chooses, however, to leave the visibility she has
in a large bank to work in the lending department of small black establishment, thus fulfilling her career goal. Furthermore, the new position will
allow her to enjoy her work. One is left, though, to ponder why a novel that
has a female protagonist begins the title with "Brothers" rather than "Sisters." It is important to note that this could be the author's choice or an editor's preference. Sheneska Jackson's *Caught Up in the Rapture* also profiles a
black professional woman. Because of her ties with some less fortunate
friends, she has many tragic experiences, but eventually becomes successful in the music industry. Briscoe's novel, *Big Girls Don't Cry*, possibly comes
the closest to representing a black professional woman with the level of
autonomy black professional women would appreciate. Although more than
one-half of the novel does not directly relate to the professional status of
the character and her success is put in the epilogue, the young woman
achieves self-empowerment both in her public and private life. She marries
the man she loves and achieves wealth and eminence as president of her own
computer firm. Significant changes in how the protagonist is profiled in a
few novels indicate that a paradigm shift is taking place, but it is seen in the
texts of only a few writers. Therefore, the question is: why so few?

The question is appropriate with the changed demographics of the
workplace, the change in emphasis and subject matter of many black women
as cultural producers, and the change in the reading habits and desires of
black professional women. Many contemporary black middle-class women
are demanding novels that are intellectually stimulating and that represent
them realistically. With their united voices, with the financial capability to
purchase the books they choose, they want fulfillment of their "Being
needs," a part of which is an adequate representation of themselves in fictive
creations.

The Salt Eaters (1980) and *Waiting to Exhale* (1992) have strategic significance, for they allow for the assessment of developments that emerge
within novels, particularly the level of agency accorded the protagonists.
Over a twelve year period, it is also possible to trace some of the endemic
causes for the failure of more recent narratives to give black professional
women protagonists a high level of self-empowerment.

In order to verify the extent to which theoretical findings reflect the
lived lives of black career women, I conducted an informal survey of 175
black professional women readers, from whom I received 119 responses. The
questionnaire sought to discover how much agency the black female cultural consumers thought the writers gave the black professional protagonists,

how satisfied the women were with the representations, and to what extent the novels mirrored the lives of the respondents. It must be acknowledged that the sample is not representative of black professional women in the United States; however, it does reflect the feelings of a significant group of women. One can deduce that these 119 responses reflect a larger group's position. Furthermore, this text is not a sociological theses that requires a very large representation; it is literary, and as such, the sample is adequate.

Using a combination of reader response and ethnographic approaches,[56] the survey partially replicates the methodology of Janice Radway's *Reading the Romance: Women, Patriarchy, and Popular Literature* (1984, 1991), and Jacqueline Bobo's *Black Women as Cultural Readers: Film and Culture* (1995). Both writers function as literary and social critics. Radway argues that the most effective way to conduct reader response critique is to directly study the subjects. Questions should not be concerned merely with the text (plot, etc.), but what the text actually says to the readers, and how it affords pleasure and utility in the readers' lives. Thus, Radway begins her experiment of white females who are avid readers of the romance by first interviewing the participants. She then infers from their answers and other visual behaviors that offer significant insights, how they transact meaning from the texts.

Jacqueline Bobo concentrates her efforts on black women subjects. She is interested in black female readers' responses to three films: *The Color Purple* (1985), *Daughters of the Dust* (1992), and *Waiting to Exhale* (1992). She finds it necessary to extend Radway's methodology in application of her study. Her rationale for the expansion is that black women as cultural consumers not only have been long ignored by cultural critics, but that critical response to *Waiting to Exhale's* extended success (film and novel) allows her to study black middle-class women's lives from more than a mere sociological perspective, as the media and some scholars previously had. The protagonists in the novel disrupted cultural notions of the black woman's inferiority.[57] She deduces the responses of the viewers not only from what they say during the interview, but their comments and other behaviors as they watch the films. Bobo's study concludes that black women viewers make up an important part of black female cultural and social activism. As such, together with black women writers, they form an interpretative community. She also concludes that the women coming from a varied socioeconomic background do not constitute a monolithic group.[58] Both Radway and Bobo are internationally renowned writers, and their works are regarded as seminal studies helping critics and other readers better understand large groups of women who have heretofore been made invisible in academia. Furthermore, their books have articulated important cultural factors that make reading possible, as well as illustrate the complexity of women's behaviors as readers.

This text focuses on the fictive representation of black professional women in the workplace. It differs from Radway's study because her emphasis is on white women readers of the romance genre. It contrasts with Bobo's study, for she concentrates her work on black female filmic viewers and their responses to three contemporary movies. This work contributes to the study of black women as cultural consumers. Because some information was gleaned from the subjects at informal social settings, the work adds some first person narratives of the respondents as they critique not only the two novels used in this study, but more recent publications. The systematic analysis fills a gap in the scholarship on black women and their response to literature.

This work is not intended as a coercive vehicle to encourage black women writers to be untrue to their craft, that is, write only what some cultural consumers desire at a particular historic moment. One significant characteristic of black women writers is the marvelous array of subjects they choose. This book provides a vehicle for cultural consumers to voice their responses to novels that represent them, and allows the women to signify why they want the novels. They initiate a call and response within the interpretive community.

This discussion does not assume that only black professional women desire novels that represent black career women; neither does it suggest that all professionals want books with protagonists that belong to this category. Black readers come from varied groups within the black community, and most of them support black women's literary production. Furthermore, this text acknowledges that one of the widest reading audiences comes from the mainstream population, both domestic and international. This text, however, does focus on black professional women as cultural consumers, since it is the representation of this group as protagonists in realistic fiction that is the subject under consideration.

This book has six chapters. Chapter One presents some of the readers' comments as to why they need novels with the professional protagonist exercising agency in the workplace and in their private lives. The respondents use different aspects of the novels to satisfy their present or anticipated needs. The answers are clustered around several foci. My analysis is interwoven into the narrative.

Chapter Two explores the factors that govern the writing process, and how these may hinder the production of more books that represent the autonomous black career woman. It involves three areas: the writing process itself, the knowledge base that is available to the writers, and the concerns women writers bring to their craft.

Chapter Three examines the external factors that impinge on the production of texts. It evaluates the response of male critics—white and black—to black women's work. It recognizes that no African American male writer to date presents the black professional woman as protagonist. Furthermore, until very recently, publishers did not promote black women's creative endeavors since editors operated on the premise that blacks did not read or buy books. Now, since the advent of Terry McMillan and her unprecedented sales of several novels, some segments of the market are making an effort to understand the black readership that purchases hundreds of millions of books each year.

Chapters Four and Five illustrate the factors that impede the protagonists from achieving a high level of autonomy in two novels, *The Salt Eaters* and *Waiting to Exhale*. These chapters help to explain why so many readers are not fully satisfied with most of the contemporary novels. Being seminal, the two function as significant markers for the development of black professional women as protagonists with some level of agency.

Chapter Six presents the results of the ethnographic segment that was designed to confirm or refute the theoretical findings of the literary analysis. This chapter records from the survey the specific characteristics the respondents like in the novels they read, the degree to which their desires are met, and the extent to which the protagonists are self-actualized in *The Salt Eaters* and *Waiting to Exhale* (and to a lesser degree in more recent publications). But more importantly, the chapter identifies those characteristics the survey subjects prefer to see evidenced in the lives of the protagonists that represent black career women. These traits, they believe, are a reflection of their own lived lives.

My findings reveal that the protagonists fall within a continuum regarding the level of agency they demonstrate. Furthermore, internal and external factors impede a greater production of these novels with protagonists as self-empowered. The work identifies four interlocking factors that hinder the characters from having agency on the job. It acknowledges that the readers have very specific expectations, and that their needs are only partially met since the protagonists do not reflect the lived lives of many of the readers.

~ ONE ~

Consumer Desire for Self-Empowered Black Professional Women Protagonists

Despite the momentous upward mobility of black women within the last thirty years, and despite the ever-increasing power they are achieving in the marketplace and in their own personal lives, most contemporary realistic fiction writers seem hesitant to represent black professional women as having achieved a high level of autonomy. In fact, only black women writers choose them as protagonists, although not without apparent limitations. Yet, with the noticeable rise of black women into the middle-class ranks, a corresponding shift in expectations surfaces. These financially privileged professionals want to see themselves mirrored in novels which act as markers—pointers, if you will—that evidence their trail of success. Two important questions need to be answered here. Why do these women want novels with black professional women protagonists exercising agency in the workplace and in their personal lives? Do the texts satisfy their expectations?

According to responses gleaned from the survey and from informal public discussion sessions, contemporary middle-class professional black women readers want novels that portray the protagonists as having their version of the American Dream. For one respondent, it entails "a strong sense of self-fulfillment, a stable and comfortable home life, a good income allowing for [a] substantial diversified portfolio of short and long-term investments and sufficient benefits coverage for the entire family, high visibility in nontraditional careers for black women, and a secure feeling of well-being." These readers understand that two of the overriding imperatives of the 21st century are financial security and empowerment in their career fields. Groups such as the "Go On Girl Book Club"[1] have discovered their power to negotiate with publishers through their united voices in an effort to secure the novels they desire.

A sense of urgency is echoed by some of the respondents' comments. One offers this critique, which mirrors many of her peers' concerns:

> As I read the contemporary novels, at least seventy percent of each text focuses on the problems rather than the successes of the black women protagonists. The only exception is McMillan's *How Stella Got Her Groove Back,* and that is real make believe for most contemporary black women. Could it be that our unhappy historical past is so etched on our consciousness, or that our present problems hold us such captives that we cannot remove ourselves from them even in fiction? I stand in awe of Morrison's *Beloved* and *Playing in the Dark,* which have earned a rightful place in the canon and the respect of the international community. But our Nobel Prize recipient is yet to write a novel that reflects the self-empowerment she enjoys. I am not asking for a Cinderella story. I know of the intersection of gender, race, class, age; I am forty-one years of age. But I am yet to read a novel in which a black professional woman actively participating in her job is basically happy, and who consistently acts throughout the course of the text as if she is disciplined, intelligent, efficient, financially astute, independent, basically content with her profession, and fun loving. I am one of many such professional women.

As an international icon, Morrison plumbs uncharted regions, which allows her audience to re-remember the past, understand the present, and possibly anticipate the future of African Americans and their society. Now some readers anticipate a fictive representation of Morrison, herself, black professional woman exemplar.

Another respondent is very candid about why she rarely reads fiction by black women writers:

> I hardly read the novels anymore because they rarely represent professional black women. They continue to represent undereducated, insecure women who cannot survive without a man. These are characters who do not reflect me. Professional black women are rarely represented in novels *to their fullest potential* such as the ones who are educated, hardworking, independent, sophisticated, intelligent, secure within themselves, and ambitious. Until that time comes, I will continue to read creative nonfiction, education texts, and write poetry, in hopes of writing a book of my own someday.

The respondents give a clear indication of why many middle-class professional black women cultural consumers read or do not read realistic novels written by black women writers. Although most are unhappy with the novels as adequate representation of who they are, the readers are willing to be selective of what they focus on, and so are able to take from the text those aspects they find useful. The areas they appreciate also suggest what they wish to have fully developed throughout the narratives. Although primarily a homogeneous group with respect to what they are looking for on a macro level, there is differentiation between what the readers want on the micro level. For example, 2 of the 119 respondents state they read a variety of novels simply for pleasure. The majority are more involved in the texts and articulate what they find enjoyable; but more so, what they would like in the texts (see Appendix C, Chart 7).

Before examining the expressed wishes and how the participants experience the texts, I want to suggest a psychological base for the need. In the Introduction, I suggested that Maslow's theory of "hierarchal needs" may help to explain the abundant and exceptional quality writing that has flowed from the pens of black women since the 1980s. However, since Maslow believes that full self-actualization is experienced by about one percent of the population (others have "peak" experiences of less frequency and shorter duration), his theory alone may not be adequate to account for the millions of black women readers who are demanding books of high quality, and for black professional women whose lives are empowered.

Perhaps an added dimension from another humanistic psychologist, Carl Rogers, and and from cognitive psychologist Albert Bandura, will further explain the behavior of the larger group of black women readers. Briefly, Rogers believes that the single overriding motive that impels us to fully develop our innate potential is the "actualizing principle," which is an outgrowth of the individual's "self-concept." Self-concept here means what one believes herself to be and the principles that foreground that self-image. To have a positive self-image, the individual must receive "unconditional regard" (love) consistently from childhood, so the actualizing potential will be realized. In this environment, the individual experiences "congruence"—harmony within the self. He then operates from what Rogers calls an "inherent motivational system" and consistently chooses what is best for him. However, if the society's perception of the person conflicts with who she or he innately perceives the self to be, and the person receives only "conditional regard" (loved only as long as he or she pleases others), that person will experience "incongruence," in which the positive sense of selfhood conflicts with the actual lived experience. These extended disharmonious experiences, Rogers believes, cause one to become psychologically unhealthy. On the contrary, the fully functioning individual is characterized by "self-confidence, self-trust, risk-taking, conscientiousness, and flexibility."[2]

How does this theory apply to the black woman's desire for novels of the self-actuated black professional woman? First, Rogers' premise that the need for positive regard is "innate"[3] "universal ... pervasive and persistent"[4] corroborates with the desire of black women for consistent positive portrayals in these novels. One could say the texts provide a kind of surrogate environment that offers this "persistent" unconditional regard. The novelists do not give the protagonists adequate autonomy, but the writers are invested in the portrayal of black professional women as a group. Contrary to black women novelists, from the initiation of slavery up to the 1960s, blacks received neither unconditional nor conditional regard from the mainstream society; they were treated mostly with disdain or brutal violence. The pervasive portrayal of blacks as less than beautiful, intelligent, or even human conflicted drastically with who blacks innately knew themselves to be. They consistently strove against almost immeasurable difficulties to maintain their self-worth, and resisted not only the invisibility that disregarded their achievements, but how pseudo-scholarship and the media analyzed and presented them. When the aesthetic consciousness of blacks nationally was enhanced by the slogan "Black is Beautiful," this "unconditional positive regard" allowed more blacks to move from incongruence toward congruence, at least within the black community. Thus, black women as a group were better able to manifest the qualities of fully functioning individuals with a stronger and more positive concept of the self. This image they now seek in novels.

The development of positive self-esteem alone, however, cannot account for the tremendous strides black women have made in their reach for professionalism within the last thirty years. Their demand for novels that honestly represent them is one aspect of their career personae. One of the theories espoused by Albert Bandura provides a complementary explanation of the phenomenon of the urgent desires of black women's readership.

Social cognitive theory acknowledges "reciprocal determinism"—that is, all aspects of our lives are interdependent. Our thoughts originate through contact with our environment. The social and cultural influences of our communities affect our behavior; we, in turn, self-regulate our thoughts, feelings, and actions toward the environment. Taken together, our cognitive skills, our potential, and our attitudes create a "self-system" which determines how we act and appraise our behavior in any given situation. The most important aspect of this "self-system" is the belief of "self-efficacy"—the strong will to trust our abilities to successfully deal with any encounter.[5] The firm belief in one's "self-efficacy" is one of the driving forces behind the need for the black middle-class self-directed women readers' demand for novels that adequately represent the protagonists as having agency.

One principle inherent in the concept of self-efficacy is that one imaginatively effects one's future goals. Black career women's behavior suggests that they accept reciprocal determinism to some degree; that is, they can self-regulate the cultural production of novels about the black female career protagonist with agency by purchasing, reading, critiquing, and articulating their need for such texts. These black professionals are exerting much effort to further change the cultural landscape regarding how black professional women are represented. Their behavior manifests some aspects of Carl Rogers' "actualizing principle" as well, for they unequivocally know what it is they desire in the novels they purchase. Journalist and civil rights activist Francis Beale argues, "Once you have caught a glimpse of freedom or experienced self-determination, you can't go back to the old routines."[6] Many black professional readers, having achieved a high level of agency in their lives, seek fictive representation.

Professional black women readers desire novels in which they can see themselves fully reflected. Narratives with characters performing their jobs within the texts function as an affirmation of the individual and the community of sisterhood who have achieved profitability of their market skills. In the survey, 78 percent of the subjects said they liked these books because they partially confirm their sense of self-empowerment. The novels acknowledge and celebrate their presence in the professional work force. The efficient, visible, and well remunerated protagonists also underscore the success of these qualified black women who are working hard and are proud of their achievements: that is, those who have broken through the glass ceiling, or better yet, the brick ceiling.

America's belief in meritocracy has not been uniformly and consistently applied to black professional women in determining kinds of jobs, in-house training, and rewards for work well done. For example, black women comprise about 12 percent of the student population in college, comparable to their representation in the national population. Additionally, as early as 1992, they earned more than half the doctorates awarded in the black community, including more law and medical degrees than black males.[7] Despite these significant gains, the United States Department of Labor reports that in 1996, full-time black women workers with comparable credentials at all levels earned only 88 percent of the salary earned by black men, 85 percent that of white women, and only 62 percent that of white men.[8] The novel that captures the achievement of the black career protagonist acknowledges her strenuous climb and acts as a cheerleader for the readers. One respondent cites Marita Golden's The Edge of Heaven (1999), in which the professional protagonist is successfully assimilated into the corporate arena. An accountant, she spent three months in Europe "auditing banks in Switzerland, London, and Amsterdam and staying at four-star hotels in every country ... I was a black woman in Europe and I felt like I belonged to and could conquer the world."[9] The survey participant comments that ironically, the primary focus of the novel is not on the success "in" but on the fall "from" corporate America due to domestic concerns, but the novel acknowledges such advancement. This response is a classic example of how the readers surveyed seem to negotiate the novels they read.

These respondents want novels with self-actualized protagonists because the narratives offer the women a collective means of immortality. Since the West privileges literacy over orality, these women desire to have their newly acquired place on the professional and economic ladder of success encoded. One respondent writes:

> One hundred years from now, black people should be able to look back at us and say, we are proud of our female ancestors. But if the novels are not accurately and creatively done, if we focus too much on the negative side of our story, and if we do not ensure that they remain in print, our hard work could easily be forgotten. More black women are involved with reading, for the books they want are becoming available. Furthermore, they are building libraries to bequeath them on to their posterity.

The desire for sustained recognition, even a communal one, is reflective of people in all cultures. One participant explains that once the texts are read as classics and remain in circulation, fewer readers will see black women represented as "reified sex objects." Good literature is defined by cultural studies analysis[10] as any text that a particular group of people acknowledges to be significant to them. Novels that reflect black professional women exercising agency in the workplace and in their personal lives is one body of valuable literature the participants of my study want to enjoy and preserve.

Additionally, the protagonists must be portrayed as having moved beyond the observer status to the inner circle of corporate America. One respondent is critical of some contemporary novels:

> The characters act as if they are visitors to the corporate scene. Do the characters in the banking industry ever use computer programs such as Excel, or do they still use the old calculating machines? Do CEOs ever use PowerPoint to create their presentations? Do professors ever use Blackboard? Do physicians use palm pilots? No mention is made of e-Books. What I am emphasizing is, are professional characters ever going to catch up with the current technology of this Information Age?

She acknowledges that technology changes so rapidly that a novel need not jeopardize its readability over a long time span by using too much technical terminology. However, even the most current novels usually mention only the extensive use of the cell phone. References to the computer is nebulous. Black women want novels that show the protagonist familiar with the job culture and skilled enough to successfully negotiate the ever expanding global marketplace on a daily basis. A few writers, like Bebe Moore Campbell in the banking scene of *Brothers and Sisters*, are attempting to do just that, but too few novels reflect the current changes taking place in the workplace.

In wanting to see the complexity of corporate lives reflected in the protagonists, the subjects desire the texts to portray the central character regularly negotiating a multilayered world in which she was not raised. This level of complexity is different from the overt oppression encountered before the 1960s. It often requires that she maintain a macro and a micro identification, a public and a private persona that function in the mainstream culture and in the black community. Such hybrid socialization W.E.B. Du Bois calls a "double consciousness."[11] The difficulty with this professional hybridization is that the black professional woman must be able to make the transition and function in both worlds with minimum conflict. Deconstructing some aspects of the self when she is on the job and re-constructing them when she is with some members of her native community require an enormous amount of energy because a daily transformation is often required. *Our Bodies, Ourselves for the New Century* (1998) records a woman saying she resigned her position after she was told by her boss to either not wear braids to work or leave the establishment. The woman's comment is, "It's asking people to change who they are," and to conform to a prescribed and desired look in the marketplace.[12] Novels that celebrate the black professional woman negotiating the complexity of the corporate world function as a kind of reward offered, for some of the respondents.

Books that dramatize the protagonists interacting in their culture are desired, for they directly reflect the lived lives of the respondents. The two novels extensively analyzed later in this book have the protagonist and other women bonding together. In *The Salt Eaters*, Velma has a group of women activist friends who work and share cultural experiences with one another. Furthermore, the protagonist belongs to an arts organization, the Seven Sisters of the Grain, whose members travel together for their varied performances. Similarly, in *Waiting to Exhale*, all four protagonists are friends and support one another. The narrative allows for cultural bonding by presenting a similar experience with women readers who share a familiar frame of reference. The black woman cannot function fully in an ahistorical setting.

Novels in which the protagonist belongs to a community, with some aesthetic that foregrounds the individual, comforts the high-ranking black career woman. She can enjoy the privileges of both worlds, black and white, despite the psychic discomfort that she may occasionally encounter. Since she participates in the mainstream ethos daily, one respondent is glad the books written by black women sometimes use the black vernacular, mention the names of other black writers or significant events in black history, and have allusions, that is, "signify" other texts. Catherine Ross confirms that many women read to understand their history and ancestry from different perspectives, and so "read themselves into the story and then read the story into their lives."[13] Black women readers do not want to feel alienated from the texts.

Another very important way that the novels function as a mechanism for "bonding" black women readers is through the formation of hundreds of reading clubs across the nation. One respondent writes:

> I can always expect an uproariously good time when our club meets twice a month. No matter what we read, we are dead serious when we begin to analyze the work. I do not know how it is possible, but we all read so differently. And no matter how we may want to bring some closure, some nice consensus to the table, we cannot always mesh the ideas together. As I drive home, my mind is looking at the book from all four directions and then some.

Another subject writes that what she particularly likes is to watch how people's minds work when a new idea is put on the floor. In a way, you can almost visualize how the electrical impulses are operating in the brain:

> The ideas ricochet from so many angles. They strike the bull's-eye, they rebound, they circle the issue. Once in a while a bomb explodes, then we regroup. Most of the time it really is fun, a peculiar kind of fun where everybody is really listening intently to one another and answering. We always get lots of laughs and even hugs sometimes. It is my time off from husband, kids, and work, and I wouldn't miss it for anything.

Not surprisingly, several of the women want the books with professional characters, since their continued publication allows their book club activities to continue.

Furthermore, black professional women desire novels that render them truthfully because they want to evaluate new possibilities and themselves. The fictive representation allows readers to understand and avoid the errors of the protagonist; likewise, they can visualize how a character successfully

negotiates a difficult work situation. The novels with self-empowered protagonists can function as motivators for future behavior. One respondent
explains:

> A narrative with a high ranking personnel can sometimes provide
> new awareness. The reader may not be a stockbroker, but by read-
> ing a novel about a successful black female professional, she has a
> sense of how her peer fares. The career is taken out of the world of
> abstraction and put into the world of possible reality. Images help
> to concretize abstraction. Reading about a black female senator par-
> tially demystifies those different worlds.

For her, a convincing portrayal of an episode on Capitol Hill can create an
interest in politics and thus, more potential career options.

Realistic novels about autonomous career women also provide other
teachable moments for the professional. If books and other forms of mass
media fail to give black professional women a positive reflection of who
they are, then it is difficult for some to identify themselves as fully functional.
If we believe that it is through the responses of others that we, to a large
extent, come to know who we are, and if we do not feature positively in the
cultural myths and symbols of corporate America, then people, and here
specifically some black women, may have difficulty defining their functions
in the world of work. Fortunately, some individuals have the ability to reject
the media version of what a black woman is imagined to be. One respondent writes that Terry McMillan's "fictive and filmic renditions of black professional women may not be deemed serious scholarship, but they do
publicly acknowledge that someone called a black professional woman exists.
Between her, Toni Morrison, Mae Jameson, Oprah Winfrey, the black professional woman cannot be rendered invisible anymore." Black middle-class
women readers specify the kinds of books they prefer because they are seeking avenues by which to identify space for themselves.

Sometimes the novels serve needs that the respondents rarely articulate. One of these needs I will call the "generational dream deferred" motif.
The concept was first publicized in Langston Hughes' poem "Harlem,"[14]
and later found full dramatic development in Lorraine Hansberry's *A Raisin
in the Sun* (1958).[15] The novels about contemporary successful black women
record in one sense the fulfillment of a dream unrealized by many of the
professional women's mothers, who nevertheless channeled their energies
and funds into educating their daughters. The mothers worked and prayed
to facilitate their children's success in the mainstream work force. These
novels demonstrate that these nonprofessional mothers did not labor in vain,
and that their offspring in turn fulfilled their parents' expectations. This

theme, as discussed by Critic Dorothy L. Dennison, appears in Paule Marshall's short story, "Reena." At her college graduation, Reena represents "not just a personal accomplishment," but a triumph for both her mother and father and their parents before them. Reena comments: "It was as if I had made up for the generations his people had picked cotton in Georgia, and my mother's family [had] cut cane in the West Indies."[16] Black women are not the only ones to express this sentiment. Richard Ford writes that he, too, came from a working-class background, and that his parents "slaved" so he would not have to undergo the hardships they encountered. He acknowledges that his success, which allows him to write at leisure, is a testament to his parents' success.[17] For both the older and younger generations of black women, then, the texts function as a cathartic vehicle to celebrate what they have accomplished. The narratives also allow a crossover readership to vicariously identify with the experience in the novels, and take pleasure in their own achievements.

In a thirty-year span, these black career women I surveyed (and others) have achieved a high level of success, which makes an even brighter future for themselves and their children seem realizable, and so the respondents want these possibilities captured in novels they read. Many black women have a perceived status in the workplace. The operative word here is "perceived." Some form of "assistantship" is attached to their titles, which suggests that their autonomy is limited to some extent on the job. These participants in my study want books that will function as forerunners of what they and their children may achieve in the job market. Scholar Edward Said, in *Culture And Imperialism*, critiques the novels of the British Empire in the 19th century. He argues, "Empire follows Art, and not vice-versa." Novels of Jane Austen, for instance, were not mere pieces of genteel culture. Rather, they created the environment that schooled the British to find it natural to expand their colonizing practices so that they could boast that the sun never set on the British flag.[18] If empire follows art in a negative way by enslaving millions for the profit and comfort for a few, it is reasonable to assume that novels that positively articulate the career woman can position her historically as having fulfilled the Dream, thus allowing others to dream and so enter the bargaining and decision making tiers of corporate America.

The theme of the "generational dream deferred" finds full expression in the artistic rendering and publication of very few of the texts for which the respondents (and no doubt many others) clamor. The informants want the novels that reflect a contemporary manifestation of their ancestral heritage. I want to cushion this heritage of creation potential in Alice Walker's exultant paean to the mothers and grandmothers and ancestral mothers of black women readers and writers.

In "In Search of Our Mother's Gardens," Alice Walker traces the genius of black women writers to what she believes to be their creative source, the foremothers. She writes that although black women's creative talents were denied outlets, the women nevertheless yearned, even if it were in vain, for varied avenues to unleash their artistic abilities. They experienced the terror and pain of untapped genius. Walker asks the reader to imagine the loss and bewilderment black women of extraordinary capabilities must have endured during slavery and Reconstruction. The cruelty was of such violence it is "enough to stop the blood." If one can imagine the famous blues women singers "muzzled for life," then he can have a glimmer into understanding the mental and spiritual tortures of these stifled artists. How did they endure the perpetual rape and consequent nearly annual birthing, the commerce in their children, the bloodstained lash intended to frustrate their need to be painters, writers, sculptures, and poets? Walker then asks if the collective "you" had such an ancestral mother.

Yet, amidst this nightmarish milieu remains a riddle: how did the foremothers transmit their artistic ability and craft to their progeny? Their creative flowering took different forms. For the many who lacked educational opportunities, they transferred that flow into quilting, flower gardening, floral arrangements—any avenue that became available. Few, like Phillis Wheatley, shone forth through their brilliant poetry that continues to receive international praise. Walker comments that the ancestors have, "more often than not, anonymously handed down the creative spark, the seed of the flower they themselves hoped to see; or like a sealed letter they could not plainly read." Fortunately, the long, vicious chapter of servitude did not destroy the innate creativity of black women, as evidenced by the tremendous outpouring of later generations. As a consummate artist herself, Walker discovered that the stories she and all the other women write are indeed a continuum of "my mother's stories."[19] Walker personalizing the experience does not diminish the collective source, the foremothers.

What I emphasize here is the creative potential of the foremothers, not their supposed ability to do superhuman work and perpetually nurture others while being forced to ignore their own individual needs. These early women were compelled into debasing roles during slavery and later as maids, but that their remarkable minds allowed them to create art in whatever form they could suggests that they loved themselves enough to surround themselves and their families with beauty, especially the art of their own making. Trudier Harris argues that it is primarily the physical and emotional aspects of "strong black women" always used in the service of others that is replicated in many books. Among other texts, she cites Alice Walker's short story "Every Day Use," in which the mother is given overt masculinized strength.[20] However, even here, the mother demonstrates her love of the beautiful in the exquisite quilts she creates. She offers the most artistically designed and envied one, not to adorn a wall of a home or museum, but to be used daily for the comfort of her less materially successful daughter who has a deeper sense of spirituality, and who better appreciates the masterpiece.

The generational dream deferred, with its potential for even greater possibilities, must find fulfillment now through varied productive avenues. Based on my survey, the readership wants novels that were the foremothers alive (most blacks believe the ancestors are alive in a very real sense), they would be pleased that such books give flesh to what they had envisioned. These desired books would be a testament that writers and readers alike have maintained the creative spark. Langston Hughes' prophetic vision in his poem indicates that the "dream [too long] deferred" may express itself in many less productive ways, but he was insightful enough to say "The Dream" was not *dead*, merely *deferred*.

So far, it could appear that black career women want novels for narcissistic reasons only; however, that perception would be false. Eighty-seven percent of the subjects in the survey want protagonists who can function, even minimally, as models for women who do not readily have professional role models. In *Days of Grace*, Arthur Ashe comments that the persistent need for a model or leader is indicative of the black community's "lack of power and organization." However, he acknowledges that there appears to be a need for successful blacks to live commendable lives. He instructs his daughter not to "beg God for favors," but rather ask for wisdom to make right choices. He proudly and affectionately tells her that he has left her an inheritance which will allow her "more material advantage" than most children in the world, and that she is to use it prudently.[21] One wonders if at twelve years of age or later, Ashe did not regard men such as Ron Charity as role models, since they taught and championed his cause to the white establishment, requesting he be allowed to play on the better tennis courts whites controlled in Richmond, Virginia.[22] It is possible because tennis is a highly individualistic sport that Ashe may have had less tolerance for those who need communal support. His sense of independence is echoed in his advice to his daughter and reflects the upper-middle class social status he enjoyed as he was writing his book.

On the contrary, the middle-class respondents to my survey are enthusiastic for role models. They feel successful professionals can become icons for the millions of young black women who are yet to join the ranks of career women, especially those whom these women cannot reach regularly on a one-to-one basis. They acknowledge also that books about black women can offer insights into longevity and deeper levels of happiness.

What kinds of books best function as providing models for women in general, and black women in particular? Writer Shelby Foote believes that women purchase about 75 percent of fiction books, but "they mostly buy bad books. I mean, most of the bad books are sold to women. I have always had an idea that it was men who bought Hemingway, Fitzgerald, Faulkner, and Dos Passos."[23] Foote's sexist comment not only attempts to diminish women's ability to choose books intelligently, but suggests that only men enjoy good books. Furthermore, by not including a woman writer to the list suggests that only male authors produce good books, and that women readers do not support the cultural production of women writers. However, a third year female African American medical student suggests that novels about the black career woman with a strong sense of autonomy can "be an inspiration to young people and provide the impetus for action." She explains that she voluntarily visits girls who are incarcerated, and they need every possible encouragement that is available. A senior at an ivy league institution finds that novels, because they are fun to read, can allow young people a means of "non-coerced" identification with the protagonist. Thus they can move beyond the mere "idolizing phase to at least the internalizing stage."

Other women attest to the positive influence of books, including novels, on their career paths. Critic Barbara Sicherman discusses how the intense enthusiasm for books by Minnie Thomas, former president of Bryn Mawr College, led her to deconstruct texts, to emphasize "the possibilities of female heroism," and to eliminate all differences based on gender. Thomas, and others in her social circle, understood that their "dreams of glory" could only materialize if they had an excellent education, prominent jobs, and agency in their lives. Sicherman argues that reading can intensify one's imaginative capabilities, and thus allow the reader to vicariously experience success. The reader can then examine her thought life and change her feelings since the reader can "appropriate" the meaning as she understands it. By Minnie Thomas "inserting" her person imaginatively in the works, she was able to say, "Knowledge is power ... and I, for one, am going to do my best to gain it." Eventually, her goal for leadership materialized. Her small group of "progressive" and professional minded women of the 19th century urged each other to pursue their dreams, and by so doing, created a new consciousness of female possibility.[24] Granted, these women were from elite backgrounds, but their goals were radical given the social context of their times.

Books can have a positive effect on the lives of very diverse people. Gordon and Patricia Sabine, after interviewing almost fourteen hundred readers who attest to the positive impact of books, record their experiences in

Books That Made the Difference: What People Told Us (1983).[25] They report that texts help people regain their health after catastrophic illnesses, comfort others in grief, help professionals save their careers, assist women to find and give emotional fulfillment, and save others from their addictions.[26] Furthermore, one respondent to my survey writes, "Sometimes I have a tendency to spend more money and time on my family than myself. As I read *The Edge of Heaven* (1999), I couldn't help notice the way the protagonist liked 'the glide of silk across her skin,' having two massages per month, and dining well. It reminded me not to forget myself. Now I do more for me."

Some of the most memorable comments come from someone involved in pastoral counseling. She sees novels with autonomous professional protagonists in the workplace as "paving the way" for so many black women who "don't think of themselves as being empowered in the workplace." She adds, for many "the thought has never crossed their minds for fear of the negative impact it could have on their job security." She feels such novels offer "inspiration to let us know we can succeed; to give us something to look forward to; to help us set goals." Whether the novels women read are regarded by critics as trash or quality literature, frequently the texts positively influence the lives of many black women.

Black women readers want novels in which beautiful black professional women protagonists demonstrating self-empowerment serve not only as icons for the young, but also as icons in the cultural mythos, thereby replacing the Aunt Jemima symbol in the national consciousness. They want the bandana removed and the "elegant" black professional woman put in her place, thus encoding the black career woman in literary history as counterstroke to the Sapphires and Lilieths so often depicted in the media. Since writing itself is a powerful act, the increasing number of novels by black women writers in recent years suggests that black women are gaining momentum as a group, and their impact is influencing the mainstream perception of who they are. However, there is still a need for characters with agency to have their very names and images etched on black women's psyches.

Women reading in groups can effect change. One lawyer notes that in recent years, the only activity that has brought together black women from different socioeconomic backgrounds is the reading of books by black women authors. She adds, "The concepts of self-actualization and sisterhood are catching on, but not among the poor women in the community. They see women serving in secondary roles, for example as 'back up' in many rap music videos and films. The problem is how to get these sisters to read these novels." The idea that reading helps black women is emphasized by Jacqueline Bobo. She argues that the novels by black women writers provide "a coping mechanism, enabling black women to recognize the array of forces controlling their lives." She adds that the texts "nourish and sustain" the women and provide the impetus for them to make changes.[27] A woman may have to read several novels, however, before her consciousness is awakened to the possibility of change.

Many of the women respondents want novels that appeal to a crossover audience, which they hope will help "further-along" the bonds of sisterhood that are being forged with women of other races and nationalities. However, some writers need to have enough sovereignty over the black characters they are portraying before they write about others. One respondent, a writer and reader, comments on this issue: "I think right now we are writing primarily about ourselves to better understand what we have been through, what we now experience, what we hope to achieve." She adds that she has many white college friends and working colleagues, but she has not *"lived* long enough with them" to avoid writing in a superficial way, that is, representing them merely in a work-related relationship. Although she does have four white women friends with whom she can have serious "sleep-over kinds of discussions, it wouldn't be fair to write about my friends at this point. I think once we writers have explored ourselves fully, we will be better able to write about others as *kin*."

Another reason yet exists why the readership is demanding fiction that depicts the profile of the black career woman. The novelists, themselves career women, are telling their own story. They echo Walt Whitman's "I celebrate myself, and sing myself."[28] Fifty percent of the questionnaire subjects expressed how wonderful it was to have black women write about black women, that is, "articulating the self." Detailed descriptions of their physical features, skin, hair, dress, style, charm, sexuality, and their intellect are all equally significant. Black women no longer want to read novels in which they are compared to mainstream standards of beauty. They want their own novels that depict them as they perceive themselves: beautiful and happy with themselves. Such texts are not written by outsiders who may see black women as mere objects of their analysis, but written by subjects—the black professional women writers, whose art is evidence of their own subjectivity. Black women must write their own song or book or risk misrepresentation.

Writing the self allows for a greater appreciation of black womanhood. An older participant wants the novels that project the professional because "some of them depict us as champions who have won against difficult odds." She adds: "We need the fighting spirit to survive as we did during the 60s. Some things have changed, but the powerful structures and ideologies that control our society have not undergone a significant enough transformation. We need to pass on the torch of championship to our children." One hopeful sociology student comments, "Despite the many difficulties black women experience, we can be proud that we are women, black women with accomplishments." In the same tenure, a medical intern feels: "We are making strides; quite a few of us are here, and we are beginning to make a difference. The novels are lagging behind."

If realistic narratives are to reflect the lived lives of all black professional women, then they should be fully inclusive. One respondent wants books that address the age range of the contemporary scene. She expresses concern that hardly any writers are portraying black professional women protagonists with self-empowerment as belonging to the baby boom population. She adds: "We are here, efficient and adventurous, and yes, attractive. We too want representation." The critique is poignant. Most of the recent realistic fiction features young women professionals, while the older generation is represented either as uneducated or working in jobs traditional for women. Addressing issues of solvency, inheritance, retirement, the high divorce rate, health, and longevity are areas some respondents want to be treated creatively.

Some participants of the survey, whose fields are less traditional for black women, enjoy the narratives and recognize their value in portraying the career protagonists. They do have some reservations about the emphasis put on fiction. They are pleased that the texts are raising the consciousness level of black women who read them. However, they see the popularity of the novels merely the beginning of what is needed to change the perceptions of black women held by those in the "inner circles of the power structure. Rarely does any novel have the shock effect of *Uncle Tom's Cabin* by Harriett Beecher Stowe" (1852). They argue that novels of popular culture are perceived as having very little permanent value; that is, they are produced for mere entertainment. Thus, if read, the novels are not given any serious consideration by those with the power to make the most profound legislation and policies that govern minority populations. They point out that the stock market crash ended the Harlem Renaissance in one stroke, so marginalized were the writers. Black intellectuals, including novelists, must seek to influence those in power to have a vested interest in black women's cultural production as a whole, while continuing to satisfy the desires of the traditional white and black readerships. What these respondents would like, along with narratives that represent career women protagonists, is very serious critique of the accuracy of the representation of the women characters, and to what extent the portrayals restrict or empower black women. One lawyer comments: "I couldn't go into a court of law and quote a novel as scholarship worthy to defend my case. I am better served on a professional level by the scholarship that results from intellectual discussions on these works. We need both kinds of texts: the narrative and the critique."

The respondents are echoing, in a different vein, Michele Wallace's concern. She sees the remarkable success of recent novelists as a kind of bittersweet experience. The novels are focused on black women, which is valuable in itself. However, because a very large amount of black women's intellectual production is fiction, the black novelists must articulate their experiences in "allegorical and coded language." The problem is due to racism. Because black women are marginalized to begin with, their texts can be doubly marginalized due to audience reception. Thus, black women's fiction narrows the scope black women scholars can use to develop theories regarding human behavior within specific cultures.[29] Fortunately, the novels' crossover appeal is beginning to have a positive effect on some readers outside the black community as well.

Black women writers themselves want fiction about the black professional woman, but they do not report these narratives as crucial, as the other cultural consumers do. They read for fun, for a knowledge of the market, and for the techniques others use. Nancy Flowers Wilson explains that she looks for the "'old' in the 'new'" or the idea that has been "hazily circling in her brain." Another writer-reader comments that she reads novels about the black professional woman because that is what the black cultural consumers want the most. By staying current, she can avoid taking an angle in her presentations that others have already used.

Furthermore, black women want novels with career protagonists because they love good stories, especially ones that tell about themselves. One woman writes: "It's simply a pleasure to read a scene that is similar to your own experience." The readers want intriguing characters and interesting plots that allow them to "lose [the] self in a fantasy world." Realistic fiction is, after all, a world of make-believe, and even though the novel will recognizably represent the black community with its pleasures and pain, a novel's primary goal is to entertain its audience.

Women readers of all racial groups seem particularly attracted to stories that incorporate romance into the novel. Alain de Bottom suspects that there is a connection between unfulfilled love and literature. He finds that books speak to us as passionately as our lovers; therefore, literature about love is a good substitute when our own love life disintegrates. He quibbles that although love may be good for our physical well-being, unhappiness best serves the publishing companies as well as the continuation of novels.[30] The need for the novel to end happily is partly responsible for the success of Terry McMillan's books. In her stories, the conflicts are pleasurably resolved. Many women, unable to find lasting, fulfilling relationships, seek that fulfillment in fantasy. One respondent remarks: *"How Stella Got Her Groove Back* sold in the millions because Terry told women that love was possible if they were willing to break conventions, such as the ban on marrying younger men."* The desire for protracted, passionate romance is rarely sustained at a continuously high peak in real life, so readers come back for the next novel. Not all readers respond positively to romance stories, but many women writers incorporate romance as an important aspect of their texts.

I was pleasantly surprised with one response to the questionnaire: "Black women want the books because they give us the satisfaction of knowing that they exist." The comfort level of having one's own cultural watershed to drink from at will, and of knowing that the source's intent is to offer intellectual and emotional sustenance, is in itself cause to linger and invite the soul and senses to savor those hours spent reading.

Black women readers insist that novels representing autonomous black professional women in the marketplace must become readily available. The demand is palpable. These books must offer literary truth about black women's lives so they will have longevity. Presently, many middle-class professional women identify with the characters in very limited ways. They become very critical of texts they feel do not represent them accurately. Unlike other groups in the United States, the negative images of black women have a staying power that is difficult to counter. So in one sense, these novels with professionals in them are wonderful stories for the women to enjoy. On the other hand, they resonate on the visceral level, that "nerve cutting" edge of what they perceive themselves to be as opposed to how the media often profile them. The portrayal of black professional women, then, is not just a story or an abstraction; it is a way to self-identity for some readers. The representation of the protagonist exercising a high level of agency allows for not only the enjoyment of the texts, but makes possible a heritage for future generations of readers.

~ Two ~

Craft and Culture: Challenges to Black Professional Women's Representation

There is a market for novels that represent black professional women exhibiting agency in the workplace; however, there is not a corresponding supply. Impatient readers could find the paucity of such novels irritating since writers of romance and other popular genres often churn out a novel a year. Even though they understand that romance writers follow a formulaic pattern, they may still have difficulty understanding the lag between publications of these realistic texts. One reason for the scarcity is, crafting these novels superbly to accent the subjects realistically poses several challenges for the writer. This chapter discusses some creative issues that directly relate to the writing of the narratives.

The problems inherent to the craft of writing that black women novelists encounter fall into three categories. The first difficulty comes from the theoretical constraints of the act of composing. The second relates to sensitive issues about black women that are reflected in the lives of professional protagonists. These characters with multilayered psychology require not only keen insights, but also the language necessary to avoid re-enacting stereotypes or sentimentalizing them. The third relates to the sociology and the historical moment of the writer, particularly the knowledge base from which the composer invents her characters. The writer may want to respond favorably to the desires of her readership, but may not be able to fulfill their expectations as regularly as they anticipate.

One dimension of difficulty in producing more novels that represent the black career woman is technical. Writing itself is a very complicated task because it involves metacognitive processes that do not always allow the writer complete control over the finished product. As the writer records the ideas, the mind behaves like a little inquisitive child who goes for a walk with her parent. The bundled-energy youngster surges forward to explore an interesting sight ahead, then returns to the parent's side to ensure all is well, then lags behind to examine some object(s) she thinks she has missed, then once again she bounds ahead—loitering long enough to enjoy a quaint discovery, before heading off to seek yet some new adventure.

Similarly, while an idea is being recorded, the mind leaps ahead, forcing the writer to keep the writing progressing, then retraces its steps, compelling the eye and hand simultaneously to analyze what is being written. Then the mind darts in multiple directions expanding the idea, thus enriching the text and allowing further progression of the work. Some ideas are epiphanies; others seem so illusively transmitted that if not instantly snatched and recorded, airy-like they fade into the fairyland from which they came. Others are gems, but the conceptual iridescent jewel—the ideal gem in the mind—resists and often eludes the naming word. Theoretically, although the writer begins with an idea, during the creative writing process the script takes on a life of its own, for the mind is busily engaged with imagining other scenarios, occupied with issues of intertextuality, and remembering events other than the one being recorded. The writer must synthesize all these operations as well as continue recording the text. Therefore, although the novelist makes an effort to exercise some level of control over the manuscript, the end product does not necessarily replicate the original plan.

The writer of realistic fiction who deliberately attempts to harness every stage of the writing may become frustrated and may find the work forced. Terry McMillan encountered such a predicament when writing *Waiting to Exhale*. Originally, she created one of the characters as biracial (African American–Chinese). However, she ran into difficulty "because I was trying too hard with the Chinese part of it, to show these mixed cultures."[1] She eventually edited the chapter and published it as a short story. The mind must be allowed to play its games; consequently, a writer does not know how a character will act until it is given rein to develop itself when placed in a certain environment. Responding to the paradoxical question of whether a novelist can effectively control the ideas in her work, writer Diane Johnson comments that when the characters are allowed to evolve on their own, they unfold in such remarkable ways that the writer is surprised at the outcome.[2] Additionally, journalist Roseleen Brown reports that she cannot know beforehand how her characters will respond in the midst of conflicts or solve their dilemmas.[3] Thus a novelist's original intent to portray a black professional woman may not come to fruition in a particular text.

Even when the writer controls the material without doing damage to the manuscript, the topic must be one she finds engaging. That is, it must resonate profoundly with her, impelling her to tell her tale. Rarely is a novel completed in a few months. Zora Neale Hurston's masterpiece, *Their Eyes Were Watching God*, is one of the few exceptions. Writer Maureen Howard explains that writing is not about the euphoria of a first love. Rather, "It is like a long marriage." It is about fortitude, ardor, wearisomeness, and a compelling drive.[4] Many readers are to be reminded that a novelist usually lives with her characters for two years or more. The successful novelist loves the creative process involved in writing, but the long hours invested in the production of novels are lonely and often frustrating. In *When People Publish*, fiction writer Frederick Busch comments that writing is the most difficult job he knows except loving another person.[5] Because of the time and effort required to create an excellent novel, the writer can only derive pleasure in writing if a subject is significant to her.

A writer's selection of topic is neither always randomly nor freely chosen as readers often think. One cardinal rule of writing is that most writers write best what they know. This "knowing" is identical to acquiring information gathered at the library and storing it in one's long-term memory, so it can be reproduced for an examination or business meeting. The writer must become so acquainted with the knowledge that she has a playful familiarity with it. Novelists must transform their personal experiences imaginatively into realistic fiction. Fred Chappell, when asked where does one begin a novel, replies that the choice depends on the particular genre. One may begin with a "central idea, a philosophic notion ... a visual imagery ... a memory of a character, some from—hell ... from personal experience."[6] The self is like a constant, and that self can interpret events and experiences, whether they are internal or external, only as the self perceives them. Busch, after analyzing the novels of various genres by famous novelists such as Charles Dickens, Herman Melville, and Sir Arthur Conan Doyle (unfortunately, no females included), comes to the conclusion that "the narrator is a side of that writer, partly his shaping spirit, who organizes the telling of the story of the storyteller."[7] The novelist writes the self.

Upon examination, we see a similar pattern in the novels of some black female writers who write about the black professional woman. In Paule Marshall's works, for example, the impact of Marshall's absentee father foreshadows a missing father or father figure in most of her texts. Marshall claims that the conflict Ursa, her protagonist in *Daughters*, has with her father, Primus McKenzie, is an attempt to resolve her own difficulty with her father's abandonment of her as a child, though in a transformed manner.[8] If novelists are comfortable and engaged by the professional scene, they are more likely to create characters from this group.

Another tier of difficulty associated with the fictive subject of the black professional woman having agency in the workplace is that the writer is working with a portrait that for many women, and here particularly black women, is still in the process of being defined. Are women primarily home-makers and mothers and secondarily professionals, or are they able to effectively harmonize the roles? Many women may avow that they are career women first. However, if one measures the amount of time, including tho-ught time, that these persons, especially mothers, spend with childcare, part-ner-care, house-care, and even pet-care, the results challenge the notion of the career as primary. Both personal and public life are important for the well-being of the individual, but unlike most professional men, women are inordinately subjected to the private sphere. Consequently, the women often experience role confusion.

Sometimes the confusion is attributed to the disparity between stated social values and actual practice. For instance, psychologist Erik Erikson suggests, "Childbirth is woman's 'labor' and accomplishment."[9] However, the work force does not privilege motherhood. It is difficult for women to successfully integrate this incongruity. An identity is not a ready-made entity; rather, it is forged over time through a gradual "accruing" of the self-image that one's society allows.[10] Since black career women in large numbers became a cultural phenomenon just one generation ago, there are still conflicts about what the black professional woman's role is, and how the different aspects can function harmoniously to create a professional iden-tity. Writing the black professional woman protagonist is very difficult, for some women are in the process of defining themselves.

Another area related to the writer's craft is the issue of self-love. No reader can deny that McMillan's How Stella Got Her Groove Back is playfully narcissistic since the writer delightfully incarnates the life of her protago-nist, Stella, in marrying a young Jamaican male. Busch suggests that some writers are self-lovers more than lovers of their characters or their audience. He suggests that art allows many opportunities for the artist to "mak[e] love to oneself; writing can be frictive as well as fictive." The writer must be con-scious to maintain a delicate balance when fusing autobiography and the imagination in order to produce real art.[11] Although McMillan's delightful self-love in her fourth novel brought her fame and fortune, her second novel, Disappearing Acts (1989), brought a $4.75 million lawsuit from her former lover, Leonard Welch. He argued that several parallels exist with his life and that of the character Franklin, and that readers could associate him with the fictive persona. The case was dismissed because the most damaging behaviors were not representative of the plaintiff.[12] However, the episode showed the delicate interface between life and art.

A writer of realistic fiction is not strictly controlled by what she liter-ally knows. A novel is not history; it is imagined truth. A writer may invent a novel character or event, yet her frame of reference is partly lodged in the experiences she has had. Indeed, she can describe what she sees in her mind's eye, but she will often only superficially catch the nuances of the subcul-ture of someone who lives in a class different from the novelist. In her writ-ing she is thinking, she is being; therefore, how the black woman writer views, approaches, selects, and even fears her subject matter determines the final outcome. If she cannot seamlessly effect a transformation between the knowledge she has gleaned in her research and her imaginative rendition of it, then the texture of the text will have a disconnect. Every successful writer takes chances and pioneers into unknown territory, but only some effect a believable transformation.

Successful novelists also have a good eye for details. They delightfully capture the misused words, look of contempt, touch of elegance, raw humor (as the occasion warrants), a graceful stride, or a painful moment. One such moment occurs in *The Edge of Heaven* (1999). A husband leaves his wife because he is threatened by the high level of agency she exhibits in her career, and he is yet to receive prominence in his field. He secretly applies for funding, and then leaves the family to further his career. After the acci-dental manslaughter of the child, he pushes for legal separation while his wife is in jail. She is eventually released, but the pain and guilt become unbearable, and she begins to neglect herself. The surviving teenage daugh-ter looks on as the father, who returns to visit and continues to remain with them after the funeral, attempts to bathe the mother. She reports: "My father sat on the toilet, holding my mother's body in an awkward yet res-olute embrace. I saw no pity, no affection on my father's face. My mother could have been a stranger he'd rescued from the side of the road. I turned from my father's impassive stare."[13] While acknowledging the vividness and forcefulness of the language, the reader may be disturbed by the subject mat-ter and wonder why a black novelist describes such an ugly scene between a black man and a black woman that will be made public. The novelist is vindicated because making reality palpable through details is the writer's task.

In addition to the constraints the novelist encounters with the techni-calities, there is the psychological challenge facing black women writers. Along with representing the successes of the black professional protagonist that reflect the lived lives of career women, a writer must also explore some sensitive areas that impact them. In *The Edge of Heaven*, Marita Golden's teen protagonist is asked by her mother what it was like for the girl while the mother was away in prison. The protagonist's aside is, "I have discovered, you don't tell because you can't. You lived it. And that is more than enough."[14] The naïve teen narrator's inability to articulate her experiences is acceptable to the reader. However, the novelist has to work through the pain and write that story of taboo, that of a black professional woman responsible for the death of her young daughter, albeit unintentionally.

One of the most difficult areas to represent sensitively is how black career women may sabotage their own success in the workplace. Not many would challenge that the principal factor contributing to a significant number of black women's lack of financial success is external oppression from the economic and political systems. Arthur Ashe relates that because he was often the only black in certain social settings, he became fully aware of the behavior that blacks refer to as "racial 'tipping.'" He explains, "In many white circles, blacks are accepted as an element only if they comprise a certain small percentage of the people involved. Beyond that number, the presence of blacks threatens whites, the organization or group begins to lose whatever cachet it formerly enjoyed, and a sense of doom taints the atmosphere." In other words, "We African Americans are perceived as acceptable in a token amount, toxic beyond it."[15] He notes that the practice can be seen in housing. Fortunately, this behavior is changing, but black women still face challenges in the job market. Of course, all people, to some extent, sabotage their potential for greater success in several ways. However, the subject is here discussed because black women's marginalization highlights this behavior, and because this work concerns black professional women as represented in fiction. One important aspect of this topic will illustrate the dilemma.

Women writers, in presenting characters, often find it necessary to confront the childhood socialization of girls, which sometimes conditions women to prescribed modes of behavior. As professionals, though they acquire high levels of education and professional status, they often reenact these gendered roles. Some aspects of female childhood acculturation are not conducive to continued significant success in the corporate world for the individual or for the collective selves of black career women. These behaviors are quite complex, and the writer needs a very keen awareness of the social dynamics to create characters that reconstruct these behaviors. No novel can highlight all the potential ways black career women may inadvertently hinder their progress; however, by scripting how the thought, life, and actions of the protagonist impact her well-being, the novelist examines some of these moments of self-sabotage.

To understand how black professional women may repeat negative behaviors compulsively, it is necessary to consider how we learn. Psychologists Hockenbury and Hockenbury give us an intriguing overview of some theories of learning. One is that we learn through our senses by responding to stimuli from our environment. The brain recognizes and processes the stimulant and matches it against experiences, while simultaneously receiving new experiences. However, sensory experiences do not automatically become a part of our learning. Most of these stimuli are fleetingly recognized and then discarded. When the brain determines that certain information is significant enough to benefit the individual's survival and pleasure, or if the person actively repeats the behavior, then the brain stores and classifies the data first into short-term memory, and after extended meaningful exposure, into long-term memory. This process includes not just facts and skills, but also social encounters and the circumstances under which they occurred. One of the problems with memory is that not all information can be easily accessed, but memory does influence behavior. When one retrieves memory, it is reconstructed memory, and so some important details are lost. The reconstructed retrieved memory is susceptible to distortions, especially if a schema—the habitual way of understanding events or situations—interferes with re-memory, or if suggestions from reading, watching a movie, incidents, or words of the media are viewed as a part of one's experiences.[16]

In addition to raw data, one's emotional makeup—the unconscious and subconscious—factors into how one behaves, and becomes a strong driving force behind one's actions. How we respond in childhood, for instance, to certain places, words, and actions; how we observe significant others responding to similar situations; or how we create our imaginative worlds depends significantly on our temperament. Today many thousands of black women have earned middle-class status, and at an intellectual level can eloquently articulate their desires for agency, success, and wealth. However, on the emotional level that often propels their actions, some of the behaviors learned in a working-class environment, though valuable in themselves, do not have a one-to-one correspondence to what is required or preferred in the corporate workplace. This is true because some of their deepest and most valuable knowledge is forged in childhood, and is lodged in their long-term memory. On the other hand, much of this information is quite priceless.

Ruth Simmons, president of Brown University, remarks that although her parents were sharecroppers and her mother did other people's laundry, their high regard for themselves, others, and work well executed taught her as a child to respect herself, others, and her career. Her mother's strong work ethic, evidenced for instance in how she scrupulously ironed around buttons on garments, taught her a respect for details, hard work, aplomb, and magnanimity, attributes necessary for success as president of an ivy league university. She notes that some young people lack the nurturing and sense of "communal membership" she received.[17] The results is an undisciplined lifestyle that allows for less desirable cyclic behavior.

Certain components of home life could be perceived as constraining to black professional women. I chose the issue of single parenting because the two novelists used in this text addressed that subject. In *The Salt Eaters,* Bambara, while addressing the problems within the nuclear middle-class family, mentions teen pregnancy and single parenting. McMillan's *Waiting to Exhale* emphasizes the issue by having one upper-class and two middle-class protagonists as single parents. Many women writers question whether they need to consistently depict the nuclear family as the only ideal structure that can represent the black professional woman's household as being healthy, financially secure, and fulfilling. These novelists reflect contemporary reality. In 1995, there were 8.1 million black families in the United States. Women headed forty-six percent of these black family households,[18] either by necessity or by choice. In these family arrangements, there is traditionally a pattern of extended family, which usually provides a sense of security and support for its members. In the majority of these homes, children are happy and their physical and emotional needs are met, despite the absence of one parent. This family pattern is not deemed appropriate by mainstream America, although today there are more single headed households in all racial groups in the United States than nuclear ones.

The novelists, in their attempt to provide clues as to what may sabotage the goals of their protagonists, must be careful not to fall prey to societal schema they have internalized as the norm: that of a mother, a father, and 2.5 children. In a disproportionate number of homes, the mother is the primary source of stability: financially, emotionally, and educationally. Admittedly, the same gendered parent can make the transition into adulthood easier for the young girl, and if professional, can establish a trend of a professional lifestyle. However, the mother's role in the home may condition the girl to be less professional than she could be in adult life. Even though the mother is professional, the child sees less of her parent functioning in her career role than as homemaker. After school pickup, mother rarely speaks of the chemistry breakthrough she presented at a conference; rather, she is concerned with domestic responsibilities such as events at school, homework, and stopping at the local grocery. Additionally, these mothers are frequently financially strapped because despite their high salaries, the relationship with their ex-husbands or fathers of their children, especially in terms of child support and enrichment, is often adversarial. Most are chronically exhausted, for in addition to taking care of the family, the black community makes excessive demands on them. Whether the mother is paraprofessional or professional, the adult black career woman today watched her mother share a disproportionate amount of parenting, homemaking, and charitable concerns.

The second generation of women from the mid–'90s to the present, though more professionally and economically advanced, could follow a familiar path. Many of them have little time for professional activities. The potential young black professional woman who has watched her mother's overextendedness for twenty years has it firmly etched in her consciousness. She decidedly does not want to be like her mother in such a capacity; she desires options that are more contemporary. She may even resent her mother. Nevertheless, unconsciously her mother's image becomes the primary model from which she patterns her behavior, unless there is some outside intervention. Therefore, she follows the pattern without being fully conscious of the behavior.

A potential behavior of sabotage to this young woman's chances of success in the corporate arena is here given. A sexually developing young woman may subconsciously find the schema of the extended family (offering care of children) a solution should she become pregnant. She has heard discussions of single households operating with the extended family as African in origin. Furthermore, many of the homes she knows are single-headed ones, and they appear to the onlooker to be perfectly functional. Additionally, her peers may argue that their sexual behavior is of their own choosing and not to be dictated by puritanical standards to which preachers themselves do not adhere. Consequently, she allows herself to be pressured into unprotected sex or she occasionally chooses to be careless in her lovemaking, and thus she produces a child before she is fully able to responsibly shoulder family concerns. Erikson, in discussing the Freudian concept of "repetition compulsion," suggests that certain behaviors seen as "mistakes" are unconsciously yet deliberately contrived because the individual alone cannot change his environment.[19]

What is overlooked here is, the professional world of this young woman has changed in significant ways from her mother's. Professional women are staying longer in the work force since the retirement age increases to correlate with their longevity. The extended family support the daughter has observed previously offered by grandparents may not be so readily available. Furthermore, in the Information Age where one's skills, not one's loyalty to a firm, are preferred, and in a market where mobility is privileged, a single young professional black woman with an infant is often perceived as a liability by her company. Since the black community suffers to some degree from fatherlessness, this young woman's chances of having a father who is highly professional remain in the home and support his youngster until the child completes the undergraduate curriculum is lessened. Furthermore, fewer women who get pregnant before marriage, marry. Because of her home environment, the young professional may compulsively re-enact her mother's lifestyle, even though on the intellectual level she resists the difficulty of the single parent household.

Even if this young potential career black woman in an extended household is offered assistance (and sometimes it is not to the degree the young woman imagined), she cannot concentrate on her career single-mindedly as will her competitive peers in the marketplace. Funds that could be budgeted for professional activities are directed to childcare. Time needed for mandatory overtime and professional socialization must be sacrificed. Energies necessary for dealing with new procedures and technological advances, conflicts, and difficulties in the workplace are diverted to child rearing. The mother, though loving and wanting her child, must also deal with the feeling of having behaved impulsively. This professional woman will experience much frustration both at home and on the job.

Herein lies the difficulty for the black woman writer. How will she present the desire for children by black professional women, most of whom are single and will remain single for the rest of their lives? How does the writer define the black professional woman having agency in the marketplace as compatible with single motherhood? The novelist has to be forthright yet sensitive to the issue. Pregnancy is not a crime or an immoral act, but it does carry its own peculiar burdens and joys. During difficult moments of parenting, the mother may feel the hardships outweigh the happiness that children bring, especially if the income is sufficient only for the basic needs. If the mother chooses to privilege motherhood over her career, she may at a later date acquire the educational or professional training she needs; however, because she received it later than her peers, she probably will not have financial parity in areas such as retirement investments. Even if she does, it will cost her pecuniarily much more than her counterparts. Representing the potential for sabotage of one's career in light of the communal experience of single parenting in the black community is difficult, for it could be interpreted as a rejection of the lifestyle of the mother figure in past generations. It is a complex balancing act that some black women have not resolved in their lives.

For a successful professional woman to aver that she does not want children is sometimes looked at with askance. In *The Edge of Heaven* (1999), Golden deals with the problem masterfully. Her professional woman, Lena, debates with her husband, who desires a second child: "How would I handle another baby, Ryland? I'm swamped at work. But I don't want to give it up. There's no time for a baby." Her statement is interpreted by her husband to mean that she has no confidence in his ability to someday become a successful artist and contribute to the finances of the household. He then pressures her into fulfilling his desires. As a result, "She willed herself to forget the lies that day," and she acquiesces. But while having unprotected sex with her husband, she is questioning herself about the potential outcome: "Could she love another child?"[20] However, it is Ryland's later abandonment of the family that precipitates the death of that unwanted youngster. One questions whether Ryland wants a child or rather the destruction of his wife's successful career, which overshadows his. Ironically, Lena was raised by her mother, and although she is a professional and married at one point, the choice she makes, contrary to her better judgment, contributes to her becoming a single mother. Representing how characters negotiate this difficult yet important role of motherhood is vital, for it is one of the most crucial factors that impede a woman's reach for agency on the job, and readers who share the privileging of motherhood may reject the character.

The potential danger of repetition compulsive behaviors offers black women writers fertile ground for imaginative work. Although a difficult area to fictionalize, if oiled with gentle humor or irony, it offers different levels of awareness that could reduce potential resistance some readers have toward the writer's angle of representation. Many readers say they want realistic fiction that captures the black professional woman in the workplace, but they may not be fully aware that for the protagonist to function as an autonomous and successful black woman in mainstream America, the character has to shed some compulsive habits and behaviors that resonate quite powerfully with them. This discussion does not suggest that the writer needs to become didactic. However, her insights into human psychology, particularly how infantile experiences affect adult behaviors, enable her to recognize that transactional analysis (the understanding of the dynamics of power relations that occur during human interaction) realistically shows the complexity and struggle of integration of the self.[21]

In addition to the technical problems of writing and the delicate handling of certain topics, a third major component of difficulty relates to the novelist's craft. It involves the milieu of the writer. Books are not written in a vacuum. All writers are shaped by the socioeconomic backgrounds of their families and the communities in which they live and work. Particularly, the environment determines the knowledge base the novelists can access in creating scenes and character portrayals. A limited exposure in itself may not restrict the richness of the text a good writer produces, provided she stays within the world she knows. If she moves into a less familiar social structure, it becomes more difficult to capture the subculture: the manners, the mannerisms, the esoteric language, the flair, the nuances, and the gestures effortlessly displayed by the in-crowd. Fortunately, for some black women writers, grants, research and writing fellowships, and income tax deductions make the accessing of information much easier than thirty years ago. Still, many black women novelists do not have the means for extended research. Many implications may be drawn from this dilemma.

Few of the novelists now in their mid-thirties and older during their early childhood had parents who belonged to the ranks of the upper middle class. Most, therefore, had limited meaningful interaction on a regular basis with this segment of the community. It is safe to conclude that this group's exposure will be colored somewhat by lower middle class and working class attitudes, values, and interests. It is understandable that people the writers know best will be imaginatively transformed into characters in the fiction they produce, simply because they are the ones who will resonate more profoundly on a deep level with the writer. She can best depict their language, mannerisms, and their idiosyncrasies, for she has watched and listened to them for many years. This is a positive, for all peoples are equally valuable. As a girl, Paule Marshall listened to the colorful patois of her mother and West Indian friends as they talked in her mother's kitchen about different political and native island issues. In "Shaping the World of My Art," Marshall recounts some delightful conversations and portraits: "C'dear, how I could forget Eunice Ford from Rock Hall, and that woman had a face like an accident before it happens."[22] Only one of Marshall's five novels, *Daughters* (1992), represents the black professional woman protagonist as highly skilled, and Ursa exhibits limited agency in her career or private life until the very end of the text. However, a minor character, Vinney Daniels, is more representative of the autonomous black professional woman.

Ella L.J. Edmondson Bell and Stella Nkomo find, however, that the black professional women who are not from middle-class backgrounds have more difficulty initially adjusting to the administrative tiers of large corporations. They were not accustomed to the "associated indoctrination [of] the cultural and social conventions" operative within this group. One of their respondents comments that her middle-class background gives her an advantage since she is "conversant with the rules of success."[23] Interestingly, the rules of success here do not necessarily relate to ability or hard, innovative, or efficient work. One of my respondents humorously reports one such rule she observed on the job: "If thou shalt be so imprudent as to exceed they boss in any innovative task, thou shalt make sure that thy success is so presented as not to injure his ego, or thou shalt pay dearly and perpetually, so long as he remains thy supervisor." Fortunately, many managers welcome the productivity of all their employees, for it, in turn, boosts their chances of an even higher promotion. Real life experiences usually have a correspondence in art.

Many black women professionals today are twice removed from the center of power in the workplace: first, because they are women, and second, because they are black women. Therefore, these writers cannot appropriate the scene without difficulty. Few belong to the first tier of large international corporations of the major industries such as petroleum, automobile manufacturing, and telecommunications networks as advisors. In addition, the relative newness to and partial distance from the boardroom deny the frame of reference necessary to create the rich texture of a slice of Wall Street from an insider's view.

To get firsthand knowledge to write about a particular professional, a novelist can immerse herself in research until she gets not just the knowledge about a career, but a sense of the job culture as well. To acquire this new awareness, she must have the resources and the leisure to accomplish this task. Even then, she might encounter a dearth of resources and data available on black professional women. As late as the mid–1990s, folklorist Daryl Dance, in researching black women's humor, argues that although the data on humor is abundant in America, black women's humor is ignored. She concludes, "Insofar as treatments of humor are concerned, all the Americans are male WASPs, all the women are white, and all the African Americans are men."[24]

Admittedly, substantial material on black women in general has been produced through the collaborative work of black and white feminists. One significant text is the 1998 edition of *Our Bodies, Ourselves for the New Century: A Book By and For Women.* The writers unequivocally state the negative impact of the intersection of race, gender, class, and ageism on black women and other minorities concerning areas such as health and sexuality, violence, economics, and the workplace. For example, the writers acknowledge that in corporate America, the very dark-skinned woman with pronounced African features has greater difficulty than white or fair-skinned women proving she has integrity, is efficient, and is intelligent. They also acknowledge the difference on very micro levels, such as women of color having more back ailments since they are delegated jobs that require them to lift heavier weights than other women.[25] The search for knowledge on black women, therefore, has made considerable strides since the 1970s, when the information known about them was mostly the stereotypes perpetuated to deny the agency in their personal lives and in the workplace.

Despite the progress made, not enough research on black professional women's lives exists. Concerns such as the unique problems these professionals face in corporate America, the strategies that work best in the corporate arena, and the non–job related skills that are privileged for survival at the top levels need to be collected and analyzed. One text, *Work, Sister,*

Work: Why Black Women Can't Get Ahead and What They Can Do About It (1993), addresses some areas of which black women need to be more aware. It reminds black professional women that they must articulate their goals, plan their career paths, become "cooperate street smart" (that is, know where the center of power lies), get in touch with the major players of the game, and understand the dynamics of power politics.[26] The tone is energetic and functions to motivate black women to want to succeed in their careers.

Despite these observations, the text is primarily a "how to manual." For example, one of twenty-six recommendations in four and a half pages reads thus: "'Write Your Own Ticket': Toot your own horn. Look for ways to put more power in your own hands or to put you next in line on the corporate ladder. You don't have to be nominated to get your name on the ballot. Lobby for positions that you want. Create a new job for yourself."[27] The text fails to adequately analyze the complexity of the corporate structure. It is glibly optimistic for one's success without actually giving the necessary advice as to the requirements, for example, of creating a job for the self in a multi-layered industrial complex. Few aspects could become problematic for black women. In a section on good grooming, the writers make obvious suggestions that one may occasionally forget, such as "no run-over heels," and "no dandruff showing in the hair." However, one of the "No No's" is *"No nappy roots or split ends"* (emphasis mine). The intent is positive; hair should be carefully coiffed. However, to refer to black women's natural hair as "nappy" reflects the same stereotype of the mainstream culture. Even more damaging is the fact that this information is placed in the same list as "No dirty laundry" or "No fly girl wear."[28] Despite its limitations, the text is one of the few that focuses on the professional woman in the corporate arena.

A recent and scholarly text, *Our Separate Ways: Black and White Women and the Struggle for Professional Identity* (2001), specifically addresses issues concerning black managerial women. Edmonson Bell and Nkomo argue that several texts discuss white professional women in Fortune 500 companies, but these works omit the successes, contributions, and problems of black women in the executive tiers. Their observation verifies my contention that very little scholarship exists that focuses on the representation and concerns of black career women. The Edmondson Bell and Nkomo's text illustrates that when studies are conducted on managerial women, black subjects remain "invisible." These professionals are subsumed under the categories of either "women" or "blacks, or minorities." Their book provides an in-depth assessment of areas such as the entrance adjustment period, the problems inherent in the tasks and the work culture, the factors affecting performance and criteria for evaluation, and the level of success achieved by black women executives.[29]

Many serious concerns impact black professional women in management; one is the obstacles to advancement. Persistent images of the racialized self adversely affect the promotion of highly qualified black women. They are prejudged incompetent to lead white men. The problem here is that from childhood, many white men and women learned from the behaviors they observed in their homes: black female maids receiving supervision. Stellar performance is interpreted as the "flower blooming in winter"— the exception to the rule, rather than the norm for those who receive quality training and job appointments. Thus, the stereotypes of black women as "incompetent and unqualified" remain unchanged.[30] The women are constantly bombarded by and with racism. When they are viciously and verbally abused by their peers in meetings or in social gatherings, their white counterparts either remain silent or pretend the attack is not racist. The perpetrator is excused or mildly reprimanded, and the lone woman is encouraged not to take action.[31] Nevertheless, the performance record of these career women denies the falsehood of black women as incompetent, even if they receive minimal recognition and reward.

Another management issue is the isolation the women experience. Edmondson Bell and Nkomo write that often they are the singular administrator in a very large department, so each woman rarely gets to know others of equal rank, or receive mentoring from other black women. Furthermore, black female managers and their work are scrutinized more scrupulously than their white colleagues. In addition, they are rarely invited within the inner social circles of their peers. Closely associated with the isolation is the hurdle of racial privilege—access to "resources, culture, and capital." White women must break through a glass ceiling, which is at least fragile enough to break. They can see what is on the other side, and are cognizant of what is required to penetrate the barrier. Black women must "climb over" a "concrete wall," which is not breakable, and is opaque. Worse, those on the inside are not even aware of their presence. The writers interviewed some company CEOs who revealed that they did not know these managers exist. Not surprisingly, in 1988 the researchers discovered that no black woman was included in the 25 top managers of large United States corporations. Equally important is the fact that a few of the black women administrators in interviews with the writers attest that it was neither their credentials, spectacular performance, nor company policies that allowed them to move up the ladder. Rather, it was "an individual" within these companies who acknowledged their hard work and who championed their cause, and so they were able to get the promotion they deserved.[32]

To survive successfully, the women in administration devise strategies to meet their goals. Some include working much harder than their peers, having more credentials and experience, sometimes minimizing the African American presence while maintaining a noticeable image of their racial self, being willing to change jobs or careers, and remaining in touch with their culture.[33] This study is seminal, and it suggests that black career women functioning at the professional level do have some amount of agency despite the problems they face.[34] It is these black professional women whom the novelists have difficulty representing, especially since the women in corporate America come from different classes and varied backgrounds.

Antecedent to the lack of information is the limited use the writers themselves can sometimes make of the data that is available in government, industry, technology, and sports. This handicap is partly due to the area of concentration the writers chose in college. Many novelists are trained in the fine arts—that is, in creative writing, drama, literature, music, English, and art—and a few in the social sciences. The graduation requirements include minimal hours in business and economics, technology, or the psychology of work, and no more than two courses in mathematics and the sciences are essential.

This wealth of knowledge outside one's discipline does not readily lend itself to possible inclusion in realistic fiction. How much astronomy, biology, human physiology, chemistry, physics, psychology of human relations, and command of the language of NASA must the writer know, for example, to convincingly capture Mae Jameson, the astronaut? How much knowledge of business valued at one billion,[35] mass communication, human psychology, as well as the ability to articulate, interview, and charm an audience over a twenty year period is necessary to understand what Oprah Winfrey does so as to render her artistically gratifying to the reader? How does one write of the Williams sisters, Venus and Serena, the first set of siblings in tennis history to win consecutive Grand Slams? Venus is the winner of four Grand Slams, the French Open, the U.S. Open, Wimbledon, and the Australian Open, and "by the end of the year [2002 she had] "a tour—leading eight titles and $3.9 million prize money." She is one of six females to "hold all four tennis major championships at the same time in the history of tennis."[36] Her sister, Venus, is a four-time Grand Slam winner and holds numerous gold medals. Venus is Number Two in the world of tennis, second only to her sister, who wears the accolade "the world's greatest tennis champion." Imagining protagonists of this caliber will require a significant amount of research and lived-in experience for a writer to become immersed into the culture of these professions. Understandably, novelists shy away from them.

One cannot deny that the issue of economics is operating here. Finely crafted novels usually take years to write, and every novelist is in competition since most publishers are concerned primarily with profit, not whether the text is formulaic or original. The black woman writer who wants to be true to her craft as well as produce texts at a rapid rate may find the challenge daunting. Yet, the reality of the situation requires her to transcend the difficulty, and so create meaningful texts on a fairly regular basis that entice her readers to wait hungrily for her next novel.

An equally important reason for the lack of novels representing the black professional woman having agency in her career and personal life is how much autonomy the writers themselves perceive the black career woman to have. The issue for some critics is whether a black professional woman can claim an authentic self in a culture where she has negligible control over production, social institutions, and the media. In many establishments, excellent work is just one requirement to upward mobility in corporate America. Many black women in higher management levels are outside the informal networks that allow for mentoring, sponsoring, and inclusion on projects that are necessary for advancement. Since, according to Edmondson Bell and Nkomo, at this level corporations function as a "fraternity;" being outside the buddy system excludes the women from entering the "armpit track," and consequently from the promotions they deserve.[37] Additionally, many of these women novelists are painfully aware that their own works are at the mercy of editors and what little influence the black community can exert on merged publishing conglomerates in terms of lobbying and purchasing power. Nevertheless, that the writers themselves are producers of culture argues for a certain amount of agency. Edmondson Bell and Nkomo indicate that of the midlevel management personnel they interviewed, 23 percent reported they were ahead of their expectations, 28 percent said they were where they expected, and *all* reported having achieved some measure of success.[38] Clearly, nearly 50 percent in this study is experiencing some difficulty, but a large number of women are claiming an authentic self and having security in their professions. They provide models for women writers.

Other issues are responsible for the lack of novels with autonomous black career women. Some black women writers have difficulty renouncing one stereotype that has been used to represent the black woman. I speak of the recurring image of the excessively strong black woman as overextended. Although the use of this image by black women writers was initially intended to praise black women for surviving slavery and maintaining their humanity, unfortunately it has contributed to black women's overextendedness. Critic Trudier Harris offers extensive critique on this issue.

Historically in the United States, the image of black women as being very large and as having big bosoms was invented by white writers who needed justification for slavery. She was asexual when serving as Mammy in the kitchen and as nurturer of whites, but excessively sexual when in the slave quarters. She supposedly tempted the white master to infidelity, although her actions were constrained and her movements controlled by her owners. In this scenario, the sexual abuse she endured was her fault, and therefore she was not entitled to any legal redress.[39] As "Other," she was unfeminine, that is, unlike the aristocratic white woman, the ideal. But Harris complicates the issue by illustrating that the image of the super strong black woman is also characteristic of African and African American literature. She is represented in some texts as the bearer of burdens: she walks very long distances with heavy loads on her head, fights in wars, cultivates fields, produces children, and serves extended families in large compounds. This portrayal of the African foremothers is intended to be positive, since except for duties that are biologically restricted, they are equal to men.

Harris argues that African American women writers wanting to critique the negative stereotypes of black women being less than their white counterparts as created by Euro-Americans, and wanting to replace them with strong women who can survive as their foremothers, are caught in a bind.[40] The pendulum appears to have shifted only in terms of who is serviced. The image of the black woman is that of a "tower of strength" that unites and protects the black community, resists the abuse of spouses and children, provides for the family primarily through domestic work, and supports the black church. Harris insists that black women writers collude with the white writers in presenting a false image of black women. Furthermore, she notes that both on stage and in film, the plump black woman becomes the desired figure. For instance, both Claudia McNeil (1959) and Esther Rolle (1995) who starred as Mama Lena Younger in A Raisin in the Sun were big women. Gospel singers such as Ethel Waters have the same physique. Harris believes that some black women themselves are now "soothed" by the image.[41]

Harris further believes the stylistic device of intertextuality provides a vehicle by which black women writers perpetuate the stereotype. As texts signify others, the image of the black woman as excessively strong has been perpetuated for one hundred fifty years. She concludes that black women writers seem invested in the image, and are unwilling to relinquish it since the myth of the foremothers appears to create a promise of future success. She suggests that the motif of excess strength needs to be re-evaluated.[42] Black women should not be represented as perpetual sacrificers.

Harris's critique underscores this text's concern with the representations and social customs that seduce black women to overextend themselves in the service of the black community, whether it is family, church, profession, or politics. It could be that the heroic efforts of black women, specifically career women, to remain competitive in corporate America are misread as the superwoman, but what is intended is focus on the additional expectations that prove overwhelming. Many executive-ranked black women credit their professional success to the legacy of perseverance and hard work they learned from other "strong" black women. Their "high resolve and resilience in the face of numerous obstacles ... their motivation and personal agency stemmed from distinct early life lessons and experiences."[43] A large number of these highly successful women paid a very high price (one woman gained 80 pounds and worked 110 hours a week for an extended period to finish her project on time) in seeking to prevent the establishment from signaling their performance, or lack thereof, as cause not to promote other black women.[44] The image of the overextended woman mitigates the creation of realistic novels with black women as professionals since few can maintain agency over protracted periods under these circumstances.

The scarcity of protagonists having a high level of agency is also due to some misgivings writers have about not representing the less fortunate. Dramatist and critic Alice Childress reports that, although she was encouraged to write about those who were winners in order to "inspire" others, she deliberately chose to portray the less fortunate and unsuccessful masses, because the well-popularized ones cannot be a substitute for the whole group.[45] A similar notion of writing about the less professionally and economically successful black woman is heard from feminist writers Gloria T. Hull and Barbara Smith. They argue that in the early phase of black women's studies, courses centered on celebrated "individual black women" such as Harriet Tubman and Sojourner Truth. They feel that focusing on the renowned few is the perpetuation of an historic elitist attitude that ignored and suppressed other equally talented persons within the group.[46] Because of the efforts of black women scholars and critics, today the experiences of black women from different economic and social classes have rightly found their place in the curriculum. Professor Cheryl Wall correctly asserts that our hierarchal society structured on race, class, and gender lines ensures that poor black girls are the weakest and are the most likely to be destroyed.[47] Hence, novels such as *The Bluest Eye* (1970) by the Nobel Prize winning author Toni Morrison are rendered brilliantly to make the world understand that these girls are valuable in themselves and their unjust plight worthy of being depicted in our finest literature. The dedication of these narrators and critics is vital to the struggle of seeking autonomy for all black women and by extension all people, as well as to remind the black readership of its history.

Perhaps another underlying reason for the paucity of novels with protagonists demonstrating self-empowerment on the job is operating here. Professor Sybil Lassiter suggests that in some circles, to be recognized as middle class is sometimes understood by some members of the black community "as a threat to the political progress of black people." If the media makes authoritative pronouncements about all blacks, "the black bourgeoisie and intelligentsia generally remain silent because disagreement might assign one the label traitor or 'Oreo.'"[48] As the 21st century progresses and more black women professionals enter the middle class, writers should feel comfortable representing this group as well.

Toni Morrison's earlier position on writing about one's job is instructive. In an interview with Anne Keonen, Morrison is asked if the protagonist in the novel she is writing has a job. (This interview took place in April 1980, so one can assume that the text being discussed is Tar Baby [1981].) Morrison's response is, "No. A job is not anything that stimulates anybody [emphasis mine] to write about it."[49] One must ask why not, especially since working outside the home, rather than inherited or amassed wealth, has been the primary means of black women's social mobility. The United States Commission on Civil Rights finds that work is a vital component to raise a black woman's financial status—even more so than her white counterpart— since the black woman's family's well-being is substantially dependent on her income.[50] Also, historian Elsa Barkley Brown confirms that traditionally, black women's wages were especially crucial to the economic stability of the black community, for it was their earnings that made possible the development of churches, mutual benefit societies, and eventually the banks.[51] In our contemporary society, black women find work outside the home equally imperative as did their parents and grandparents.

The importance of a job and the drama it provides are not synonymous. However, a job offers fertile ground for examining movement and drama or conflict within a character's life on the contemporary scene. Bebe Moore Campbell's Brothers and Sisters (1995) is a classic example, since the plot focuses primarily on the protagonist's work as regional bank manager and her goal of entering the lending department. Indeed, Morrison's latest novel, Paradise (1998), in which a character takes over her father's establishment after his death, suggests that Morrison is developing her range of concerns. Women as professionals are not the focus of the text, but the job is minimally represented when a schoolteacher at a church event reminds a student that he has an appointment with her about academic matters.

One of the reasons Morrison may look askance on the notion of a job as subject matter is her critical attitude of white middle-class work ethic itself. The willingness to work hard to achieve one's goal is not Morrison's contention. Morrison's achievements are quintessential for women nationally and internationally. Susan Willis agrees with Valerie Smith that Morrison's novels show middle-class life as usually alienated from the Southern black culture. Morrison articulates the lifestyle of the majority of her middle-class characters as problematic.[52] For instance, in *Song of Solomon,* the middle-class character, Malcolm Dead, is portrayed as insensitive and grasping. Morrison's critique of elitism and greed of upper-class blacks is valid, for many of them speak disparagingly of poor blacks and exploit them. What is of concern here is that there is not a happy balance of positive protagonists who are middle-class, financially secure, or happy with their jobs.

In his interview with Gloria Naylor, Charles Rowell raises the issue of a possible black middle class in the South and why no one writes about this group. Naylor acknowledges the brilliant literature of Ernest Gaines and Alice Walker, who wrote graphically of the poor, but she also proposes two reasons why novels about the middle-class Southern blacks is negligible. First, writing about black "roots" in the South is alluring precisely because it is the closest relationship African Americans have to the Motherland of Africa. Second, writers have become misguided into portraying the poor as the primary subject for colorful and dramatic representation. She adds, however, that there are other equally valid subjects, including the internal drama. It's not all about the "South"; and it is not all about "cotton."[53] One respondent in my survey observes: "Writers seem to prefer writing about the uneducated or the poor black women or those who are recovering from some type of adversity or trauma." Naylor's comment on romanticizing the South and the "folk" clearly identifies one reason why there are so few novels on the empowered black professional woman.

Another black female writer, bell hooks, romanticizes the poor South as the watering place of black culture. In *Sisters of the Yam: Black Women's Self-Recovery* (1993), she acclaims the South in passages with reference to "the culture of poverty that led to the development of a strong ethic of communalism among the black poor."[54] It is inspiring to learn that blacks in the South developed a ritual of communal support, and noteworthy that many African American writers are culturally associated with the South. However, within the text, hooks fails to emphasize the emergence and sustenance of black culture elsewhere in the country. Gloria Naylor comments that there is no monolithic black cultural experience. The black, poor Southern ethos has been made to seem as the "classic black experience." However, younger writers who grew up middle-class neither know nor care about it, but they too have valid insights about black culture.[55] All experiences provide fertile ground for the imaginative writer.

But there is still another reason to question this essentialist notion of where the seat of black culture resides. In *Fingering the Jagged Grain* (1985),

Keith Byerman reports that black "fiction also captures the fluid movement of ideas and forms that characterizes a folk culture which is radically different from systems that appropriate permanence to themselves." He identifies both "urban and rural" speech patterns, patterns not limited to the South, as a basic component of the black cultural art form. To perceive the working-class world of the South as the Mecca of black culture today is misguided. Byerman denies the essentializing of black experience, and argues instead: "Folk culture is antithetical to any rigid, absolute truths, particularly those that operate to exclude others."[56] Black women, professional and otherwise, have no greater champions than Morrison and hooks, and I acknowledge their aggressive stance on women's issues, as well as the agency evidenced in their very visible and successful careers. Fortunately, the emphasis earlier given the Southern black experience (which was true until to the Harlem Renaissance), and Morrison's comment on jobs as not an interesting enough subject for writing are being re-evaluated.

Another women's advocate, Angela Davis, having been in the trenches of the Civil Rights Movement, offers a different perspective. In *Women, Culture, and Politics*, she quickly identifies economic sufficiency as integral to empowerment, and discusses the factors that hinder the fiscal success of black women. She boldly declares that the political strategy to effect women's economic power must clearly involve resisting any form of capitalism that denies an equal playing field for all. Davis comments that economic consideration in literature may not be as crucial for white middle-class women and their children since their offspring are less likely to suffer from irreversible effects of poor nutrition due to their mothers' unemployment.[57] Davis emphasizes the need for well paying jobs for women. The topic of a "job" and upward mobility could be a subject for consideration for black female novelists. This work, however, appreciates that each writer responds to the environment differently and brings a unique perspective to the cultural heritage.

A few writers show that the temptation to relinquish what is positive in the black community (as professionals move into upper-middle class status) becomes very hard to resist, for the very physical location of their residence allows for fewer black neighbors than were present before the integration of housing. Bell hooks feels that because freedom was translated to mean having the culture and materialistic accumulation of mainstream America, those whose skin color most nearly approximates whites were the ones to benefit most educationally, financially, and socially. Blacks internalized this attitude and intra-ethnic racism was the result.[58] Paule Marshall, like Toni Morrison, expresses concern about the consumerist practices of the black middle class, as found in *Praisesong for the Widow* (1983), and the exploitation of the poor in *Daughters* (1992).

Even more troubling is the estranged relationship between people who have uprooted themselves from the urban black community, yet still want to politically control it. Bambara critiques this practice in *The Salt Eaters* when she presents Patterson living in the predominantly white suburbs, yet he wants to run for office to represent the black community. When the urban women insist on the domicile regulations for candidacy, he questions whether they are aware of their suggestion that he disrupt his middle-class roots in suburbia. Ruby, a civil rights activist, begins to laugh hysterically and to slap her thighs. She reminds him that the residential area in which he now resides was incorporated after he graduated from law school; then she sarcastically challenges him, "You. Did. Get. Out. Of. Law. School?"[59] Patterson expects the people in the 'hood' to obey his orders with alacrity and to do all the legwork primarily for his benefit.

Equally destructive is the way the media portray the poor without dignity. Hooks, echoing Cornel West, points out that mainstream society equates black poverty with nihilism,[60] though the two are not identical. One can be poor yet retain his self-respect and find his job meaningful in some ways, depending on how much freedom he has to use his creative talents, and if there is the opportunity for economic promotion. So to a certain extent, one can understand the hesitancy for black women writers to forthrightly represent the successful black professional woman, especially since some black women are among the poorest people in the United States. The value of Toni Morrison's and other writers' depictions of African American characters of all groups within the community cannot be overemphasized. In black women's euphoria for success, the novelists remind them of their valuable past and present, the lessons they have learned, and the values and pleasures they have shared as a group.

Despite the inherent dangers of assimilation to some who enter the middle-class ranks, I must ask, if not now, when are many contemporary black women to arrive at a sufficiently high economic level where they can enjoy elegant living? There is nothing inherently wrong with accruing wealth honestly gained. Conspicuous consumption is not implied here; rather, the issue is the right for black women to have wealth and the agency that accompanies it, and to have these women represented in fiction. Most black women and the vast majority of their ancestors have worked extremely hard. They deserve adequate monetary returns for their labor. I argue that black women are entitled to wealth. They have earned it just as others have. I will further argue that although one's job is not a spiritual reflection of who one is, one's professionalism is definitely a part of the composite self.

The concept of wealth synonymous to capital, equity, dividers, and retained earnings as opposed to taxable income from a job is particularly lacking in black women's fiction. Significant for one survey respondent, is the need for many blacks to capitalize on the monetary or otherwise, successes' of their parents and grandparents. She cites several instances in which individuals of her generation have not garnered significant returns on their inheritance. In a discussion, I asked a few women to comment on what they think is the writer's role in this transference and retention of property, or how it may be imagined. The first to begin the discussion notes:

> We need to begin the conversation by acknowledging that black women as a group, and as professionals as a sub-group, have the least amount of wealth in this country—Oprah excluded. We are the first generation to have moved beyond a very minuscule and select group to be able to leave a little property for our children. We are still a very small number. Nevertheless, we, this first generation, must begin now to lay the foundation for the next one. We must.

As to how this may be done with regard to the broader discussion, one participant suggests a novel showing wealth transfer through land ownership in a family for four or five generations, and how it continues to be economically rewarding and emotionally sustaining. Another visualizes parents so living that their children grow to understand—by a process of osmosis if you will—what money is and how it works. Perhaps parents could be seen playing bank, for instance, with a five year old daughter. Someone could initiate on a regular basis children's professional day where the daughter at the mother's law firm, for example, becomes the federal judge for a Saturday in court, or considers an amendment to a law now obsolete. Students in high school could be seen involved in creating their own Wall Street. Another suggests scenarios in which elementary through middle school Girl Scout troops make money from different avenues (in addition to making or selling cookies), thus avoiding stereotypes associated with woman as domestic.

The topic led to a discussion on the ability of girls. The participants insist girls and boys can learn ownership of property by having a bank account at a very young age and being made responsible for it. Thus in novels, students in a teacher's classroom can be depicted as vicariously appropriating the behavior of fiscal responsibility during several grades, thus learning early the pleasures that come with monetary success and finding it a natural behavior. The women feel novelists can represent parents adequately guiding their children to receive the inheritance they will bequeath them—that is, both cultural and financial capital—and see the offspring handle the legacy prudently in the text(s) despite occasional mistakes. The participants believe black novelists can raise the consciousness level of their readership to understand that one avenue to wealth is inheritance, and to

understand how property is transmitted, without the text becoming dog-
matic or a sociological treatise.

Some women claim that acquiring wealth is not a priority in their lives,
nor is it a goal they have set for their children: "They just want to have their
daily needs met." One participant heard a woman caution about becoming
"greedy, for the love of money is the root of all evil." When she asked the
speaker if she knew anyone who did not love money, after hedging for a few
minutes, the woman admitted she did not. The participant then helped her
companion to understand that "desiring and enjoying wealth honestly gained
is not synonymous with greed, but murdering individuals and whole nations
in the name of God for profit is rapacity." A fear of ownership of wealth
seems to lurk somewhere in the recesses of many women's minds, possibly
because as a group, they are not accustomed to owning or controlling much
money. I suspect that the fear of never acquiring wealth is disguised under
the cloak of not desiring it. Oprah Winfrey's billion-dollar empire is beginning to dislodge, in the minds of many black women, especially the younger
generation, the notion of being satisfied with just adequate funds. The topic
of owning wealth is particularly important for a female readership, both
minorities and mainstream, for traditionally women have been taught less
than men to value capital.

An emerging group of writers in the mid–1990s is at least not denying
the desire for a good income. Younger black woman novelists, including
Terry McMillan, do not find it difficult to embrace the comforts of wealth.
Darryl Pinckney writes that McMillan's four female protagonists in *Waiting
to Exhale* feel entitled to material rewards, having earned them. Black women
do not feel guilty about promotions as they once used to; now they vie for
prominent positions through hard work and credentials. A comfortable
lifestyle is not perceived as harmful to their spiritual well-being. He adds,
"Doubts about having sold out when they get promotions belong to the
pre–Anita Hill era. A condo or a Cherokee is no obstacle to having soul."[61]
Wealth affords agency. It is not the only contributing factor to autonomy,
but it would be hypocritical to deny that wealth is power.

The discussion led the participants to address another feature of women's
financial behavior as it relates to the agency women exhibit. Although the
issue of retained earnings is usually discussed in relation to class and race, I
present it as a women's issue. Many middle-class women of parenting age
tend to focus on what their children and family need in the present and what
the youngsters need throughout the college years, but little attention is given
to building an inheritance to be passed generationally. This may be because
the average family income is sufficient only for these needs.

Yet, a very recent trend is emerging. Traditionally, women have invested conservatively while men took more chances and often became enormously wealthy. The Yankelovich Partners, under the auspices of Microsoft, conducted a survey on women's investment practices. The authors note that women describe themselves as "bargain hunters," while the men present themselves as "risk takers." In analyzing the women's behaviors, the report suggests that women "set out to reach financial goals through practical methodologies," for women are in a singular position financially. Compared to men, they have greater longevity, receive less salary, and often do not receive a pension.[62] A few women, such as Oprah Winfrey, have become icons of creating wealth.

What seems fascinating are the potential ways women novelists, minorities and mainstream, may begin envisioning not just the first or second generations, but the *seventh* generation in terms of inherited wealth. Such a dynasty could create an ideology of wealth capable of sustaining a generational hold on property with the descendants developing sensitivity to the changing economic landscape. The text could challenge the belief in the sanctity of wealth when its corollary entails the destruction of others; yet not deny the reality of competition. What may also be interesting is the beginning of a legend, a legend that will eventually become epic in which the acceptance of wealth by women and the value of human beings are dramatized. The women participants in this discussion hope a few novelists will fancy the necessity of retained earnings as staple in some narratives.

Readers cannot tell novelists where or on what to focus their creative energies, but writers can provide a healthy balance by representing all segments of the black community in fictive texts. Some respondents claim it would be a good start, just depicting a sizable number of empowered black female protagonists doing their work successfully in upper-tiered positions, and happy in their lives outside the workplace. Furthermore, writer Bebe Moore Campbell suggests that it is vital that a significant number of minority executives be in the senior position in the marketplace for the group to continue to have credibility.[63] A new paradigm seems appropriate.

The factors that deal with the actual writing of the novels that could possibly hinder the creation of texts about the black professional female protagonist having a high level of self-empowerment in the workplace are varied and complex. Different writers may not experience the same combination of these problems in the writing of a particular novel, but at some point in their career, they will have to negotiate some of these difficulties that accompany their craft. When they have successfully negotiated this tier of difficulty, another awaits them: the external factors associated with the production of a novel.

~ THREE ~

Production and Market: Social Challenges

As we have seen, factors that directly affect the actual writing of a text significantly determine the outcome of a novel. Such constraints appear daunting but for the writers' persistence and resilience. Several external factors that a novelist cannot individually control intersect with the production of narratives, and these contribute to the paucity of texts that represent the autonomous black career woman.

Until the 1980s, there were few professional women in the job market who could serve as role models. Today the workplace allows for greater participation in high profile positions, but the economic lag between black women and other, privileged groups slackens the rate at which professionals are trained, hired, and rewarded. *The Economic Status of Black Women: An Exploratory Commission on Civil Rights* (1990) presents a broad overview of how black women have fared in the marketplace and a consequent reason that few black professional women were available to writers as models in the 1960s and '70s. The authors note that black women face discrimination because of racism and sexism, and that they, like their foremothers, have been denied equal chances as whites in areas of education and jobs. Equally significant, they do not usually receive equal pay for the work they do.[1] Although extremely valuable, the study fails to name another interlocking area of oppression black women encounter: class discrimination that has its roots in the 19th century.

Because black slave women were not a part of the cult of true womanhood in the 1800s, they were not seen as fragile beauties who needed the care, provision, and protection of the white establishment. Consequently, in the early 20th century when large numbers of white women entered the job market, black women who were already in the workplace were demoted to do the more difficult, dangerous, and lowest paying tasks. Fox and Hess Biber note that while white girls of the upper and middle class were bred in "genteel refined" circles, most black girls were forced from infancy to live a life of daily deprivations, experience physical abuse, and encounter a hostile white world.[2] This oppressive environment was fostered primarily by elements of the white world that feared economic and political competition during and after Reconstruction.

A quick review of black women's status from the 1920s to the 1960s will demonstrate how economic conditions restricted the production of texts that had the black professional woman exhibiting self-empowerment in the workplace, and how changing social and political factors began contributing to the rise of black professionals since the 1970s. The United States Commission on Civil Rights reports that nationally from the 1920s through the 1940s, black women were employed primarily as farm laborers, domestic servants, laundresses and seamstresses, and few were teachers. As late as 1940, only 4.6 percent made up the professional cadre.[3] Lawyers, engineers, and computer specialists equaled 0.0 percent. However, 3.6 percent were teachers (primarily in black schools), 0.4 percent were nurses, and 0.4 percent were librarians and social workers. The bulk of the professional rank consisted of clerical workers, accounting for 1.3 percent. The Commission on Civil Rights insists: "It was neither age, religion, educational attainment [nor] location" that doomed black women into menial jobs. The problem was "racial discrimination."[4]

Historian Jacqueline Jones confirms that it was almost impossible for black female high school graduates who were fully qualified for white-collar positions to find employment "commensurate with their training. Stories of highly educated black women condemned to a lifetime of menial labor were legion."[5] Businesses associated spending money with "ego gratification." Efficient and courteous services were linked to Caucasian features. The reality of the job market corroborates with black novelistic representation of black professional female characters. Nella Larsen's *Quicksand* (1928) and Jessie Redmon Fauset's *Plum Bun: A Novel Without a Moral* (1929) show the protagonists being biracial, employable, and belonging to the professional ranks, yet they had no autonomy on the job. The middle-class fictive professional characters find a parallel with the small number of professionals in the black community. A study of the life of Alice Dunbar—wife of the famous poet Paul Lawrence Dunbar—evidences that hers was a tenuous financial position. Critic Gloria Hull shows that she endured extreme hardships both financially and emotionally. Since her social position was gained through "breeding, education, culture, and looks" rather than money, she and her peers had no financial security. Hull suggests that the understood bourgeoisie status of Dunbar and other black professional women of her group need to be re-evaluated.[6] Nevertheless, this group of professional women continued to grow numerically though marginally, but not enough to be represented in fiction.

According to the United States Commission on Civil Rights, between the 1940s and 1960s, the change in the economic status of black professionals was minimal except in two areas. In the 1940s, the average years of schooling for black women between the ages of 25 and 65 years was 6.2 years; however, by 1960, it was 8.4 years. The second important fact is that the percentage of professional black career women increased from 4.4 in 1940 to 7.7 in 1960. This 3.3 percent rise was primarily in the clerical workers area.[7] Jacqueline Jones provides specific details. For instance, women employed as clerks doubled between 1940 and 1944, but the 2 percent of black female workers in this category often "remained invisible to white business customers and were concentrated in government jobs around Washington D.C."[8] However, during the same period, only a very small number of black women entered the other career tracks. For example, only 0.4 percent of black women were in nursing.[9] Systematic discrimination kept black professional women employed in careers far below their qualifications. So pervasive were the discriminatory practices that none of the post–Harlem Renaissance women writers represented black women characters in careers that allowed for a high degree of agency.

By the early 1960s, the black community saw little change for the majority of black women; 37.7 percent were working as domestic help. The prolonged injustices in the work force spawned the Civil Rights Movement, the Black Power Movement, and the Women's Movement. All of these groups made demands for justice through national marches, sit-ins and speeches. As a result, the Civil Right Act of 1964 was passed making illegal discriminatory policies against minorities *and women*, and the Equal Employment Opportunity Commission was created to uphold these laws. The federal government created programs such as Equal Opportunity and Affirmative Action, which succeeded in bringing more black professional women and far more white women into the work force during the years 1970 to 1980. According to the United States Commission on Civil Rights, whereas in 1960 only 7.7 percent of black women were in the professional and technical ranks, by 1980 the figure had risen to 16.1 percent, while white women's positions were 20.1 percent. It points out that high school graduates ("20 percent with 12 years of schooling, and 30 percent with 13 to 15 years") found jobs in the clerical areas, and college-educated women began to filter noticeably into the professional areas of nursing and library science, social work and religious work, among other careers.[10] For the first time, the occupational gap narrowed marginally between educated black and white women, but the gap was still wide among uneducated groups of women.

Civil rights laws did not affect as many black women entering the professional ranks as they could have. Jacqueline Jones demonstrates that "only a select group" of young and educated black women profited since only 6 percent of black women, compared to 17 percent of white women, had college degrees.[11] Hazel Carby confirms this analysis. She argues that Affirmative Action allowed the workplace to assimilate and advance only those who were already of the higher social bracket in the black community,[12] and the majority of them had Caucasian features. Despite the gap that existed, the black professional woman did make some significant strides.

The United States Commission on Civil Rights concludes that continued educational achievements, changing demographics, and relocation contributed very little to black women's advancement into the mainstream world of work. It was primarily the reduced racist practices that made their success possible. The early 1980s saw a strong emerging professional group of black women, totaling 16.1 percent.[13] It is significant that this numerical rise of the black professional woman is captured by Toni Cade Bambara in *The Salt Eaters*. Velma Henry, the computer analyst, was the harbinger of other fictionalized representations of the black career woman.

Because racism within the workforce itself remained endemic despite government intervention, many black professional women who were already in the mainstream workforce understood that after they were employed in an establishment, they would have few opportunities for promotion or for breaking the glass ceiling. Penni Crabtree, writing in the *Memphis Business Journal*, finds that some women executives leave corporate America not only because of racism, classism, and sexism, but because of seniority issues with much older executives choosing to retain their positions which hinders women's chances for becoming CEOs.[14] Additionally, Laura Dresser, a Harvard University professor, demonstrates that although all workers experienced setbacks during the turbulent 1980s labor market, it was black women who suffered the most. She adds that although the most educated women gained the greatest advantage, black women received far fewer gains than did their equally qualified white counterparts.[15] Blacks had no choice but to protest the unfair treatment that threatened their newly earned economic gains.

The economic condition for blacks worsened during the Reagan administration. The first problem was that fewer black professionals were hired. Columnist Fred Block writes that Reagan's notion of full employment was to "create tax loopholes for the rich, eliminate safety regulations, and downsize social programs to enhance private investment that created menial jobs. His version of full employment is a 'Coolie America,'"[16] in which most jobs are blue collar and therefore, not compatible with the academic gains of many black women. Reagan also opposed the Civil Rights Restoration Act that legislated against discrimination of minorities, women, the aged, and the physically and mentally challenged.[17] Hence, journalist Carolyn Jacobson reports that during Reagan's tenure, unemployment of minority female teens rose to 12.8 percent, and that Reagan not only denied the validity of the women's movement, but despised it as well.[18] With less funds available, working-class teens who had to contribute to their educational expenses had to delay entrance to college. Thus, the growth rate of the middle-class professional group slackened.

The erosion of legal perimeters implemented earlier to protect employment opportunities for blacks and women further curtailed the economic growth of black professional women. In 1965, President Lyndon Johnson passed Executive Order No. 11246 to stop race and gender discrimination. It stipulated that for businesses to get government contracts, agencies had to reserve a certain percentage of the job for minority firms.[19] However, the Reagan Justice Department argued that civil rights laws were reverse discrimination against whites, although the measures protected the gains of white women who also benefited from them.

The economic repercussions proved debilitating to black professional women. In 1984, the average black female household income was about three-fifths that of white women. Consequently, 62 percent of white women's families owned their own homes compared to 43 percent of black women's families. The average household wealth, debt, and net worth for the black working family was $26,997, compared to $77,132 for the white working family.[20] The United States Commission on Civil Rights concluded that racism was the primary cause for the discrepancy between the economic status of black and white women, and the even much wider gap with white men. Discriminatory practices concerning hiring, referrals, and promotions continued because they were difficult to prove in a lawsuit. It recommended that more and forceful measures such as the periodical investigation of firms and employment agencies would be necessary to eliminate biases from the workplace.[21] It is in the midst the economic upheavals of the early 1990s that McMillan attempts to capture the successes and the many problems her protagonists face in corporate America.

In the 1990s and 2000s, hundreds of thousands of black professional women participate in a wide variety of fields in the corporate world, including some who operate their own firms. A corresponding positive literary change has taken place since the mid–1990s. With the greater visibility of black professional women in the workplace, in such areas as television, medicine, law, and politics, there is a trend to give greater autonomy to black professional women as characters in novels. Bebe Moore Campbell's novel *Brothers and Sisters* (1995) is a case in point. The newness and unfamiliarity of the professional job market of the 1980s and early 1990s have become less inhibiting for the generation of writers since the mid–1990s. They do greater justice to the autonomy of the black professional woman than writers who had fewer models to portray. The protagonist of Connie Briscoe's *Sisters and Lovers* (1996) evidences this high level of awareness.

Another external factor that influences the scarcity of novels reflecting autonomous black professional women is the way black career women are perceived in mainstream literature. Until the 1980s, the literature of Western Europe and the United States was primarily Euro-centric and controlled by white males. During that period, blacks were portrayed as "Other"; hence, the representation of black women has been unsavory. Numerous critiques, including *Playing in the Dark: Whiteness and the Literary Imagination* (1992) by Toni Morrison, argue that white America needed the "Other." The writers who created the ideology and the literature that informed the national character and influenced later literature deliberately positioned the African American as the very antithesis of what is American. African Americans were the "unfree" in a land that proclaims its commitment to people's natural rights. Their "Otherness" became the focal point of interest, that is, their menial slave status and color.[22] Later popular texts such as Sinclair Lewis' *Babbitt* (1922) and F. Scott Fitzgerald's *The Great Gatsby* (1925) either represent the black woman as domestic, or ignore her presence. The expectation of a large segment of white America about the portrayal of black women, including black professional women, remained unwholesome until the 1980s.

The media have been consistent in denigrating black women. Sondra O'Neale, professor of African American literature, reports that in the national consciousness, they represent illegitimacy, welfarism, and the serviceable mammy. She continues that politicians opposing social services conveniently exploit the image as fraudulent of social programs and excessively sexual. O'Neale concludes that if the larger society chooses to deny black women's true humanity, and if black male scholarship is unable to dislodge the negative images from the national consciousness, it is left to black women cultural producers to create and maintain a positive image of black womanhood.[23] Black women writing about black professional women goes against the grain of what is expected by a large segment of society. The topic creates animosity within certain enclaves of the white establishment, and a level of discomfort even among individuals of black communities.

Lack of scholarship, lack of life models, and perceptions the mainstream society maintains of the black professional woman are not the only external forces that prevent the creation of novels about black career women. The way black male writers position black woman characters also contributes to the paucity of such novels. Selwyn R. Cudjoe, professor of African American studies, comments on the seeming inability of many black male writers to create autonomous black women characters. The ones they imagine are usually unable to live for themselves, but live rather for their family and the black community.[24] Perhaps that is why Anita Hill, a dignified, articulate lawyer and Yale graduate, shocked the American concept of what a black woman is supposed to be. That many black women supported Clarence Thomas rather than Hill in the 1991 incident of sexual harassment demonstrates that a large number of black women have bought into both the racist and sexist ideologies of oppression. It appears that some people, in order to maintain their socioeconomic status, find it necessary to erase or deny the presence of successful black professional women.

Most African American male novelists do not represent the black professional woman as having much agency. One such contemporary black male novelist is Ishmael Reed. In one of his novels, *Mumbo Jumbo* (1972), for instance, no female character is put in a high ranking position or in a non-traditional field for women, and few are represented as consistently loyal to the cause of black liberation. Irene Castle at first supports Pa Pa LaBas, but turns against him. LaBas's helpers, Earline and Charlotte, eventually leave, and Charlotte goes to the "plantation house" and wants to use the *loa* for profit. In the text, the Haitian black Madonna is honored, but it is a mulatto secretary who leaks the military strategy of rebellion to the white marines, leading to the massacre of black soldiers in Haiti. It is possible that the historic position of black women in the workforce may have contributed to the lack of self-empowered characters in the novel.

Reed has defended the works of writers such as Zora Neale Hurston and Gwendolyn Bennett against unfair critics. Though helpful to black professional women writers at the beginning of his career, by the time *Reckless Eyeballing* (1986) was published, that relationship grew strained. Some critics interpreted the text as a deliberate attack on black women writers. Professor Deborah McDowell, analyzing the antagonism between black male and female writers in Reed's novels, says of *Reckless Eyeballing*, "Ian Ball is a clear self-portrait whose story allegorizes Reed's now well-known and predictable perception that the work of talented black men is being eclipsed by the power block of black women writers midwifed and promoted by white feminists." McDowell insists: "The bodies/texts of black women" have become the turf(s) over which black and white men compete for power and control.[25] Reed's animosity is probably directed less to women per se than to what he perceives to be the negative image of black men.

Reed now seems to have a positive work relationship with his female colleagues. Daniel Max, a contributing editor to the *Paris Review*, reports that although Reed is very outspoken against male bashing by black women writers, he has befriended and helped McMillan.[26] That assistance was offered, according to Paulette Richards, when McMillan was one of his students at Berkeley, and he encouraged her writing aspirations.[27] It is heartening to hear that a constructive relationship is being forged between successful black women writers and successful black male novelists such as Ishmael Reed.

One contemporary African American male novelist who represents the black professional woman favorably is the popular writer E. Lynn Harris. In none of his novels is the black woman a protagonist, but he gives the important women characters full development. In the trilogy *Invisible Life* (1991), *Just as I Am* (1995), and *Abide with Me* (1990), the black professional female, Nicole Marie Springer, is for a while the lead performer in *Dreamgirls*, a Broadway musical, and she performs in nightclubs as well. She is represented as a beautiful dark-skinned woman, having been a first runner-up in the Miss America beauty pageant. Nicole is seen performing her role on stage. In *Invisible Life*, the male protagonist speaks of her: "I saw Nicole step to the microphone. She looked stunning in a white sequined evening gown.... Chills took over my body as Nicole sang 'Poppa, Can You Hear Me?' from *Yentl*, bathed in the shimmering hues of the stage lights.... The lushly arranged ballads she sang unfolded like scenes from a romantic movie."[28] The reader senses the writer's emotional investment in the character.

In *Abide with Me*, the women characters belong primarily to the professional ranks. One is a fourth-year medical student, and two are lead performers on Broadway. Though one important relationship is marred by bitter rivalries, the other female characters maintain strong, lasting friendships. Here Harris unveils the contemporary reality of black professional women as the innocent victims of male homosexuality, yet balances the exposure with others who refuse to be the objects of male desire. So, although the novels are primarily concerned with the homosexual lives of the male characters, Harris's sustained positive representation of black professional women suggests the beginning of a paradigm shift away from the traditional stereotypical portrayals of black women by black male writers.

This text demonstrates that novelists other than black women can write about black professional women. Harris has successfully captured a large segment of the black women readers' interests, for he shows black women as professionals. Characters such as Nicole Marie Springer are solidly placed in his novels and are given nearly equal space with the central main character. We applaud Harris's respect for black professional women. However, as wonderfully sensitive as he is to the black women characters, the black career homosexual male is always central in these texts. A brief introduction of the two most important characters in *Just As I Am*[29] will help the reader understand how the characters are configured. On the first page of the text, the protagonist identifies himself:

> My name is Raymond Winston Tyler, Jr., second-generation attorney. The son of attorney Raymond Winston Tyler and Marlee Allen Tyler, an elementary school teacher.... I had a happy childhood, growing up deeply ensconced in the black middle-class.... I returned home after law school and several years of successful practice in a large New York firm. About a year ago, I moved two hours South to Atlanta after a two-year stint of running my pop's law firm while he followed his lifelong dream and became a member of the Alabama State Senate.[30]

In Chapter Two, Nicole identifies herself:

> My name is Nicole Marie Springer, former beauty queen, Broadway actress, and sometime word processor. Thirty years of age, but that's twenty-five in show biz years. Born and raised in Sweet Home, Arkansas, right outside of Little Rock, population five hundred and eighty-five, and one stoplight. Daughter of cotton farmers James and Idella Springer.... A small-town girl with big-city goals.
> They say in every life some rain must fall, but I've just come through a couple of years dominated by thunderstorms. Right now my life is cloudy and overcast, anxiously awaiting the sun.[31]

In these excerpts, the issue of identity and a sense of agency are crucial. The male protagonist identifies his name, which carries the bloodline of his father; his lineage, the generational middle-class position of his parents; his schooling and apprenticeship in the prestigious Northeast, his present status in his father's law practice in a large metropolitan center; and his father's ambitious political goals. Nicole, the female character, also identifies her name, but what follows is not her genealogy, but her erratic acting career, which forces her to moonlight, and her title as "former beauty queen." The environment from which she comes is not just rural, it is one far removed from the amenities and sophisticated technological advancement one expects in a prosperous farming community. Her parents are cotton farmers, and given the historical background of blacks in these underpopulated rural areas of Arkansas, they were either tenant farmers, or at best small farmers. The contrast is not just limited to the past. Unlike her male counterpart, she is presently depressed and anxious for her future. What we have here is a picture of power versus powerlessness.

In all fairness to the writer, the protagonist experiences some very painful disappointments, and for a while works for a law practice headed by a black woman. But the remarkable contrast in the identities of the self at the beginning of the text prepares the reader for a power struggle within the text, and clearly who will win. In fact, the cover of the text shows two men completely enamored with each other, while the hurt and isolated Nicole looks wishfully at them. The writer must be given credit for having the female character tell her own story and maintain her space for nearly one half the text, but it is secondary to the male's.

The inequitable presentation in the narration appears almost natural. Carol Tavris explains the difference between gender equality and gender sameness. Gender sameness means men and women have the same biological needs, personality traits, and abilities. But there is no gender equality in life (and in most novels), for men have more money, power, and access to other resources. She adds: "By ignoring these real differences in men's and women's lives and bodies, people who take the normalcy of men for granted have fallen prey to the third error" that men's lives—primarily white middle-class men—are the norm by which all others should be measured.[32] The passage in Just As I Am illustrates the need for gender equality. Black women writers and readers may want to create their own identities that consistently suggest agency, or critique even the best intended portrayals that present conflictive characteristics.

Another external reason why so few writers celebrate the black professional female protagonist is the negative review—a penalty many mainstream reviewers and publishers impose on writings that do not satisfy their cultural requirements. If the black woman is to fulfill certain expected norms, works that disrupt that status quo suffer the consequences of not getting published. Michele Wallace in Invisibility Blues quotes Trinh T. Minh-ha as saying that some readers and critics perceive "difference" as inauthentic or bungling. The rejection of what is not traditional suggests a refusal or reluctance to assimilate. The ramification for the writer is psychic betrayal, humiliation at having to disavow one's voice. A writer's repeated attempts to un-say what is her own reality leads to frustration. Eventually she realizes she must be true to herself, and not say what is deemed acceptable. She must, or have others define her in their terms.[33] Writing is difficult, but when one wastes creative energy trying to be untrue to her vision of reality, the craft at times may seem impossible.

Mainstream critics are not the only hindrance. Wallace offers an example of how black male reviewers often respond to the literature about black women. After being asked by a black magazine, Emerge, to interview and create a profile of Henry Louis Gates, Jr., she tries to incorporate feminist writers such as Hazel Carby, Deborah McDowell, and Hortense Spillers into the text. She discovers that the same elitist measures used by some white critics are operative with this publication. Her black feminist editor explains that the biographical sketches of the women writers would be totally unacceptable to her black editor-in-chief because they not being contributors to the *New York Times* he does not know them.[34] The pressure, then, of having to craft one's novel so as to minimize the possibility of rejection on the basis of traditional societal expectation is true for writers. However, it is a force all black novelists, and especially black female novelists trying to create space in the competitive market, must contend with in producing their texts.

The exclusionary policies that position the black women unfavorably are not only operative in literary circles, but also hold sway in the film industry. Tania Modleski, in *Feminism Without Women: Culture and Criticism in a "Postfeminist" Age* (1991), concurs that producers and scriptwriters reinscribe sexual oppression on black women. She analyzes the representation of race in several films, including *Blond Venus, The Jazz Singer, Crossing Delancy, Clara's Heart,* and *Fatal Beauty.* In *The Jazz Singer,* although the role of the black woman is minimal, she is made to represent the embodiment of sexuality, though sex is never referred to in the film. Furthermore, the scene is framed to emphasize the subordinate position of the black woman. Referring to *Crossing Delancy,* she comments that if films produced by white women sexualize the bodies of black women and substitutes them as mother figures who behave as the "Mammy," then what expectations can we have from others?[35] Movies provide multiple sensory experiences, so the persistent negative images of black women have a strong hold on the viewers' consciousnesses, which in turn inform their responses to novels of the black professional women. Since the reviews of texts are a powerful contributing factor of a book's initial reception, writing about black women having agency could restrict a text's longevity.

The final reason there are few novelistic portrayals of the black professional woman from the 1980s to mid–1990s is the impact of the market. Beginning with the Harlem Renaissance of the 1920s, only a few publishers such as Harcourt Brace, Alfred A. Knopf, and Harpers[36] were willing to publish works of African Americans. Knopf, for instance, has published eight texts of Toni Morrison. However, until recently, most publishers remained skeptical of black women's cultural production. In an interview with Joyce Pettis, Paule Marshall, now a MacArthur Fellow, recounts a conversation with Bennett Cerf, publisher of Random House. Marshall reports his comment about her novel, *Brown Girl, Brownstones* (1959): "This kind of book rarely doesn't do that well." She comments that what he meant was, "Though the company was publishing it, he really didn't consider it part of American letters or me a part of the literary establishment. There was that kind of disregard, certainly for black women writers."[37] In a subsequent interview, she explains that the text went out of print because: "There wasn't the kind of climate within the literary community to be open and receptive to a book like *Brown Girl, Brownstones* at the time, [and because] books by women and about women were not taken seriously." The demise was also because the publisher did not "do the kind of promotion and publicity for the book that would have, perhaps, launched it to the public." However, in 1981, The Feminist Press brought out a new edition and Marshall says, "The book became so popular that it was one of the books that kept the doors of the press open."[38] Marshall's experience was typical until the beginning of the 1990s.

Marshall's comments are confirmed by editors within the publishing industry. DeNeen Brown, writer for the *Washington Post*, quotes Manie Barron, an associate editor of Random House, as saying that the principle governing the refusal to publish books written by black women is that the black community neither buys nor reads books. However, the real problem proved to be that the books available to this readership did not reflect them and their culture positively. Hence, they refuse to purchase books that demoralize them. With the advent of Terry McMillan, the "godhead of contemporary fiction," black women, and especially black professional women, began to buy books at an unprecedented rate since the texts partially represent them. Brown reports that publishers are now busily hunting for the "next Terry McMillan,"[39] and with good reason. By May 1996, according to John Skow of *Time* magazine, *Waiting to Exhale* "swept the nation's bedrooms, beaches, hair salons, reading groups and rush-hour subway trains, selling almost 700,000 hard copies in the process and 3 million more in paperback." Skow points out that the film version of the novel grossed $6.7 million.[40]

The marketing of books relating to the black career woman before the mid–1990s did not find a very receptive audience with publishers. *The Salt Eaters* was published partly because Toni Morrison, Bambara's friend, became her editor and Morrison pushed for its acceptance. After the novel was adopted, Morrison explains that she and her company sales representatives were thrilled to put such a unique book on the market, but the bookstores were reluctant to invest in the text. Morrison observes that first novels and minority novelists usually have a difficult time entering the market.[41] *The Salt Eaters* is a powerful novel and challenges the reader to invest time into reading and enjoying it.

Economic realities may be another reason publishing companies may overlook narratives with the protagonists as black professional women? The bottom line for publishers is whether the text will sell. Lynell George, author and writer for the *Los Angeles Weekly*, agrees with Malaika Adero, Amistad Press executive editor, that publishers tend to base their decisions on what to publish by looking at what is selling in other areas of the media. Oftentimes the information is misguided, as in the case of their perceiving the black community as "pathological," and that this pathology is what sells best. They use their limited knowledge or perspective rather than embrace new approaches.[42] Books like any other product on the market must have the potential for profit if the publishers are to invest in it.

The way publishers categorize books is important in determining whether a company will offer a contract to the writer. Janice Radway instructs on what policies the industry adopts. She writes that the paperback industry, in an effort to save money and time, chooses books that closely fit their existing catalogues.[43] If, according to Adero, the pathology of the black community sells, then most texts of the popular genre could be perceived as dealing with this issue. In the late 1960s and 1970s, a third kind of text emerged, but these could be pigeonholed as protest literature, a subset of the pathological. It is possible that novels similar to Toni Cade Bambara's *The Salt Eaters*, which were experimental and could not be labeled as merely reflecting the problems of the black community, were never published. Bambara was fortunate that Toni Morrison was her editor. In fact, the formula of pathology may even be extended to *Waiting to Exhale*, considering the many conflicts in the novel.

How publishers prepare the manuscript also determines what will be available on the market, and whether it will please the readership. Karen Angel, contributor to *Publishers Weekly*, explains how publishers handle formulaic literature. To reduce cost, publishers package books to fit them into a particular genre that has proven successful. For instance, D.H. Lawrence's *Sons and Lovers* (1913) was the "precursor" of titles such as Eric Jerome Dickey's *Sister Sister* (1996), and the success of these novels suggests that the formula works.[44]

Many black women writers of contemporary fiction (and nonfiction) are comfortable with the title and cover chosen for their manuscripts. Occasionally, however, the packaging the publisher chooses against the client's wishes creates embarrassment. A survey respondent who also writes explains how she defended, in writing and by telephone, several titles she had recommended for her first book, but her efforts had very little impact on the final decision. Because she had signed the contract giving the publisher complete control over the packaging of the text, the company did not carefully choose "the presentation and design that might reflect what the book argues for or against." Each time she addresses a group about her book, she finds it necessary to add a disclaimer.

Publishers control the symbols and the final decisions in the publication process. Unless there is some reciprocity between writer and publisher, the book may fail to attract a large readership because the presentation and design lack charm or are inappropriate for a particular audience; or the title may fail to reflect the thesis of the text or catch the eye. Generally, publishers want titles that are accurate; writers focus on accuracy and specificity, that is, titles that reflect the essence of the text. The ideal is that both parties feel at least partially satisfied with the final product. Since the primary concern for publishers is profit, the cheapest method of publishing and packaging is preferred. Recently, because the autonomous black professional woman protagonist does not fit the old stereotypical mold, some publishing houses have found it necessary to create new strategies to accommodate the radical transformation, which now accompanies her portrayal as having agency.

Today, the market responds very favorably to novels representing the black career woman. Lynell George comments that with the phenomenal sales in 1992 from Alice Walker's *Possessing the Secret of Joy* (1992), Toni Morrison's *Jazz* (1991), and Terry McMillan's *Waiting to Exhale* (1992), the world of publishing took note, for they remained in the top 10 slots on the *New York Times* Bestseller List for weeks. He compliments the black women writers as experiencing "a shining moment of vindication."[45] Linton Weeks, contributor to the *Washington Post*, adds another perspective on the welcoming reception recognized black women writers are receiving today. He reports that African Americans spent $320 million on books in 1998. Nevertheless, he quotes Faye Williams, co-owner of Sisterspace and Books, as saying that the black readership is growing and demanding more serious books, not the "girl-friend stories." However, the publishers are lagging behind in delivering what the black community wants.[46] Publishers now realize that they have a need to investigate and satisfy the readerly desires of the black community.

One significant reason for the publishers' new willingness to publish scholarly texts on black professional women is that sophisticated readers are lobbying for them. According to DeNeen Brown, the "Go On Girl Book Club" founded in 1991 by three black female editors at a New York magazine publishing company began as a gesture to celebrate the works of African American writers.[47] The women argued that until quite recently, blacks were recognized for song, dance, and sports, but not writing—that is, telling their own stories themselves. As of summer 2001, there were about 35 chapters of the "Go On Girl Book Club" in the United States, and they focus exclusively on books written by black authors. They have a strategic plan for operating. First, they read a text and discuss it. If they appreciate the content and style, they notify publishers that they are interested in it. Second, when they endorse a book, they purchase the book en masse. One of the charter members, Monique Greenwood, suggests that in order for novels to hit the bestsellers list, the books must be sold early. The "Go On Girl Book Club," numbering over 400 members, purchases the books quickly to give them a head start up the charts.[48]

With black women authors in the forefront with their record sales, space has been created for the rise of the black career woman as worthy of discussion. Max Rodriquez, publisher of the book review "QBR," comments that African American texts are not merely for a "dilettante market." A crossover readership allows the books to become an integral part of American literature.[49] Texts of writers such as Toni Morrison, Alice Walker, and Terry McMillan are staples in college curriculums.

Despite the euphoria about black women publishing, there is still an urgent need to publish more novels that represent self-empowered black women. The results of the survey sent to readers as part of this work confirm that 76 percent of them are not satisfied with the profile of the black professional woman in recent novels. Of the 24 percent who said they were satisfied, some qualified their approval by adding that there are certain characteristics they would like to see changed. Nevertheless, they support the writers, and the successes of the recent fiction about black professional women have been phenomenal.

External factors control the production of novels that represent the black career woman exhibiting a high level of agency in the workplace. With the continued proliferation of critical analyses from feminist studies, African American women's studies, cultural studies, reader response theories, and the sales of novels by black women writers, readers and publishers become more aware of conditions that create the dearth of these books. The knowledge that a market exists is a contributing factor in fulfilling on a regular basis the desires of the black professional women's readership.

~ FOUR ~

Feminism and Nationalism: Conflicts in The Salt Eaters

Toni Cade Bambara's *The Salt Eaters* is the first contemporary novel to portray the black female protagonist performing her job within the text and exercising some level of agency in the workplace. Bambara's text is informed by her life experiences and her creative grasp of how the triple oppressions of racism, sexism, and classism, as well as the incessant demands of the black community, impact her depiction of her black professional woman protagonist. Since Bambara created a character that was indeed the first of its kind, her writing from *absence*, rather than expanding on a portrayal already in existence, exemplifies how difficult it is to craft novels that adequately represent the black professional woman. Yet this text also demonstrates how ably an excellent novelist can transcend the level of difficulty such a narrative poses.

The immediate concern for this chapter is the extent to which Bambara's, *The Salt Eaters* allows its protagonist, a black career woman, autonomy on the job and in her private life. The issue of self-empowerment is important since the protagonist's story is told through her interior monologues, the reports from different characters, and the omniscient narrator. This stylistic device allows readers to grasp how the quadruple jeopardy (racism, sexism, classism, and overextendedness on behalf of the black community) limits Velma Henry's empowerment on the job. Equally problematic is how Bambara's passion for the well-being of the black community is privileged (even though marginally) above Velma's need for autonomy.

Bambara's attempt to articulate her interest for unity within the black community and in women's issues is often conflictive because of the antagonism that exists between the two sectors: women's issues and unity within the black community. What the reader discovers is a weakened image of female power caught up in the moment of the 1960s through the 1970s. The difficulty of effecting an adequate utopian vision while negotiating the two sides of the equation causes Velma Henry to attempt suicide, though she is rescued in the denouement.

Four important aspects of Bambara's biography foreground her concern for both the black community and the struggle for black women's empowerment. Born in New York City, Toni Cade Bambara (1939–1990) had the opportunity from early childhood to hear zealous, eloquent speakers such as the Garveyites, Rastafarians, trade unionists, and Pan-Africanists discuss concerns of the African American community. After receiving her bachelor of arts degree in theater arts and English in 1959 from Queens College and while working on her master of arts degree, she was employed as a social worker. Thus, her early interest in the events happening in black neighborhoods was strengthened, and this concern remained a primary motif in all her works. She was an English professor at several universities, director of various publications sponsored by the City College SEEK program, and coordinator of programs at community centers. Equally important, Bambara was directly involved in the Civil Rights Movement and the Black Power Movement. It is during the 1960s and 1970s and while on her international travels that she became active in women's issues. In 1973, she traveled to Cuba where she joined with the Federation of Cuban Women, and in Vietnam in 1975, she was a guest of the Women's Union, where she lauded the cooperation of women and men as equal partners in the struggle for freedom.[1] Her involvement against women's oppression is an important topic in her fiction and non-fiction, most notably in *The Black Woman: An Anthology* (1970), which feminist critic Cheryl Wall sees as the forerunner of black women's attempt to define the self.[2] Other critiques of her work appear in interviews as well as her own written analyses, as exemplified in "What It Is I Think I'm Doing Anyhow."[3]

Bambara has mastered the art of the short story. She edited *Tales and Stories of Black Folk* (1971) and wrote three volumes of her own: *Gorilla, My Love* (1972), *The Seabirds Are Still Alive* (1977) and *Deep Sightings & Rescue Missions*, which also includes essays (1999: published posthumously). She has written two novels: *The Salt Eaters* (1980), which earned her many awards, and *Those Bones Are Not My Child* (1999: published posthumously). In these texts, there is evidence of Bambara's unswerving loyalty to black traditions, urban vernacular, cultural art forms, and music at a time when black culture was considered highly unfavorable by the literary establishment.

With her background in social work, Bambara's writing satisfies the criteria of what Terry Eagleton calls "effective literary work"; that is, it forces the reader into a new critical awareness of his or her contemporary codes and expectations. The work interrogates and transforms the implicit beliefs we bring to it, "disconfirms our routine habits of perception," and so forces us to acknowledge them for the first time for what they are. Instead of strengthening our traditional assumptions and perceptions, an important literary text shocks our preconceived notions and forces us to learn new systems of comprehending truth.[4] Bambara's language and content violate what was deemed desirable during the 1980s, for she represents the black career woman with a high level of agency. By profiling the black career protagonist in the workplace performing her duties as a professional, Bambara fractures past stereotypical representations of black women.

The Salt Eaters reflects elements defined as "cultural work" as well as "utopian fiction." Jane Tompkins defines cultural work as writings that "attempt to redefine the social order."[5] The Salt Eaters can also be identified as "utopian fiction." Carol Farley Kessler sees utopian fiction as not quixotic, but an obtainable utopia she calls "pragmatopia,"—that is, organization or communities in the future that effect relationships and teamwork based on equality rather than the hierarchal ranking often found in male dominated societies.[6] As such, these works attempt to provide a solution to nonegalitarian gendered societies, and when coupled with realism allow for a kind of subversive politics so that new possibilities may emerge. Bambara imagines what Kessler calls concrete "transformational possibilities,"[7] that is, to change realism from merely reflecting the status quo to egalitarianism between the sexes. In the novel, Bambara creates equality within the different circles of women.

Bambara begins her career by writing short stories about characters, especially women and children, interacting with the black neighborhood. She demonstrates how the racist and sexist forces negatively impinge on them in Gorilla, My Love and The Seabirds Are Still Alive. She then critiques imperialism in Third World nations and the nationalistic movements in America in The Black Woman: An Anthology (1970), a collection of essays, poems, papers, and short stories. Finally, The Salt Eaters (1980) encapsulates her earlier concerns, but expands them to embrace "time" in terms of the past, present, future and even cosmic elements. Bambara's texts also qualify for the category of "utopian fiction" in terms of what can be understood to be her manifesto. She writes:

> There is a war going on and a transformation taking place.... Writing is one way I participate in the struggle.... Writing is one of the ways I participate in the transformation—one of the ways I practice the commitment to explore bodies of knowledge for the usable wisdoms they yield.[8]

This statement of purpose clearly materializes in The Salt Eaters.

In this novel, Bambara addresses several issues within the black community. Two behaviors undermining its progress are sexism and disharmony. In an interview with Claudia Tate, Bambara explains why she writes the text:

> Some of us have been engaged in trying to organize various sectors of the community—students, writers, psychic adepts, etc. And I am struck by the fact that our activists or warriors and our adepts or medicine people don't even talk to each other. These two camps have as yet to learn ... to appreciate each other's vision, each other's language. The novel, then, came out of a problem-solving impulse— what would it take to bridge the gap, to merge those frames of references, to fuse the camps.[9]

Bambara, active in the Black Power Movement of the 1960s, became aware of the lack of cohesiveness among blacks, which resulted in the movement's inability to create a coalition with other minority groups.

Equally important as the first two was the weakened relationship between black men and women, particularly between the professional leadership of men and women who together had the ability to create a strong co-leadership cadre. Although Bambara did not specifically mention black professional women in *The Black Woman: An Anthology* (since she felt all women are worthy, and therefore did not want to single out one group for special attention), she and other career women felt increasingly estranged from the black males who wanted to control the governance of the movement. Bambara wrote that ironically, the Liberation Movement was urging the black women within the organization to practice the invisibility which had been forced on women during slavery. She adds, "Perhaps we need to let go of all notions of manhood and femininity and concentrate on Blackhood."[10] The deliberate attempt to deny black professional women agency in the revolutionary movements had to be confronted. The novel became the conduit for exposing the sexism of the black community.

Bambara identifies other shackles from which black women seek to be liberated: "the dehumanizing system of racism ... the manipulative control of a corporate society; liberation from the constrictive norms of 'mainstream' culture ... the systematic myths that encourage us to fashion ourselves rashly from without (reaction) rather than from within (creation)."[11] I argue then, that because Bambara declares herself as both "nationalist" and "feminist" by saying "I am about empowerment and development of our sisters and of our community,"[12] and because most of the protagonists in her writing are female, she is equally concerned about gender issues. This attempt to balance the interests of the black community and women has important implications for this discussion.

In *The Salt Eaters,* Bambara creates black career women who represent the first wave of professionals to enter the corporate work force in the early 1970s. James Blackwell defines mainstreaming as a process whereby groups who previously were rejected by mainstream society are being brought into the system. Still regarded as outsiders due to their race and class, they are marginalized within that new economic, social, and political environment, and may continue to experience prejudice, as well as being subjected to exclusionary practices. Just because federal injunctions require that educational and business enterprises provide entry for the newcomers, it does not guarantee that the particular institutions will comply with stipulated guidelines or welcome the newcomers. Companies maintain certain requirements that do not necessarily deal with the actual performance of a particular kind of job. Blackwell points out two of these, which he calls "cultural assimilation." Assimilated employees must speak fluently the language of the dominant group. They must adopt many of the dominant group's cultural standards, values, and goals, or at least practice them at convenient times.[13] But what is the result of these behaviors?

According to Blackwell, the individual has two choices. She either relinquishes her own cultural norms and embraces those of the dominant group, or learns how to detach herself from her actions. She will then follow the mainstream culture in the areas of employment and education, yet daily maintain the social patterns of behavior from her marginalized group. Whichever route is chosen in the exchange for mainstreaming, the dominant group exacts a cost the initiates must be willing to pay. The cultural outsider will experience some cultural loss, but it is hoped she will gain "cultural, economic, social, and political compensation for that loss of her ethnic heritage."[14] The incorporation of two cultures sometimes becomes disabling, for the expectation from the dominant institutions is that the new employee alone is responsible for whatever adjustments become necessary.

Velma Henry, the protagonist, is a young black professional woman who has joined the working elite core of white male professions. As a computer systems specialist, she has bypassed the typical professional fields of black women, that of teaching and social work. In addition to being a full-time employee of a nationally known nuclear power company, Transchemical, Ms. Henry is an entrepreneur; she contracts her services to other companies. Her proficiency, productivity, and high visibility surprise her black professional friends who work in the black community. Since Velma had participated in the Civil Rights marches, Jan, a friend and partner in the black struggle, expresses her befuddlement at Velma's success in securing government jobs, which involve classified material. She later adds that Velma's high visibility makes it possible for her to receive important contractual jobs both outside the local area and at diverse stations throughout the city. For a black married woman and mother in the 1970s, Velma Henry exercises a great deal of agency in enhancing her professional career and income.

Velma Henry suffers from the oppression of racism both as a black person in the United States and as a black professional woman in corporate America. Velma lives in a small, segregated black community called Claybourne, Georgia. The township has a long, proud history—the forefathers established it by officially planting trees and creating sculptures to commemorate the event. It claims a middle-class element with its Academy of Seven Arts, an infirmary, recreational facilities, and businesses. The community also incorporates a segment that is mired in poverty with welfarism, unemployment and underemployment, alcoholism, crime, and teen pregnancy. A high level of tension exists between the community and law enforcement officials, both in the police force and the National Guard. Isolated as it is from the mainstream culture, it suffers from the abuse of large companies in the vicinity. One cause for continued tension is the resisted annexation of Gaylord Hill, a valuable piece of real estate where blacks live, and which the powerful Russell Estate wants.

The racism Velma endures on the job takes various forms. She repeatedly faces disrespect from her managers. Palma, Velma's sister, recounts Velma's work experiences with supervisors' attempts to execute the "shakedown samba" (140). This observation suggests that her bosses try to intimidate her job security. Consequently, Velma is tense. All employees have difficulty performing at maximum level when there is no positive communication with supervisors. Workers need to know their managers exercise fair play in terms of evaluations, training, workload, promotions, and benefits. Not all supervisors deal equitably with minority employees, and they wrongly assume that the black professionals are merely hired because of affirmative action.[15] To keep their positions, black workers are expected to demonstrate a high level of proficiency before and after they are hired.

Furthermore, Velma Henry is isolated in her job. Not once is the name of a coworker at Transchemical mentioned. Never is there mention of her socializing with any of them. She has no support group within the company or mentor to guide her. In the novel, much attention is given to a group of six engineers from Transchemical who each day frequent a café. Five of the men are white, and one is Japanese. Each day they discuss their work and there is camaraderie among them. A woman never joins their party. It is perfectly legitimate for men to fraternize and drink, but this is a daily lunchtime event, not a "men's club" affair. Clearly the "old boy network and the old lines of communication"[16] are operating here. In the 1970s, engineering and specialized areas in computer science were perceived primarily as careers for elite white men. Any woman, particularly a black woman, who entered these areas was seen as encroaching into male territories of power, and she could expect stiff competition and possible vindictive behavior.

In addition to racism, Velma suffers from the sexist behavior of her coworkers. Today, sexual harassment in the workplace is a crime, but in the 1970s, the law did not stipulate such behavior to be illegal. Although Bambara does not elaborate on the specifics of the abuse, we deduce that pervasive negative images of black women as sexual objects in the media, and the fact that her white male colleagues felt threatened by her high professional status, have motivated their behavior. This idea is suggested by Bambara, who shows that in the minds of the employers of Transchemical there is no distinction between the domestic servants and employees like Velma. While discussing the exploitive actions of the rich white neighboring establishments, she says a bus comes to the black community to transport the nonprofessional employees to the plant and to their domestic jobs. Velma is neither a factory "hand" nor a maid, but she fits the category in the minds of her colleagues as mere surplus labor, or an "uppity" Negro.

If Velma's delicate position as a newcomer were jeopardized by harassment from a boss, her stress level would be excessively heightened on the job. This unsavory working environment accounts for her abruptly changing a job without handing in a resignation, for her sister discusses Velma's employment and sexual harassment in the same conversation. Although leaving without notifying her manager is a nonprofessional way to behave, that Velma is hesitant to discuss fully the details of the harassment (this is the Velma that is not afraid to challenge the black political leadership in the black community) makes the reader suspect that the indignities were from persons in authority over her on the job site. For Velma, then, race and gender intersect to intensify her stress in the workplace. Fortunately, her expertise and the high demand of her career choice make it possible for her never to be without employment.

Velma's job creates conflict for her in other areas as well. Velma is not a one-track-minded computer analyst; she is very knowledgeable of the sciences. Representing Velma as a full-fledged liberal arts student and then professional woman, Bambara creates a novel that is prophetic and progressive. Velma is cognizant of the illegal practices of the nuclear industry at Transchemical, and is aware that the black community in which she lives is the recipient of this environmental abuse. She also knows of the potential widespread hazards the industry poses to communities beyond her township. She may wish to be loyal to her place of employment, but she also has very strong ties to her township. The juxtaposed interests create tension for her.

As a computer analyst, Velma has access to the documentation which verifies the violations that are occurring at Transchemical. Fred Holt, a bus driver, recounts a conversation with a friend, Porter. Porter showed him many articles about the high level of radiation the workers were exposed to; consequently, they were all terminally ill cancer patients. Porter himself was dying of radiation exposure from the atomic blasts that occurred at Yucca Flats beginning in 1955. He feared his generation of employees would die before anyone was able to research and to assess the damaging effects of radiation on them. Porter also confirmed that another chemical plant was being sued for willfully jeopardizing the lives of the employees. He believed the management intended to raze Transchemical because educated environmental activists were beginning to collect data on the health hazards to the employees' lungs. Velma is one of the educated insiders who is opposed to the dangerous exposure of radiation to the workers.

Although Velma is isolated at work, top management recognizes her expertise and shrewdness. When the information about the chemical plant's violations of government regulations, especially in relation to the black neighborhoods, is lifted or erased, she is not called in for questioning as someone who could provide some leads as to how the loss of the company's files could have occurred. She becomes the prime suspect for the sabotage, and therefore is put through cruel interrogations.

While in therapy at the Southwest Infirmary, Velma retraces the bitter memories that eventually pushed her to attempting suicide. She links her brutal treatment during the Civil Rights Movement by the officials at the police precinct, the "interrogation" one would encounter if kidnapped by terrorists, and being bombarded with questions in the stately office of Transchemical about an "error" (17). For Velma, all were equally traumatic.

Bambara's concern for the black neighborhood as a nuclear waste dumping site is not merely a theoretical matter of feminist women associating with Mother Nature as opposed to patriarchal science. The correlation of environmental abuse and minority neighborhoods in the United States has a long history. Lawyers Sanford Jay Rosen and Tom Nolan give a brief history of the Environmental Justice Movement. It began with the Civil Rights Movement in the 1960s, but "its current incarnation started with a 1987 report issued by the Commission for Racial Justice of the United Church of Christ (UCC) in Cleveland." The report, "Toxic Wastes and Race in the United States," concludes: "The distinguishing characteristic of communities where toxic waste facilities are likely to be sited is race of the residents."[17] They specifically identify the neighborhoods of African Americans and American Indians. Bambara's awareness of environmental racism is one of the reasons she wrote *The Salt Eaters*:

> It is a thrown-open sort of book generated by these questions.... It
> gets downright cosmic, in fact, in the attempt to sound the alarm
> about the ineptness and arrogance of the nuclear industry and call
> attention to the radical shifts in the power configurations of the
> globe and to the massive transformations due this planet in this last
> quarter of the twentieth century.[18]

According to Jan, another political activist, Transchemical has been illegally transporting radioactive waste through the black community to a factory in Alabama. Although she is not sure Velma is responsible for reporting this violation to the environmental authorities, and for destroying or lifting accounting records, Velma is the prime suspect, for she has been a whistle blower in the past. Jan confirms that Velma is in the process of getting a lawyer to defend herself.

Velma's stressful position at work is further exacerbated by community factors. She experiences a level of marginality in the black community because her expertise in nuclear waste is not readily or favorably received. She is a noncompromising negotiator when life-threatening issues are at stake. Ruby, another friend and Civil Rights activist, complains that their organization, Women of Action, is attempting to solve too many social ills such as school and prison reform, alcohol and drug abuse, domestic violence, child abuse, and rape cases. She finds it very disconcerting that Velma has successfully convinced the women to launch an attack on the nuclear power industry's abuses.

To convince the skeptical Ruby, Jan interrogates her as to where radioactive waste is transported and buried, where the testing cities are located throughout the world, who works with the contaminated products, and what are the disastrous effects on Navajo reservations. Jan then challenges her, "Cancer, Ruby, cancer. And the plant on the Hudson River and —Ruby don't get stupid on me" (242). Ruby is unconvinced of the lethal danger the nuclear waste poses, and retorts that Jan is beginning to sound like Velma. Bambara forces the issue by having Jan reply, "Hell, this is an emergency situation," and environmental pollution has persisited for years due partly to poor "Peacetime construction that has become a "death trap" (243). She ends by asking Ruby to consider whether racism and avarice are not responsible to a large extent for the unethical practices at Transchemical. She suggests that such a power configuration in the city contributes to the quality of life in both the local, national, and international arenas.

When Ruby votes against Velma's proposal to challenge Transchemical, Velma is caught between the racism of the white power structure and the ignorance of the black community. Professor Janelle Collins surmises that Velma expends an inordinate amount of energy on behalf of the black community, "but at the cost of an individual being driven to fission, disintegration, and instability."[19] The educated black young female attempting to change the knowledge base of the black community is fighting an uphill battle. Except for Velma's expertise in her field and other related areas, she is devoid of the resources that create power in white corporate America and the black community. Nevertheless, her sense of self-efficacy allows her to single-handedly challenge the white and black political and economic systems in her effort to protect the black community.

Today, feminist criticism shows how race and gender and class oppression intersect. In the 1970s, because of racism and classism of the white feminist movement, black women whom Velma Henry represents were denied membership. Thus, minority women became isolated in their fight against environmental pollution in black neighborhoods. Feminist scholar Carol Stabile in *Feminism and the Technological Fix* explains that the feminists of the late 1960s felt overwhelmed by the new technology, especially those of reproduction and environmental control. They continued to emphasize the binary opposites created earlier between the female-mother earth/illogic versus the male/culture/logic. Technology became the symbol of nuclear weapons and destruction. Thus, the women reinforced the association of the feminine with nature and life.[20] However, the activists did not deem all human life valuable.

Although these feminists were concerned with patriarchal oppression, they participated in the worst forms of racism and classism. Stabile notes that they hail Charlotte Perkins Gilman's *Herland* (1979) as one of their charter texts. They also made excuses for her statements, such as, "Insanity had increased greatly among Negroes since they were freed, probably owing to the strain of having to look out for themselves in a civilization far beyond them." These feminists, from their privileged white middle-class positions, addressed only certain environmental abuses. Stabile demonstrates that they concentrated their energies on such areas as the North Pole, dolphin survival, and the beaches where their classes visit. They totally ignored those areas where the most devastating abuses occurred; that is, the environment of poor African Americans, Latinos, Native Americans, and European Americans who had no access to the center of power. The disadvantaged women were rendered invisible by class-conscious "ecofeminists."[21]

Audre Lorde, a black fiction writer and feminist critic, interprets the behavior of these white feminists in her article "Age, Race, Class, and Sex: Women Redefining Difference." She comments that most white women publicly deny that they enjoy "built-in privilege of whiteness." As they speak of *woman* as monolithic—that is, seeing only their experience as the norm—then minority women are treated as "other," and their experience and culture is made to appear too strange and difficult to understand.[22] If it were not for the racism and classism of the Euro-American feminist movement, Velma Henry (that is, the black women she represents) could have had the support of women with more access and power to help fight the abuses of Transchemical. Their united numbers would have produced the clout needed to get better results, and might have prevented Velma's near suicide, partly brought on by feelings of isolation.

Racism is not the only force that works against the black professional woman demonstrating a greater amount of agency on the job. The misogyny of the black community is equally responsible for thwarting Velma's reach for autonomy. Velma is oppressed by her sexist husband, James Lee Henry, otherwise called Obie. He does not respect Velma's independence as a professional woman.

As a couple, they both work hard to build the Academy of Seven Arts. Obie is president, but it is Velma who spends an inordinate amount of time at the school. She is invested in building her husband's career. Velma manages the office, functions as accountant and payroll officer, supervises the office staff and ensures each employee has access to training to keep abreast of their fields. She also writes the largest grant proposals and solicits more funds than any other at the institute. After Velma leaves, it takes eight people to complete the tasks she had executed.

Unlike Velma, who has superb managerial skills, Obie lacks the administrative ability to maintain control over the splintering factions at the institute. Velma's organizational techniques keep the academy unified. When the situation is beyond control, his grudging soliloquy qualifies her accomplishments. He surmises that it was possible he was exaggerating, but he admits that the institute and their home functioned very smoothly through Velma's efforts. He assesses that her methodology is not directed toward peacekeeping as his is; rather, she maintained a well-oiled operation that prevented hostile groups from forming because she espoused an open-door policy. She successfully coordinated every aspect of the institution. How nicely the pieces fit in place with her.

Had Obie held his wife in high esteem, as president of an institution that has seven disciplines, he would have provided the staff necessary to reduce her workload. She is a veritable "mule of the world" at the academy. The accusation leveled at Obie is justified, for Velma gets no public recognition for the work she does. She is not the vice president; she is a mere supporter of her husband.

Why does Velma spend so much time securing her husband's career at the cost of her own? Conservative sectors of the black community encourage black women to support their men's careers because their manhood needs shoring up, or because society dictates that the man is the head of the household. One way to do this is to help them have a high profile and allow them to be the primary breadwinners. If the women earn higher incomes, then they allow the men to control the funds. But Velma's group of career-oriented friends have moved beyond this type of coercion. Ruby's response is: "Bullshit.... So quit the understanding, standing-by-the-man, good-supportive-sister crap" (199). Darlene Clarke Hine reports that black educated women (especially those who were single or childless as Velma was when she got married) are expected by the black community to be responsible for the advancement of the race. These educated women accept the challenge as their obligation.[23] Although the community gives them some recognition for this sexist position, it clearly frustrates their desire to concentrate on their professionalism.

Stephanie Golden adds another insight to this self-sacrificing behavior. She argues that women finding fulfillment only in making others happy is "precisely the consequence of amputating the mermaid's tail." The "Perfect Wife" or surrogate is one whose merit is calculated in relation to how much of her selfhood had been eroded.[24] Golden's argument reflects one of the dilemmas of the novel. Since the Academy of Seven Arts has an open-door admissions policy, it is understandable that Velma becomes involved, especially since her godmother, who assisted with her college education, expects it. However, M'Dear Sophie never works outside the home. Velma, the professional woman, cannot replicate Sophie's lifestyle and succeed in corporate America. Velma can only partially satisfy the expectations of others. Predictably, some members of the community have come to regard her as "always going against the grain" (252).

As a professional with some level of agency, Velma recognizes her husband's poor leadership skills. The omniscient narrator remarks that while "everything" is disintegrating, Obie is "sitting it out on the bench" (94). Successful presidents must forcefully execute their decisions. Velma confronts Obie and succinctly tells him their characters and methodologies are diametrically opposed. She has lost respect for him and is leaving him. Velma does not intend to sacrifice everything she values for her man. Feminist writer Mary Ann Weathers finds women's willingness to deny themselves career advancement to further men's careers and help them develop their self-esteem to be despicable. Such a role debases women as simple props supporting a weakling.[25] Some men exploit women through this kind of reasoning, only to forge ahead with higher status and pay in the professional world, and then they often abandon the wife left educationally and financially behind. In "The Last Taboo," Paula Giddings affirms that it is time to critique the behavior of the most powerful black men, like Clarence Thomas, who since the 1970s have become the "gatekeepers" to avenues of success in many areas of influence. She adds that men still regulate the "socio-sexual and professional relationships in the black community."[26] Velma wants to maintain agency on the job, but the conflict between the public and private spheres neutralizes her efforts, especially since her husband insists on putting his career interests ahead of hers.

Obie, having used Velma as a workhorse at his institution, expects to continue the exploitation of her as homemaker. Devalued in his eyes, she is no longer a "prize to win" (20). Velma, however, has her own career interests. This is precisely where Velma's problems begin as a professional woman in the domestic arena. Obie surmises that several factors contributed to Velma's nervous breakdown, but he is certain of one thing. His excessive demand that she maintain a domesticated role significantly contributes to her emotional trauma. Tension erupted over child rearing. Palma, Velma's sister, notes that Obie remains ambivalent about who would do the parenting. The "mother-act" (139) requires a great deal of energy, for the adopted son is responding to the dysfunction in the household, and is having difficulty adjusting in early adolescence. He experiences mood swings: he switches from being responsible to being extremely dependent to being aggressive. It is possible that Obie and Velma have not resolved the tensions resulting from Velma's earlier miscarriage, and the resultant adoption.

If Velma is to excel in her job, she cannot be completely responsible for childcare. Psychologist Hilary Lips writes that if professional women are to have power in the workplace, they must eliminate the "double-shift." Women as a group have been defrauded from having any significant influence or making any powerful effect on the world because their vital resources—time and energy—have been diverted into domesticity.[27] Obie complains that her most creative talents and energy are invested in her career; hence, she returns home exhausted. Since Obie is himself a professional, one expects him to understand that Velma's career advancement is important to her. In addition, Obie works in the black community as president of a black institution, and so escapes the daily subtle and overt racism his wife encounters. Bebe Moore Campbell writes that although the families of black professionals in higher levels of management are exuberant about their accomplishments, they remain ignorant of the tasks and the levels of stress these career partners encounter on the job.[28] Black professionals find it doubly hard, for unlike some of their white counterparts, they are often the first generation to participate in the executive ranks or work as specialists in highly technical and specialized fields. Obie ignores that Velma's job in white corporate America entails different demands than his.

Obie's resentment of Velma's career spills over into their sex life, and he uses his dissatisfaction as a weapon to control her. He complains that she is not responsive to him, but what quality sex partner is Obie when it takes him two years to recognize when his wife has an orgasm? The tension between them creates a psychological barrier for her and she finds coitus with him distasteful. Instead of recognizing that the tension in the home is responsible for the failed sexual fulfillment, he labels her frigid, and begins to have affairs.

Velma challenges his deception. She confronts him with his infidelity and tells him he has been untruthful for months. Simultaneously, Obie wants her to say: "*my* aloofness, *my* fatigue, *my* job," is the reason for the dysfunction in the household. Velma questions his attempt to distort her sense of reality and erect a "smoke screen" (230). She concludes that she is repulsed by his lack of sensitivity and prudence in his affairs. When she tells him she can no longer trust him, he inanely replies that he had always trusted her, but now she has accepted a new job without notifying him of her intentions. No one will deny that a wife accepting a new and demanding job should communicate this information to her husband, but knowing Obie's previous objection to Velma's professional activities accounts for her silence, at least until the position is secure. Obie's linking his sexual promiscuity to Velma's increased visibility and productivity reveals how threatened he is by her. His behavior is a form of reverse sublimation. If he cannot fully succeed in a socially acceptable way, having affairs is his way of proving his manhood.

Obie's insecurity with Velma further reveals itself in the way he competes with her in conversations. When they first appear in the novel, he interrupts her as she tries to speak to him at dinner. He is discourteous in removing the dishes before she is finished eating, "interrupting her story, breaking right in just as she was about to get to the good part, to tell her to put her fork down and listen" to him (21). Linguist Deborah Tannen explains that many men interrupt their wives because they resent listening; such a seemingly passive behavior suggests the subordinate position of a child or employee.[29] Because most men assume they are superior to women in intelligence and are the authority figures in society, they feel they are entitled to interject their comments or questions before a woman has completed presenting her point of view. Ironically, Obie obstructs Velma's conversation because he knows he is a partial failure and wants to improve his image. Obie's biggest cause of resentment is Velma's professionalism; he has no appreciation for her expertise as a full-time computer analyst. Eleanor Traylor suggests that the problems Obie encounters on the job have trapped him in a "chasm," which has enlarged into the home, and has trapped Velma, as evidenced in the disintegrating marriage.[30] Obie not only denies Velma the congratulations she deserves, but he discourages her.

Obie's problem extends beyond his career; he is experiencing emotional distress. He admits to himself that both at home and at work he does not "recognize" himself or Velma: "The fissures at home had yawned wide" and the once enjoyed exquisite delights have disappeared in it (94). When his problems become overwhelming, he visits Ahiro, a masseur. Ahiro tells him his back is as tough as a slab of rock, and that he is to stop acting so macho. He should cry when he needs to, for weeping contributes to good health and enables him to get rid of his "excess salt," his emotional turmoil (92). While Ahiro is coaching Obie with relaxing techniques, Obie is mentally blaming Velma for not relaxing during sex, thus limiting his pleasure. As the therapy session continues, Obie feels disoriented; yet he pretends to be in control, condescendingly telling Velma later to allow him to help her break the behaviors that entrap her. Obie cannot acknowledge to his wife that that he is experiencing problems. Dorothea Mbalia thinks that Obie is as emotionally catatonic as Velma is physically immobile, and that his problem comes from "ideological immaturity." She intuits that when he fails, he blames himself for not succeeding individually in solving the problems of the black community. Such thinking reflects an unrealistic goal that could trigger a suicide.[31] Yes, Velma is heading for a nervous breakdown, but Obie, who is not far behind, is incapable of helping her.

Bambara's concern for the unity of the black community prompts her to shore up Obie's position by appointing him leader of the Spring Festival. Ruth Rosenberg explains that the name "Obie" means not only "conjuror and sorcerer, or one who bewitches or puts under a spell," but also has the theatrical meaning of the best actor receiving an award.[32] Obie is a good actor. Having failed to exercise his presidential powers, he relies on an expedient activity to stave off the problem: he hopes the Spring Festival will be the catalyst to stimulate cooperation among the warring factions until a plan of action can materialize. The show will once again put him in the spotlight so he can redeem himself, at least in the community's eyes. It is questionable whether his stratagem will be successful with the faculty at his institution. When the festival is about to begin, Obie has yet to formulate a plan to solve the problems at his institution. Nevertheless, he convinces himself that some strategy will emerge if only he remains accessible to the possibility. This scheme would be quite grandiose for it encompasses himself, his wife, his institution, the nation, and the whole planet. Obie procrastinates, waiting for some magical intervention, but it is imperative that as president of the Academy of Seven Arts he formulates a plan and implements it.

Bambara's epistemology underpins her belief that all systems of knowledge are interwoven. Voodoo, psychic powers, physics, and thermodynamics all interplay. Hence, when Obie soliloquizes that he senses a plan, he probably means he has not yet fully grasped how to implement his ideas, or he expects to be inspired by the spirit world. Keith Byerman believes Obie (the name means "obeah man") is the appropriate leader of the spring ritual, for he is the masculine counterpart of Minnie Ransom, and this role engenders the spirit of healing.[33] Obie's symbolic role could become a reality provided he develops good leadership skills and ceases to unproductively squander his energy in hindering his wife's already developed professional career. On one occasion, he did express a desire for harmony in his life. The spring festival, symbolic of rejuvenation, could provide a clue as to how he ought to proceed. He is caught in a downpour of rain toward the end of the text and Bambara identifies an "eye" with supernatural power that has targeted him: "clarifying," "arresting" him (289). Running to investigate a phone call that will inform him of Velma's attempted suicide, he trips and falls. Symbolically, he is associated with Saul on the road to Damascus, for he later confesses he was "stripped by lightning" (292). However, Obie is not renamed. The parallel between the two incidents does not need a perfect one-to-one correspondence for the analogy to be valid; however, the absence seems conspicuous.

The sexism evidenced in Velma's marriage is indicative of the pervasiveness of sexual discrimination in the black community. In *The Salt Eaters,* the less successful men, the "boy-men," have no respect for the poor women upon whom they prey. They demand a couple dollars the women intend to use for the physical needs of their children. It is to Bambara's credit that she presents one couple, Daddy Dolphy and M'Dear (Sophie Heywood), as enjoying an egalitarian marriage. They have good communication, dance, travel, support each other in danger, and experience a common spirituality. The sexism that generally pervades the black community directly affects Velma outside the home. When Dr. Meadows mentions to a group of unemployed men that Velma is in the infirmary, one asks what is wrong with her. Before the physician can reply, the inquirer responds with another question: "He [her husband] finally bury his foot up her ass?" (188). The brutality of the language indicates the hatred of the speaker towards Velma as an independent professional woman, one who resists being dominated by her husband. In small townships like Claybourne where quite often domestic concerns are surreptitiously made public, high profiled career women such as Velma must negotiate the resentment of their less successful professional spouses, and the animosity of some unemployed males who may feel threatened by the women's financial success and the freedom it affords.

Two of the most problematic sexist episodes that Velma has to reconcile in her memory travels are those she encounters in the Civil Rights and the Black Power movements. The betrayal of the political leaders seems etched on her consciousness, and it becomes very difficult for her to dislodge. Margot Anne Kelley believes that the incidents Velma remembers, even when they happened a long time ago or in diverse places, are crucial to our (and Velma's) understanding her present crisis. She also suggests that Velma's "memories are loosely 'nested,' like framed tales-within-tales, so that four levels of action and recollection are presented as relatively simultaneous." She concurs with Douglas Hofstadter that the recollections are a "tangled hetarchy" because all the incidents are of equal magnitude, and all of them impact Velma with equal force.[34]

The frequency with which the event at the Civil Rights march occurs in Velma's descent into her memory pain, and the fact that it is the one that flashes across her mind at the moment of her attempted suicide, suggests that it was a particularly painful and humiliating experience. Minnie Ransom, the faith healer, asks her several times if she can afford to get well. It is as if she faces a wall that she cannot scale. When this event scrolls into her mind's travels, she howls in psychic agony. Minnie tells her to holler as loud as she wants or needs, and comments that she rarely encounters such psychic distress except among the cosmic forces. The two episodes have Velma trapped.

After an all-day march, despite numerous painful incidents, the protesters finally arrive at their destination. Children are crying, exhausted, and in pain; the adults are weary, massaging their tensed legs; students are singing discordantly because they are "ragged." Unfortunately, the expected amenities are not yet available to accommodate them. In the midst of the exhausted and famished mob, a fleet of limousines arrives with men dressed as for a special occasion. The arrogant, asinine, expedient leader emerges from the "cool blue of the air-conditioned interior" while Velma's throat "[i]s splintered wood." His attire is classic: his sparkling black boots contrast sharply with the dried grass he treads on; his "knife-creased" pants and jacket fit him elegantly; his lily-white shirt and azure tie make him the epitome of crass consumerism. His bodyguards, equally well dressed in silk and bullet-proof garb, follow behind him to the platform (35). Unaware of the betrayal, the masses enthusiastically welcome the so-called leader the white world has endorsed. As Velma looks at the man, she bitterly comments, "Some leader." He seems to embody three powerful African American political leaders and one folk hero. He has the physique of Dr. Martin Luther King, Jr., the rhetoric of Malcolm X, the dress flair of Stokely Carmichael, and the dark glasses of Rap. Enraged, Velma comments, "What a disaster.... Sheet" (35–36).

Susan Willis argues that indeed, the black community is misguided into accepting this person as leader. It becomes evident that other powerful forces outside the black community promoted and manipulated the representative so he would not threaten the status quo. She adds that Bambara's parable suggests: "The commodity form may well represent the most advanced stage of capitalism's colonization of the black community."[35] Velma the professional understands the deception, and feels outraged by it.

The images that remain fixed in Velma's mind are the red silk pajamas, the silver ice buckets, and the blonde white women the leader and his entourage enjoy after the speech. Velma goes to a hotel to make phone calls to get more food, doctors, medicine, and transportation for the exhausted throngs. While there, herself exhausted, unkempt, and in pain, she sees the sexual philandering of the speaker and his companions as they lavishly entertain white, nonexhausted, slender, gorgeous women acting like pedigree horses. Velma as political activist and representative of the people objects to the leader's betrayal and is consequently thrown out of the hotel. By the time she gets back to the group, she is desperately in need of care herself. Her first psychic slip begins here. Ruby helps Velma to relax, to ambulate, since she is unable to marshal her limbs and control her head, which indiscriminately rolls from side to side. At first, Ruby fears Velma's neck was broken when they forcibly exited her from the hotel. Fortunately, caring words, massages, and cool water bathing her legs have a therapeutic effect. The incident haunts Velma for many years.

Before Velma collapsed inside the hotel, and after she was rescued from the oven in which she had pushed her head to commit suicide, what hovered over her memory was "a blond hair between green threads on a field of red" (40). Velma had enough self-control not to physically harm anyone, but she had internalized the pain and the rage so that her reaction seemed to have resulted in a mini-stroke. The double betrayal, political and sexual, occurring simultaneously, was too overwhelming for her to bear. Michele Wallace identifies such occasions thusly: "Being a black woman means frequent spells of impotent, self-consuming rage."[36]

The second episode that leads to Velma's attempted suicide involves the Black Power Movement. The black men do not want the women who are professionals to have any leadership roles; they alone want to reap the rewards of the movement. Velma relives the humiliating events. Lonnie, a black male leader, tells Ruby, Jan, and Velma they are to be "cool ... give some slack, get back" lest the movement be derisively dubbed a 'woman's thaang'" (33). One night at a meeting, Jay Patterson comes with an agenda that he expects the women to implement for his reelection. Jay brings an important speaker to impress the women, hoping they will cooperate in front of a stranger. The women, however, do not succumb to such coercive action; they give the men an ultimatum. Since the male leadership will not respect women as equals, the women will no longer serve the men with their labor or money. They intend to begin their own programs that are of interest to black women. The black male leadership bitterly resents the autonomous behavior of the black professional women. In response, the women complain about their workload because the men are not fulfilling their responsibility of organizing the community.

In Velma's pained reflections, the reader gets a tiny glimpse of the intense hurt she feels. Her anguish is likened to being overworked and shedding angry tears privately at night; to being shoved to the edge of the bed and barely hanging on and fighting to get a little of the covering; to soliciting funds only to have the representative betray the community with his private agenda; to being asked to be fully supportive of policies to which she was deliberately denied input. This translates to "break her hump" in bringing to fruition what only the male cadre decides is important (25). Multiple layers of hurts, disappointments, and rage remain bottled within Velma.

The inordinate amount of time, energy, and funds sacrificed to the movements and programs of the black community literally drains Velma of the resources necessary to maximize her level of agency on her job in corporate America. Bambara ably captures the difficulty black professional women experience in effecting their empowerment and simultaneously serving the needs of the black residents.

The sexism of the black community as reflected in Velma's husband's behavior, the abuse of black men toward the women, including Velma, the misogynist practices, and the betrayals of the black leadership in the liberation movements deny the protagonist the empowerment she struggles to attain in her professional career. Susan Willis is particularly insightful in evaluating the effects on Velma, resulting from the services she renders. Willis writes that the autonomous spirit that is enabling to the protagonist, Hazel, in one of Bambara's short stories, becomes the bane for Velma, for the black community refuses to allow her to become fully self-actualized. The multiple oppressions are indicative of the scene with the red pajamas, which so frightfully damages her psychically that it constantly recurs in her memory. This happens precisely because her rage can find neither outlet nor community resolution. Consequently, she can find no peace in the black community.[37] When Obie chauvinistically tells Velma just to let her hurt go (some of this pain he himself inflicts), the reader begins to understand the gulf that exists between the couple. The statement also discloses the gap that separates the black women's from the black men's understanding of what it means for black professional women to perform at maximum level in corporate America.

The multiple pressures—racism, classism, sexism and service to the black community—drive Velma to attempt suicide because they are simply overwhelming. As she slowly begins to disintegrate emotionally, she realizes that she needs to disengage herself from the myriad obligations that are the root cause of her inability to relax. She tries to escape the angst and isolate herself for a while. Velma needs professional space, but she feels trapped. It is important to note here that Velma is not an isolated case. Other black professional women in the group feel burdened and want to disengage themselves. Ruby and Jan discuss the issue, desiring to leave the turmoil and disillusionment of the political scene for the safety and creativity of their personal careers and entrepreneurial pursuits. They want a significant level of professionalism and autonomy. For Velma, however, the need for retreat is significantly greater, since she works in white corporate America, not in the black community as these two women do. Her friends deal with black male sexism, but additionally, Velma must negotiate racism, sexism, and classism on the job.

Another problem Velma encounters is the inability many people in her community have to understand what it takes for her to succeed in corporate America. As a computer analyst, she must keep abreast with the rapidly changing technological scene in the workplace. However, members of her community, such as M'Dear Sophie, perceive her pursuit of degrees and other efforts toward professional development as useless or vain. They want that energy spent on remedying the social concerns in the black community. Black women like Velma who work in mainstream America (and the black community as well) must be credentialed. Bebe Moore Campbell evaluates the work situation. Usually, the women are the only black professionals in their department, are ignored by their white co-workers, and are misunderstood by their communities. Thus, many black women in top managerial positions are torn between their African American communities and corporate America. They experience the double jeopardy of racism and sexism, which in turn contributes to their high divorce rate. She quotes Dr. Murray, who affirms that these workers experience stress-related disorders such as "migraine and low back pain" because their rage at the overt and covert racism, if not resolved, leads to dejection and alienation. When they do not resolve their anger, the result is depression and withdrawal.[38] Velma evidences all these symptoms.

Velma's health has received much attention from critics. Writers like Gloria Hull feel that Velma's problems are due to her being "solely political and relentlessly logical."[39] This interpretation is not surprising, for M'Dear Sophie announces that Velma rejects any philosophic system that seems illogical as hers or the mud mother's, which has been forced "underground" (294).

M'Dear is Jeremiad of Velma's future. Although M'Dear, Velma's godmother, understands Velma fairly well, she is a naïve narrator in several
instances. For people immersed in the supernatural world, but not familiar
with the scientific and technological advances of computer technologies,
Velma's rational approach to solving problems may appear excessively logical. There is hardly room for parapsychology when an analyst is evaluating
the computer systems that control large cities and huge corporations. Margot Kelley agrees with Kumkum Sangari that some Third World texts have
strong negative overtones toward science. The underlying cause may be
attributed to the fear that advanced science and technology make the colo-
nized subjected to the colonizer.[40] It is possible that Velma's knowledge and
particularly the tool (computers) she works with have become a contributing source of anxiety for those who are ignorant of information systems.

   This discussion does not suggest that the world of the supernatural is
irrelevant. Bambara accepts the African concept that all knowledge systems
are interlocking. The Academy of Seven Arts over which Obie presides has
disciplines ranging from the sciences to astrology. The Southwest Community Infirmary employs both traditional and nontraditional medicine.
Furthermore, there is no question that Bambara privileges the spirit world
over the scientific in this text. Minnie Ransom, the faith healer, is given center stage, while Dr. Meadows, who recites the Hippocratic oath, is castigated until he embraces both types of medicine. Velma's career is rarely
spoken of positively; in fact, only her professional female friends mention
it. Ruby, the math teacher, is fired. Much of the text deals with the destructive force of science, and the omniscient narrator prophesizes a possible
apocalypse resulting from man's contact with "radioactive mutants" (46).
Also, Bambara emphasizes the need for clean earth through the dramati-
zation of the traveling troupe, the Seven Sisters. Carol Stabile, addressing
the technophobia of the feminists of the 1960s and 1970s, points out that
because technology is used unjustly against those who do not have access
to it, these feminists criticize techno-science while being cognizant of its possibilities to empower people.[41] Bambara understands technology's potential
for good and ill. Her protagonist is caught in the dilemma of utilizing science and technology on her job, but also using it as a subversive tool to save
lives. She reports the waste products of techno-science at Transchemical
that are harming her community.

   To counter the argument that Velma's illness is due to her being too
logical and that her life is not balanced spiritually, I will demonstrate that
she is a multidimensional artist. First, very early in the novel, Velma discusses
art with Obie while assisting her sister Palma with setting up her art exhibit.
Second, we are told she is a proficient and dedicated musician, and performs

for the Seven Sisters on their national tours. Wherever she is, indigenous music acts like a magnet and draws her to the park. She works tirelessly with Obie to establish the academy. Furthermore, she goes to the marshes to seek the knowledge of the spirit world. That she comes away unfulfilled does not mean she is completely lacking in spirituality. In fact, her argument with her partner, Jamahl, is that truth is found among one's social and ethnic groups, and that a meaningful existence cannot be had outside one's culture. Her comments testify to a deep level of awareness of the abiding value of the mores and belief systems of the black community. Strangely enough, Sophie Heywood comments that eventually Velma will come to embrace the fundamental principles of life, and thereby become an example worthy of imitation (147). Sophie appears incapable of imagining Velma, the individual and computer analyst, interpreting black culture from different perspectives; she wants Velma among the "psychically adept" (147).

Bambara deserves much credit for trying to bridge the gap between the different ways of knowing in the black community. However, the novelist's desire to provide unity within the black community through the vehicle of a black professional woman who is employed in corporate America, and who is expected to give an inordinate amount of time to the black community, does not bode well for Velma. If she is to be the "agent of change" uniting the divergent avenues of knowledge in the black community, and if she is to have her "gift" of parapsychology unfold, such as Minnie Ransom has, then Velma will not be able to successfully exhibit much agency on the job as computer analyst of the 1970s.

Another argued reason for Velma's illness, though closely related to her being logical, is that Velma does not endorse the "mud mothers" but rather flees from them. This behavior is supposed to evidence a lack of spirituality. Bambara makes it clear that it is imperative that one embraces the mud mothers: "There is no escape the calling of the caves, the mud mothers, the others. No escape" (19). Hull argues that Velma's illness is due to her "blotting out the mud mothers as a child, for seeking at the swamp with a willful spirit, and, finally for running from the answer when it stares her in the face" while looking in a mirror. According to Hull, her reflection is supposed to reflect "wisdom which is primitive, intuitive, from thought, imagination, magic, self-contemplation ... past memories and images ... passage to 'the other side'—all symbolized by the mud mothers and the mirror." She claims Velma finally makes the connection when she calls Minnie's jugs and bowls "*givi* and *zin*," words she was not aware of previously, and recognizes "silvery tendrils" of "auric light and energy extending about her" (225). Only after this acknowledgment is she able to get well. An obvious gap exists between what is expected of Velma and how the expectation is to be effected. Neither Bambara nor Hull says how Velma, the black professional computer analyst, or anyone for that matter, is to understand and appropriate all the "mud mother" knowledge from a reflection in a mirror or visits to the marshes.

The mud mothers are important to Velma because if she endorses them, they are supposed to provide mythic knowledge or ancient power that will maintain her equilibrium. Earth, mud, and water are traditional symbols that reflect the death-rebirth cycle. Susan Willis offers a different interpretation, which relates to the way television affects us. As a child, Velma runs away from the mud mothers because they link together portrayals of prehistoric communities with Hollywood's gothic overdramatized quicksand sinkings. The scene speaks to a youngster's repressed fear of being stifled by an overindulgent mother as well as to a person's fear of losing his individuality amid the mass of humanity.[42] Willis's discussion is plausible since M'Dear Sophie is overprotective and controlling and Velma is seeking individuality. Characters in the text apparently have achieved this wisdom of the mud mothers: M'Dear and her husband Daddy Dolphe, a Mr. Cleotus Brown, known also as the Hermit, and Minnie Ransom, the faith healer. Unlike Velma, these characters do not work in corporate America; they have the leisure to pursue such interests.

Velma is not completely rejecting the mud mothers; rather, she is negotiating a comfortable place for herself between the two cultures she straddles. Susan Willis introduces an important feature of the mud mothers. She feels that because the mud mothers are presented as artistically refurbishing the wall of a cave, they have become an important symbol for an unfettered mode of articulation, which escapes masculine control. Hindered from speaking and writing, they were forced to invent new avenues for artistic rendition. These innovations were long denied public acknowledgment of their intrinsic worth. Not surprisingly, Minnie Ransom's healing seeks to make Velma more integrated into the community as well as give her a voice.[43] I concur with Willis except to argue that Velma does have a voice, but it is individual, and as such, she is either misunderstood or ignored.

Velma Henry is a partial contemporary replica of the mud mothers. First, Velma uses the technology that is available to her to articulate her wishes. Because mud is not the medium of communication of her day, Velma manipulates the computer and the language skills she has learned. She clearly challenges her callous workplace (Transchemical) through her computerized methodology of reporting about its unethical environmental practice. The male leadership of the black community, her husband and other family members know that she treasures her autonomy. Like the mud mothers, her voice is unheeded. Velma wishes to be restored primarily *to* and *for* herself, albeit within the black community. No one, except Velma, grasps the significance that she has meaning as an individual first, that is, she must validate the self, and only secondarily as a member of the black community—one she works tirelessly to enhance aesthetically, economically, and politically.

Second, Velma, the artist, reflects an affinity with the mud mothers. She is the pianist for the artistic association, the Seven Sisters of the Grain. Traylor speaks of Velma: "Their songs, skits, paintings, dances, and stories articulating themes of unity, self-determination, collective work and responsibility, cooperative economics, purpose, creativity, and faith were the artistic embodiment, Velma thought, of the teachings of the Academy."[44] Velma finds no dichotomy between her career in science-technology and the arts.

During the therapy session, Minnie's spirit guide, Karen Wilder, who is far more perceptive and knowledgeable, says Velma is off "dancing." Minnie asks incredibly if it is in "the mud." Old Wife, the guide, replies in the affirmative: mud appears to be an appropriate medium for Velma (43). Indeed, mud as well as salt is interpreted as both negative and positive in this novel. Minnie does not appreciate an adult playing around for long in mud puddles. She interprets such behavior as negative, for it suggests that Velma wants revenge—a head like John the Baptist's on a charger. Wilder understands Velma's need for mud as affirming. As the mud mothers found creative expressions as painters, so it becomes a necessity for Velma.

Minnie Ransom at the beginning of the therapy session is mistaken in her approach to dealing with her patient. Her first question concerning whether Velma wishes to be well is not applicable to the patient. There is evidence that Velma *wants* to be well. Dr. Meadows comments that Velma's attempt was not a serious one; in other words, Velma did not intend to actually kill herself, but rather to draw attention to the fact that she was temporarily overwhelmed. Furthermore, Velma did seek help in the guarded manner potential suicide victims employ. Ruby reports a conversation she had with Velma, who asks her when is the right time to commit suicide. Ruby misses the cue of her friend's verbal suicide note and nonchalantly comments that Velma is "crazy." Jan immediately intuits Velma's intent and asks Ruby to assess whether Velma could have been serious about her comment. Ruby trivializes the situation, but Jan forces the issue. Could Velma have been "trying to tell you something?" (216). Ruby replies she cannot continue to be bothered by Velma's many crises, and Velma will handle her problems quite well. Ruby is dangerously mistaken.

Minnie recognizes the seriousness of Velma's case and is honest in acknowledging that she feels incompetent to perform a therapy session singly with Velma; she is incapable of matching Velma's "frequency" (42). And rightly so. Velma is a professional woman, involved in a field to which Minnie is alien. Additionally, Velma's needs are not as simple as the previous patient, who was upset about the death of her mother. This comment about a grieving child is not meant to be facetious. Furthermore, Minnie is a skilled practitioner and is known to also cure cancers. Velma's problems, however, are multiple and varied, not what Minnie is accustomed to healing in a couple of minutes. Trudier Harris confirms that Minnie herself seems to do "very little"[45] until the end of the session.

Minnie's mentor—Wilder (otherwise called Old Wife)—comes to her rescue and the patient's. First, she reproves Minnie for her lack of communication skills and her inappropriate technique in treating the patient. She questions Minnie, "What's troubling you? It ain't like you to be talking bout 'Are you sure you wanna be well'? What kinda way is that?" (45). Minnie is partly preoccupied with plans to seduce the young Dr. Meadows. Later, Minnie is seen "stalling, stalling, and failing," her hands merely lying on her client's shoulders unable to effect a cure (47). Minnie's tried and true routine of placing one hand on the patient's spine and another on the navel is not appropriate for this patient. The healing process is made more complicated because Velma, at first, resists Minnie's treatment. Minnie tells her patient that as a practitioner, she senses that Velma has not yet arrived at a point where she is ready to "dump the shit." She scolds her that adults do not prolong childish behavior such as playing in mud for an extended time (20).

At first Minnie fails to grasp that the multiple oppressions Velma has endured, which require time for the healing process to take place, even though Minnie is knowledgeable of her marital problems. Later Minnie complains to her spirit mentor that she may fail to heal the patient and hold the attention of the audience who was observing the session, unless Old Wife offers her additional guidance. She adds she cannot "generate" adequate "energy" to effect a cure. The Spirit Guide who is supervising the session encourages Minnie that all will be well (59–60). That Wilder often leaves the patient suggests that time for reflection and evaluation is crucial to Velma's healing. With proper guidance—after three quarters of the book—Minnie finds the right technique, accesses relevant information, and asks the appropriate question: The fountain of health is within you. How will you handle health once you recuperate?

The suitability of this methodology is confirmed by Michael Taussig, an anthropologist at the University of Michigan. He makes two important observations. Diseases are the combined results of physiological and social factors, but are rarely so perceived, for the interaction between the two are often unrecognized illnesses. Non-westernized healers are concerned with the sickness in the body politic as reflected in the individual patient. Taussig looks to so-called primitive medicine to understand the basis of the power struggle that often ensues in the clinical setting. He argues that the conflicts are overwhelmingly a vehicle to dominate society. In modern medicine, the medical profession acts as if it alone has the power to heal the individual. Thus, it maliciously prevents the patient and doctor from forming a bond that allows for healing.[46] Bambara fractures the capitalistic vise on medicine in Western culture, and through the faith healer, tells the patient that she has the power over her own health. By associating diseases with stressors of the culture at large, the individual pressures Velma faces on a daily basis tie in with the black and white communities in which she interacts, and which impede her reach for agency on the job.

Velma must choose health, but that health is dependent on her ability to avoid undue stress when she recovers from this particular trauma. This is the crucial stage of the patient's therapy. After she revisits the old hurts and has released or forgiven them, the primary dilemma remains. How will she direct her life when she becomes physically and emotionally healed: her husband's unreasonable demands on her as wife and mother, the black community's expectations, gains in her own productivity and visibility in corporate America. If she decides to keep her position, she will need to concentrate more energy on her career. Bebe Moore Campbell writes that blacks seeking visibility and power must make choices, such as whether to hang around with their old pals from the black community, or socialize with their business partners at local joints and plan business strategies. They may have to choose between visiting their social clubs and societies or working overtime.[47] Velma's outsider position, that is, her absence from informal networks, keeps her away from the center of power where important decisions about upward mobility are made.

Minnie and her Spirit Guide choose a remarkably effective medium to reach Velma. Music therapy is recognized in cultures to work well with patients undergoing psychiatric counseling. What is especially remarkable is that the healers confer and tailor the music precisely to Velma's needs. They choose "sassy twenties" blues in which the performer stirs Velma's senses with "Wiiild woman doan worrreee, wild woman doan have no bluuuuzzzzzz" (262). Velma responds immediately, and says, "Day of Restoration" as she feels Minnie's warm breath on her. Minnie, now fully in tune with her client psychically, offers Velma that which is necessary for her own emotional breathing space (264). As Velma mentally interacts with the folk characters of the black community in the songs, her spirit is lifted as if in dance. Interestingly, the Spirit Guide has to give Minnie the imperative twice before Minnie fully grasps the significance of Velma's artistic inclination as a vehicle for her recovery. She instructs: "Let her go, Min," since dancing is her path to knowledge. "Let her go."

Music is a successful therapeutic tool for several reasons. Velma is a professional musician. Daryl Dance confirms that the music from the park intersects with Velma's healing. She points out that the Pan Man has been trying to teach people in this country the "meaning and wisdom of the pan" and at that crucial moment plays with all his being (168). Since Velma responds to the drums, Dance writes that as the music reaches Velma, it penetrates her "kumbla"—a kind of depressive tomb.[48] Velma hears another kind of music; Minnie and her group of twelve supporters (The Master Mind) lovingly sing around her. Eleanor Traylor senses that as Velma is immersed in the music, and as Minnie speaks of her cultural heritage, Velma's emotional pain is reduced, so she can begin to respond to healing. Velma's mind is released and she soon stands on her legs, a "burst cocoon" (295).

The particular music played for Velma can eventually produce a paradoxical effect. It disrupts the appointed role as peacemaker or supporter that Bambara and the black community impose on her. Black women blues singers of the 1920s were the wild women who migrated to find more congenial places in the North or midwest. They challenged the stereotypical maternal and conjugal expectations, and refused to be hampered by anyone else's agenda, or to be hindered in their careers or successes in the recording industry. Furthermore, they challenged racism, classism, and sexism in their songs. These are the women being offered as a model for Velma. Hazel Carby mentions women such as Josephine Baker, Alberta Hunter, and Mamie Smith who sang in clubs and cabarets and who were associated with prostitutes on their vaudeville circuits. Carby argues that the blues women intersected with the physical and social contemporary problems, and offered radically new ways to meet the challenges of their day. Their focused and unconventional lifestyles provided examples that inspired other women to effect their own dreams.[49]

The paradox lies in the fact that Velma was perceived as "wild" during her college years. Velma, who has since been socialized to be less wild, has lost some vital coping mechanisms that served her well during her young adult years. As a socialized black professional woman in corporate America, the spirit, the demeanor of the "wiiiild" sisters is offered as a model for Velma to embrace. If the wildness in the earlier Velma is tapped, it should restore her effective coping skills. Velma needs the sassiness of her former self to insist on her right for space to function as an autonomous human being.

One of the powerful signs that suggests the pressures Velma faces are tied to her health is centered on her menstrual cycle. On occasions that cause her emotional anguish, she does not have the sanitary items she needs. The incident of betrayal with the black politician finds her unprepared at the end of the march. Here at the Gulf station they are boycotting, Velma has only a frayed and useless tampon. Her confrontation with Jay Patterson and the Black Power leaders who objectify the black professional women in the group is another incident in which she attempts to use a wad of toilet paper as a temporary sanitary item. When her estrangement from Obie becomes so intense and she is getting more anxious, she continuously leaves her residence with more of her belongings, while simultaneously misplacing her supplies. Velma's inability to be adequately prepared for her menstrual cycle is also related to the stressors of her job. When Palma, Velma's sister, mentions Velma's unpreparedness for her periods, she discusses Velma's many job offers outside the area in the same incident. Daryl Dance suggests that the problem with her menstruation is not merely the issue of having the sanitary articles to absorb her menses. The incidents are representative of bleeding from other injuries that are life-threatening: an awareness of being clitoridectomized in a dream, a flashback when her head hit a concrete floor in a jail cell for participating in the Civil Rights demonstrations, when she miscarried.[50] The protagonist's life is overshadowed by physical and emotional pain. Yet, as a black professional, Velma has to be twice as proficient on the job to succeed. She needs to be both physically and psychologically strong to maintain agency in the ever-changing field of computer technology.

As Velma gathers her fragmented self into a whole person, she has to decide where her priorities lie. Velma's problem is not due to a lack of spirituality; it is not due to a lack of centering in her traditions; it is not due to being too rational. Velma has important characteristics of the mud mothers: artistic sensibilities and the insistence of finding her creative voice and using it. She is not ambivalent about being well, as Minnie Ransom at first mistakenly thought. Velma does profit from knowing more about the survival aspect of the self that the mud mothers and other folk characters are be able to teach. The important point here is that Velma must claim what she wants. As her healing progresses, Bambara has Velma dancing in the streets with folk creatures: "winti, coyote, and cunnie rabbit" (246). During the therapy session, Velma readily or concomitantly develops a greater appreciation for her black cultural heritage. The crucial element is that Velma needs to harmonize these folk images with her own worldview. As utopian as *The Salt Eaters* is, the conflict within the text remains unresolved despite the hurried end with Velma, the protagonist, healed to return whole to the community.

The end of the novel hints that Velma will choose a career that does not involve corporate America, and will have more time to serve the community. The world of the spirit as opposed to the world of the mind gains ascendancy. Frantz Fanon argues that as writers and other artists attempt to break free from the colonizing influence of their oppressors, they find it important to seek out a national culture that was viable before colonialism. It is wholesome for them to discover that their ancestral past has cultural legitimacy. However, he cautions that the past by itself will not be helpful to the immediate present and its problems, unless the artists bring the folk material to bear on the present issues. It must be relevant to the lives of the people.[51] Although it is important to respect and value the Minnie Ransoms in the community, the Information Age, in conjunction with the global economy, requires highly skilled professionals in the corporate arena. There is a need for space to be carved out for black professionals who, if they are to survive whole in the West, will find it necessary to embrace the empirical as well as the spirit world without having to subsume one for the other. A dichotomy or even the privileging of one over the other can create fragmentation, as is evident in Velma Henry.

A serious dearth of black professionals exists in high-level positions of engineering, biochemistry, mathematics, nuclear science, and technology. Julianne Malveaux in "Sisters in Science" reports that in 1998, 500 degrees were awarded in the social sciences and the humanities, and although 600 were given in education, only 102 Ph.D.s were awarded to African Americans in the physical sciences, another 102 in engineering, and 290 in the life sciences. She points out that people such as astronaut Dr. Mae Jemison and Nuclear Regulatory Commissioner and MIT graduate Dr. Shirley Jackson have confirmed that black women are capable of entering and succeeding in the fields of science and technology.[52] The black community must positively embrace and promote science and technology if it is to control its destiny in the 21st century. This discussion does not suggest that *The Salt Eaters* published in 1980 is irrelevant to us in the 21st century. What is important here is that Minnie Ransom's cure, even though effective, can only affect a few. In fact, even if the united community listens to Velma and puts pressure on Transchemical, only a few hundred thousand residents will be rescued from the deadly exposure to radiation. These citizens deserve protection, but other minority and poor white communities remain at risk also.

Blacks as an aggregate dare not withdraw themselves into the mythology of the ancestors as a substitute for knowledge necessary for contemporary times. The ancestors, who primarily lived in tribal communities, effectively used the technology and the knowledge they knew to fashion the basis of a valuable and life-giving culture. However, each successive generation must respond to technological changes if it is to prosper. Today, for instance, the world confronts the advent of cloning. The black community will need many highly skilled geneticists, physicists, biologists, computer engineers, and financiers to represent their perspective. It is wonderful to have access to folk knowledge that can give us clues to understanding the world around us. We need the continued artistic performances by groups such as the Seven Sisters of the Grain, who call themselves by such indigenous names as Daughters of the Yam, Daughters of Corn, and Daughters of the Rice, to remind us of folk art, native cultures and medicine, and a clean earth. Fortunately, Bambara's prophetic vision allows her to appreciate both, even if she privileges the spiritual over the scientific.

Bambara's intuition is a good example of how a profound faith in indigenous folk culture can harmonize with science in some areas. A recent development in the food industry allows the reader to see another aspect of how *The Salt Eaters* addresses contemporary issues. Bambara intuits that there are different food pyramids of equal value for various cultures, although the U.S. Department of Agriculture in the 1980s and mid–1990s publicly recognized and endorsed only one Euro-American food guide pyramid. Respecting the marginalized food pyramids of countries she visited, such as Cuba and Vietnam, she symbolically acknowledges these cultures with the names of the performing arts characters: Daughters of the Yam (African American), Daughters of the Corn (Native Americans), Daughters of the Rice (Asian Americans), Daughters of the Plantain (Caribbean/Latino American), Daughters of the Fruit (African). The Boston Women's Health Book Collective reports in 1998 that different food guide pyramids reflecting different cultural eating habits have been acknowledged and are now being promoted. It names an Asian pyramid (including rice), a Mediterranean pyramid (including pasta), and a Latin pyramid (including plantain).[53] African and Native American pyramids are still omitted. Perhaps these two are understood to be subsumed under one of the other pyramids, although their diets are quite different in important ways, with maize and tubers being staples. One could argue that agricultural science and technology have yet to catch up with Bambara's recognition of what is a healthy diet, and that the African and Native American diets be added as viable pyramids. It is this split between disciplines and ideologies Bambara hoped to heal.

Bambara, as a utopian writer, endorses technology by having her protagonist become a computer specialist, but Bambara has not moved far enough to have that career choice get full recognition. Velma as brilliant computer analyst is not prominent enough in the text. Her foil, Minnie Ransom, has a strong voice but she cannot stay the devastations capitalist America creates in black communities, as described by Fred Holt, the bus driver.

It is the professional woman, Velma, with her scientific and computer knowledge, that brings to light the nuclear predicament within Claybourne. It may be that Bambara, among the first wave of black professionals to enter the corporate workplace in the 1970s, is speaking of Velma as computer analyst from an outsider perspective. Having lived in a working-class environment during her youth, she can capture Minnie Ransom as faith healer more graphically than she can the newly initiated black professional in a nontraditional field for black women.

As a professional and feminist, Bambara is aware that black career women have a responsibility for their own well-being. So despite the multiple discriminations Velma experiences, Bambara represents Velma as contributing to her own emotional collapse. Velma overworks herself. Ruby thinks she is "Driven, Compulsive" (193). Velma is impelled to give back to the community what she has received, for she understands its urgent needs. Can the reader justly fault Velma for her involvement, for instance, with Transchemical? She may also be responding to an inner drive to excel for her own gratification. Self-empowerment and the desirability of success are compelling forces within many women. Nevertheless, Velma owes herself health and needs to curtail her communal, family, and even work involvement.

In the conflict between the interests of the black community and the individual, Bambara privileges the community's wants above those of the protagonist. While contemplating Velma's suicide attempt, M'Dear Sophie, who represents the black community, verbalizes her wish that after Velma becomes well, she will submit to spiritual instruction. Margot Anne Kelley writes that Velma's future memories (seen in the flash forward) infer that she was able to fuse her emotional and spiritual aspects of herself and thus effect social change.[54] If Velma is to have the means to reestablish the balance of the Academy of Seven Arts, champion the social needs of the black community, and unite the split between the black men and women—especially that with her husband—it becomes highly unlikely that she will be able to effect any agency on her job in corporate America. To make this seem as if unity has been effected, Bambara employs *deux ex machina*—the supernatural. In about ten minutes, thanks to a healing session led by Minnie Ransom and her Spirit Guide (and a gigantic thunderstorm), Velma's wounds are miraculously healed, the overwhelming depression that had induced her catatonic state has been successfully reversed, she stands upright and well balanced, and throws off her shawl, reborn.

I find the ending unrealistic. Bambara is being very creative in her combination of stylistic devices. The omniscient narrator, fast-paced flash-forwards, and the massive thunderstorm meant to rejuvenate the lives of all the major characters do not, however, satisfactorily tie up the loose ends. Critic W. Maurice Shipley believes the healing is not literal but a symbolic rebirth of the Goddess force on earth.[55] The healing does function on a figurative plane, but Bambara makes it clear that the wounds on Velma's wrists are literally healed. Accepting this miracle requires complete suspension of disbelief in this realistic fiction. Since Velma had put her head in the oven and was resuscitated, she is better associated with the phoenix rising from the ashes. Unless all the major characters (except Minnie Ransom) are suffering from some form of communal psychosomatic disorders, it is difficult to understand how they could undergo a significant transformation due to the unusual thunderstorm. Yet, all will recount a spiritual renewal.

Other critics discuss the significance of the ending of the novel. Eleanor W. Traylor thinks that Velma is the only vehicle by which we understand Claybourne. It is by Velma's final acceptance of reality and her search of future hope that we see a rebirth of the community, and the potential for rejuvenated powers among those who can effectively balance the varied aspects of their lives.[56] I question whether it is only through Velma's consciousness that all this information is filtered, since we hear voices in the text. What is important here is Bambara's concern for the salvation of the community at Velma's expense, which makes the end of the story problematic.

Elliott Butler-Evans provides a more plausible explanation. She interprets Velma's suicide attempt as a means of dramatizing resistance against the sexist discrimination she and the other women experience, and by so doing, she attempts to rebuild her life.[57] Velma is suffering from severe depression. The problems that precipitated the suicide attempt have not miraculously disappeared. In the flash-forward to many years hence, we are told that she would laugh at how minor her past problems were compared to those she would encounter in the future. She could not have predicted one half of what was in store. We do not know what experiences await her, but it is reasonable to assume that if unresolved problems at this healing were glossed over, they may resurface. Another possibility is that she had difficulty accepting being another Minnie Ransom despite a *loa's* interest in Velma.[58] A third alternative is that Velma accepted the colossal challenge of balancing both a professional and psychic career.

I want to believe that Velma accepted the recommendation of the "Wild" blues singers and did her *own* "thaang." Choosing her own course involves finding a happy balance between those elements that satisfy *her* desire. Paramount among these elements is a fulfilling and successful career as computer analyst. It is understandable that Velma will experience many problems later, such as possible separation from Obie (as Minnie hinted in the healing), if they cannot resolve their differences.

The style of the novel is cause for deliberation. Bambara succeeds in creating a work of art that involves risk-taking. Artistically, it is a masterpiece. Elliott Butler-Evans comments that the text is not only centered in the folk culture; it also provides philosophic principles by which people live.[59] Bambara transmits to her readership African American culture in the worship of the ancestors. Minnie Ransom sets water and food for the loa each day, and Fred Holt claims wisdom from his sessions with the hermit of the salt marshes. Gloria Hull adds that the novel functions on varied levels of reality: "Time (synonymous with timelessness) is not fixed or one-dimensional or solely horological; instead, it exists in fluid manifestations of various dimensions. Past, present, and future are convenient, this-lane designations which can, in fact, take place simultaneously."[60] The novel's style is eclectic. Critic Margot Anne Kelley applies the principles of "chaos studies" to the narrative. The text diverts interest from individual persons and private self-governance to whole systems of thought—community, wellness systems—of which the individual is a part, and thus allows for a question and answer method of inquiry about connectedness.[61] This makes possible healing to move from the center, where Velma and Minnie Ransom are, to the rest of the community.

As wonderfully symbolic as Kelley's analysis here is, Bambara's use of chaos principles prevent Velma from having as much agency as she might have in the workplace. The focus on the community is a staple in African American narratives because of the marginalized position of blacks in the United States. The individual occasionally gets put on the periphery or becomes sacrificed for the good of the whole. I find it ironic that although Bambara is a feminist who works hard to achieve in all her works the empowerment of women, it is not Obie's or Cleotus Brown's (the spiritual hermit), or Doc Serge's career that is sacrificed for the unity of the black community. It is that of a woman's, Velma Henry. Yet, a woman may be Bambara's best choice of subject, since she wants to effect harmony within the community and capture the reach for, and frustrations to, autonomy of professional women during the 1970s and 1980s. The novel suggests that leaving corporate America to embrace the "gift" similar to Minnie Ransom's is the preferred alternative for Velma to find happiness. It seems the quick, impromptu ending effects a career path not consummate with the character who struggled throughout the text to be a computer expert exercising agency in her life.

Velma as individual cannot achieve autonomy amidst her many conflicts. If we apply Maslow's theory here, Velma is in the process of becoming self-actualized. She has moved beyond the basic and psychological needs.

It is Velma's "Being needs"—the urge to fulfill one's highest potential and thereby become fully creative[62]—that are not allowed to reach full fruition because of her environment. Janelle Collins believes Bambara's belief system requires a more unified and different political vision than one finds in the Claybourne community. It places women, Velma and Minnie—on center stage in the text, rather than the immature men and deceitful political leaders. She adds that what appears to be disharmonies—the brief and incomplete discrepancies of events, the nonlogical use of varying points of view—all suggest a feminist writer's attempt to create a new ideological position. The style, she believes, indicates the disharmonies in women's lives, and the writer's attempt to draw attention to the disunity in the community that negatively impinges on black professional women's reach for self-actualization.[63] One accepts the novelties of style as intending to complement the plot, but in this particular instance, Velma's choice to give up her profession to happily become another Minnie Ransom seems unrealistic. Yet, fiction, by its very nature, requires the suspension of disbelief.

Bambara is a trailblazer and the first feminist writer to imagine the black professional in corporate America actually performing her job in a nontraditional field, and being so proficient at her work as to pose a threat to the establishment. However, Velma finds it difficult to maintain the agency one would expect given her educational level and training, because of the multiple jeopardies that strangle her reach for self-empowerment. Nevertheless, Bambara's daring break from the negative stereotypes of black women, and her creation of the black career woman exercising some level of agency in the workplace and in her personal life, leave a model that is endearing to black women writers and many readers. In Abraham Maslow's theory of "Hierarchy of Needs," the self-actualized individual (as Bambara evidences) has periods of illumination, periods of "pure delight" during which the artist envisions and effects her wonderfully original ideas.[64] Toni Cade Bambara evidences all the characteristics of the fully self-actualized artist whose epiphany, taking form in *The Salt Eaters*, has become a legacy upon which a younger generation of black women writers continue to build, and a treasure to all readers, especially professional women whose sense of agency it affirms and encourages.

~ FIVE ~

Re-thinking Agency in
Waiting to Exhale

Terry McMillan, an internationally known popular fiction writer, created a sensation in the publishing industry when her novel, *Waiting to Exhale*
(1992), remained on the *New York Times* Bestseller List for several months.
It has sold 700,000 hard-cover and nearly 4 million paperback copies. Pocket
Books bought the paperback rights for $2.64 million, the second largest pur-
chase of its kind in publication history. In 1995, Twentieth Century–Fox paid
$1 million for the screen rights and made the book into a movie.[1] McMillan
has published four other novels, *Mama* (1987), *Disappearing Acts* (1989) (a film
production), *How Stella Got Her Groove Back* (1996) with Twentieth Century–Fox paying $2 million for the screen rights, and *A Day Late and a Dol-
lar Short* (2001). For *Mama*, Simon and Schuster eventually paid $81,000 for
the paperback rights, with 1.2 million copies in circulation.[2] She also edited
an anthology, *Breaking Ice: An Anthology of Contemporary African American Fiction* (1990). At present, McMillan has outdistanced any other African American writer in the number of books sold and the consequent remuneration.
Her phenomenal success motivated Mayor Jerry Brown to honor her by
proclaiming December 4, 2000, Terry McMillan Day in the City of Oakland, California.[3]

McMillan's literary successes with *Waiting to Exhale* and *How Stella Got
Her Groove Back* are partly due to her giving the professional protagonists a
level of agency in their public and private lives. All women living in a patriarchal society can appreciate the gesture, so McMillan is able to appeal to a
crossover audience. Her superb use of the vernacular that captures the nuances
of the urban black community, her drive for success, and her knack of capi-
talizing and enlarging the already hungry black readership created by Alice
Walker and Toni Morrison allow her to cater primarily to a black audience.

126

McMillan's *Waiting To Exhale* offers a combination of familiar and new issues regarding the representation of black professional women. It satisfies, to a greater degree than Bambara's *The Salt Eaters*, the desires of black professional women because she profiles the contemporary characters having a much higher level of autonomy in the workplace. McMillan and her readership form an interpretive community which challenges the stereotype of the black woman as unprofessional. Economist and writer Julianne Malveaux observes: "I see popular culture as the creative manifestation of that which is happening in the economy."[4] If correct, then the phenomenal sale of McMillan's text is indicative of the growing presence of black middle-class women in the professional ranks.

McMillan differs from her predecessor, Toni Cade Bambara, and from most black women writers in two significant ways. McMillan is not an academic writer, but a popular one. As such, her literary approach is fundamentally different. Francis Stead Sellers argues that many black writers follow the typical ideological-philosophical track of writing that is designed for the academy. McMillan's focus is to entertain the populace with sexy novels as Jilly Cooper and Danielle Steel have been doing for years.[5]

McMillan does not appreciate her work being associated with Cooper and Steel since she wants to be understood as a "serious" writer.[6] Nevertheless, there is validity to Sellers' observation, since McMillan's presentation of female sexuality reveals similarities with those popular writers. John Leland adds another dimension to McMillan's departure from presenting serious academic discourse. He claims that because she does not focus on race issues, she appeals to different types of readers and earned criticism from a few black reviewers. He adds: "Elizabeth Nunez, who heads the National Black Writers' Conference, expresses concern that McMillan's success could suggest to black writers that to have wide appeal, they should not write about race issues which still is a crucial factor of black life."[7] McMillan's creating space for the concerns of black women apart from racial matters, especially black professional women's concerns, was at first not well received by some academic critics or by groups within the black community.

The problem is due to a misunderstanding by critics regarding the paradoxical nature of the characteristics of popular culture that make the genre successful. John Fiske explains that popular cultural commodities satisfy contradictory needs. The economic system that produces popular culture has to reap enough profit so that the system can continue to meet the demands of the readership. To ensure this profit, the books and other cultural forms must be able to reach a crossover audience. On the other hand, because many citizens in capitalist societies are subjected to and oppressed by that economic system, these art forms become necessary to subvert the capitalistic ideology, for therein lies the fluid matrix of social dissatisfaction and the possibility of creating allegiances. Popular culture transforms the cultural factors of discontent, reshapes them imaginatively into a cultural resource that offers multiple and pleasurable interpretations, yet are transgressive of the hierarchal and policing values and standards imposed on form and content. Popular culture invades and violates established criteria of art.[8] McMillan, to be successful while subverting the most blatant stereotypes of black women, finds it necessary to appeal to a crossover readership. Some critics see aspects of her text as pandering to the publication industry and capitalism, but that millions of black women readers positively respond to the text indicates that the novel appeals to them on multiple levels.

Because McMillan uses a different rhetorical context in her writing, critics have difficulty assessing her work in terms of traditional academic discourse. The problem stems from how academia categorizes texts as belonging to high and low culture. Alice Walker and Toni Morrison, for instance, are established literary icons both nationally and internationally, so their work is a part of the national canon. Bambara is also classified among the producers of high art. McMillan's work is pop culture and perceived as low culture. Because she is the first internationally acclaimed black popular writer, critics need to create a new body of scholarship that is outside the established criteria as they evaluate her work. Critic Janet Mason Ellerby argues that the majority of academically renowned writers have ignored McMillan's work as mere entertainment, characteristic of popular culture. She adds that McMillan may not create polished masterpieces as Walker, Morrison, and Naylor, but her work does deserve academic inquiry.[9]

What may appear to be inherent weaknesses in McMillan's texts when compared to academic works may not be literary flaws, since the same criteria used for evaluation is invalid. Fiske explains that critics unquestionably assume that good literature is a chiseled art piece to be highly praised and archived. On the contrary, pop culture is understood as a commercial product designed for immediate consumption and therefore is often not necessarily well crafted. He agrees with other critics such as Bourdieu that the debate about aesthetics is simply a convenient attempt whereby the middle-class assumes control of cultural production by determining whose cultural capital is viable and therefore profitable.[10] McMillan's text resists the strictures of aesthetic control.

The theoretical assumption of art on which the evaluation to McMillan's works is predicated has been questioned only within the last thirty years. Raymond Williams' fundamental premise about culture provides a cultural studies perspective by which *Waiting to Exhale* is better understood. His revolutionary definition of culture insists that "culture is ordinary.... We use the word culture in these two senses: to mean a whole way of life—the common meanings; to mean the arts and learning—the special processes of discovery and creative effort.... Culture is ordinary in every society and in every mind."[11] For the proponents of cultural studies, there is no valid distinction between what is deemed high and low art. All creative writing is an art form, although the media, areas of interests, and the language used vary. It is yet to be determined if the evolutionary nature of the literary canon will endorse McMillan's work.

McMillan also differs from her predecessors in that she has had a longer time frame in which to recognize the significant demographic shift in the number of black people who attained middle class status, and so intuits the needs of black middle-class women. When Bambara published *The Salt Eaters* in 1980, blacks were beginning to be mainstreamed into the larger American society. By the 1990s, the group had grown considerably. In 1995, 22.1 percent (1,515,397) of African American women employed were in managerial and professional specialties.[12] The growth allows McMillan to represent all four female protagonists as professional. Mark Lowery suggests that this expanding professional class with access to more education, finances, and political power is more sophisticated, and secure both in white-collar professions and middle or upper management. He adds that their upward mobility is hindered by racism, for a $9,000 median income differential exists between white and black college graduates.[13] It is this group's interest that McMillan captured. Critic Francis Stead Sellers adds that *Waiting to Exhale* is designed "for and about" black career women who escaped the unsavory aspects of poor neighborhoods for affluent communities, yet who attempt to maintain their black cultural heritage.[14] McMillan validates their presence by representing them as upwardly mobile in the American class structure: three as middle class, and one as upper class.

McMillan's readers express their appreciation by purchasing *Waiting to Exhale* (and the other novels) in the millions. Fiske identifies them as pop culture fans who read the novels compulsively, become intensely involved in the texts, and prefer this kind of reading material.[15] Both the characteristics of her fans and the popularity of the text(s) confirm McMillan's position as a popular writer. Her philosophy of writing is aimed at capturing her readers' multiple needs. She believes "good fiction is not didactic, but pleasurable, informative, and stimulating."[16] McMillan learned from her predecessors the concept of black women having autonomy, but it was McMillan's radical departure from them that ensured her immediate international recognition.

McMillan's originality evidences itself in her extensive use of the urban vernacular. This device generates controversy. Through the characters' free use of expletives, the writer is perceived by some readers as re-inscribing black women as crude and unintelligent. Few would argue that the behavior is not excessive in many instances. One explanation for the use of the urban vernacular is that popular culture does not fall under the rubric as academic texts, and the same conventional rules do not consistently apply.

For some readers, the unbridled audacity of the language, which seems to violate all rules of propriety, provides novelty. For others, it is the women speaking candidly and casually about their sexual behavior that appeals to them. John Fiske addresses both issues. He argues that although popular culture is vigorously criticized as debasing the language, it adds fresh vigor to, rather than devalues it. He points out that because popular culture has a tendency towards superfluity, popular culture is attacked as vulgar and inordinate. Its excessiveness is the very quality that makes it difficult for any ideology or required standards to control it. Popular culture appeals to the millions who are not recipients of the American Dream, and those who feel powerless.[17] This critique is appropriate for McMillan's text, and many of her readers are of the working class.

The language the four protagonists use prove embarrassing or delightful to different segments of McMillan's readership. More than 60 percent of the respondents in my survey did not appreciate the excessive use of "four-letter words." Most of the 60 percent argue that their occasional use to vent frustration and anger is admissible, but it is as if the women did not take "the energy to speak decently to one another." Since the survey participants would not use this language with other professionals they respect, they perceive it as inappropriate to use it among friends. Another describes the language as "tainted." One respondent shows her mixed reaction to the language when Savannah angrily rejects Kenneth:

> I was truly shocked to hear her say, "Fuck you, Kenneth, and the horse you rode in on." Maybe I was surprised because I have never heard the expletive before, and possibly because I could never imagine myself ever making such a comment. I do not know any black professional woman who uses this kind of language so consistently. Graphic though it may be, it is truly appalling.

About 10 percent of the respondents say they enjoy the shock effect of the language. They argue that it is precisely because the women are very close friends that they dare speak to one another in this manner. One reader comments:

> I must admit that when I heard Savannah tell Bernadine, "I will I will I will.... Bye, you rich bitch," I laughed so hard. But as I looked at the text closely, the expletives are used when the women are under the greatest stress or angry at the political/sexist system. The vernacular offers an avenue to deal with events that are made unjustly difficult for them. It's their way of feeling they are subjects. In fact, when McMillan's first publisher refused to promote her first book, her immediate response was "Fuck this." Her angry response helped her generate enough energy to do her own legwork and today she is a phenomenon.

One respondent confirms that she and her friends speak like this on a regular basis, particularly as it relates to oppression of women in a patriarchal society. It offers them a "comfort zone where any discussion is possible, and because it is shocking—different from what we used to speak before we understood how oppressed we are—it provides laughter and so reduces our stress."

One useful aspect of the vernacular is its creativity; it confirms Fiske's theory that popular culture invigorates the language. When Bernadine asks the others to contribute to the pizza at the sleepover, she says, "Church up, ladies" (320). Here the standard noun, church, is used as a verb, but the word "church" is metonymic. It is the practice of several denominations in the black community to collect more than one offering in a single gathering. "Church up, ladies" suggests the communal participatory action that is common among friends. The technique of using the first person narrative or dialogue gives immediacy to the vernacular; it reflects the anger or pleasure in the women's voices. Paulette Richards suggests that part of the creativity of McMillan's speech is her ability to merge familiar mainstream slang terms with the black vernacular. For example, the mainstream American slang term "ass" becomes "simple-ass husband"; "hunky-dory" becomes "hunky-fucking-dory," and "gets-on-my-nerve" becomes "gets-on-my-last-nerve." These improvised word groupings are consonant with the "blues aesthetic," for they reflect one form of African American philosophy of resistance that is not polemic.[18] Although the text has four black middle-class professional women, the language appeals to some black middle-class and working-class readerships, for both groups experience marginalization and discrimination financially, socially, and politically. It also appeals to a crossover readership.

Waiting to Exhale evidences the triple oppression of race, gender and class as well as the expected dependency of the black community on black women, but the presentation is less direct than in Toni Cade Bambara's *The Salt Eaters*. McMillan refuses to deal with "the problem," claiming her work is not a sociological study. She appreciates the role protest literature has served in the black community, but is aware of a paradigm shift away from race-centered texts since the 1970s. She finds some readers and critics who still insist that artists address sociopolitical issues.[19] She refuses to discuss the "Middle-Class Blacks' Burden" as Leanita McClain, writer for the *Chicago Tribune*, vividly describes: "I run the gauntlet between two worlds [black and white]; I am cursed and blessed by both; I can also be used by both. I am a rope in a tug of war.... I assuage white guilt. I disprove black inadequacy and prove my parents' generation that their patience was indeed a virtue."[20] McMillan sidesteps the incessant tensions affiliated with racism, and deals primarily with women's issues. By placing her characters in a fairly comfortable economic bracket, she eliminates the effects of racism encountered below the poverty line. This comment is not consistent with other novels such as *Mama* (1987) and *A Day Late and a Dollar Short*.

Because of McMillan's assertion against nationalistic claims, and the readability of *Waiting to Exhale*, it is easy to miss the politics that inform her representation. The novel creates space for dialogue and ideas not articulated because of the earlier focus on the racial "other." John Leland records one reader's response: "Terry talks about problems, but with humor and fun. I laugh through the tears. That's what I need."[21] McMillan deconstructs the race, gender, and class issues by presenting them in the text only as they impact the lives of black professional women.

In the novel, McMillan emphasizes the career concerns of the four characters, allowing for a more detailed analysis of their professional status. She endows her protagonists with the necessary characteristics to compete and have a measure of success in corporate America or in their entrepreneurial pursuits. All four characters are college graduates living in Phoenix. Savannah Jackson, Robin Stokes, and Bernadine Harris (for a short duration) are in the middle tier of their firms; Gloria Matthews is the successful proprietor of a beauty salon, Oasis Hair. McMillan gives them some level of agency on the job. Savannah's performance is a good example.

At the beginning of the novel, Savannah, a thirty-six-year-old black professional woman, has had four different jobs in different locations within fifteen years. She is goal oriented and a problem solver. Unhappy with her position at a gas company in Denver, she applies for a job in the publicity department of a Phoenix television station. She is hired. Savannah is a risk taker and is willing to accept a $12,000 reduction in pay to achieve her dreams. Although on the edge of jeopardizing her financial security, she hopes her gamble will effect her goal of advancing to the "production" department (3).[22] Later, she encourages Bernadine that every noble or progressive act is accompanied by an element of fear. Savannah has the ability to independently design her goals, choose a strategy to achieve them, and adjust that strategy when necessary to ensure success.

Savannah has very definite career aspirations and is assertive enough to express her goals to the interviewing committee. She wishes to produce television programs. Later, on her way to Phoenix to begin her job, she is confident of her ability to excel in her field. She confides in her riding companion that because she was successful in the job in Denver—she had successfully produced several "public service announcements and instruction films" (115)—she knew she would be selected after the interview. She had capitalized on the gains of her varied experiences.

Savannah's professional profile illustrates a progression from the paradigm shift that Mary Helen Washington creates with her idea of the suspended, assimilated, and emergent woman. Savannah's mother is not a professional, so she does not understand what activities inform a successful career. She counsels Savannah that if she exerts as much effort on finding a husband as she does on her professionalism, she would have been married for many years. Savannah's mother has found a sense of fulfillment in marriage. This difference in foci creates tension in the relationship between mother and daughter, as was seen in *The Salt Eaters* when Velma Henry resists her godmother's expectations to focus an inordinate amount of time on community activism. Here, Savannah centers her energies primarily on her career. She, like her mother, wants a companion, but Savannah seeks a meaningful relationship while maintaining her sense of autonomy. McMillan transgresses the patriarchal assumption that the female identity is linked to the male's.

Savannah, like most black professional women in corporate America, wants to attain a high level of productivity, have visibility, and reap substantial economic rewards. Her career had already peaked in Denver, so she evaluates her position. She contrasts the reduced salary of the television crew manipulating the cameras with the much higher remuneration of those who interact directly with the public. She plans to seek the best opportunities and is careful to make wise career choices. Savannah conceives two strategies. She decides to "work my ass off" (115). Then, sidestepping immediate self-gratification and maintaining a margin of economic security, she reallocates her investment portfolio to meet current expenses of her mortgage and her mother's support. This plan allows her long-term goal a good chance to materialize. Savannah's attitude and behavior are diametrically opposed to notions that black women lack financial acumen. McMillan is offering an oppositional gaze to the well-established stereotype, begun during slavery, that black women are dependent creatures.

One of the most endearing characteristics of this black professional woman is her level of self-efficacy: the ability to envision her goals and actualize them. En route to her new job, she enjoys the majestic heights of the mountains, which symbolize her career aspirations. The same determination that characterizes Terry McMillan to have her books marketed is replicated in Savannah's career behavior. When Savannah is given the assignment to work collaboratively to produce a program on a "trial basis," (246) she explains to her mother that the project entails an enormous amount of work, such as detailing newspapers daily to find ideas for a new program that will address African American concerns. To help her mother grasp that much of this research is to be completed away from the office, Savannah uses the familiar word "homework."

Savannah's work habits, which include extensive reading, are confirmed in the survey I sent to professional women in which I asked them about their reading habits. Persons in law, medicine, academia, engineering, and administration read 60 to 35 hours per week. Forty-six percent of the respondents said that three-fourths of their reading is work-related. Savannah's promotion is not due merely to affirmative action quotas, but hard work. Here again, McMillan disrupts racial stereotypes.

McMillan is purposeful in establishing the professional skills of her black career women as well as the daily activities and problems their jobs entail. Bernadine Harris, for example, works in the finance department of a real estate firm. The omniscient narrator's voice portrays Bernadine examining the "control sheets" opened at her station, looking at the adding machine, and wondering what item she last recorded. She is having difficulty concentrating on her work because she is preoccupied with her children and their response to their parents' divorce. Bernadine's job forces her to make an ethical decision. Having settled her divorce case for one million dollars, she considers quitting the firm. She recognizes that this action would create a dilemma for the company, since leaving management in peak season disrupts the flow of activities such as payroll. She makes an ethical choice to adhere to her friend's philosophy of life: to maintain the blessings of "good karma" (399). Bernadine's behavior evidences discipline and sound moral judgment, a contemporary woman's version of grace under pressure.

McMillan portrays what another character, Robin, does at an insurance company, and shows her attempts to advance her career. Robin is exceptionally good at obtaining profitable contracts, and is proud she did the underwriting of a "ten-million dollar account." She is aware of how profitable such a contract is to her firm in late December, for it ensures the company will remain in the black. She also knows that it should enhance and solidify her position with the firm. The reader applauds her, and is glad she will finally get a bonus. Robin, as a black professional woman, knows how to concretize a promise made by her boss in the heat of the achievement. She asks him immediately after his public announcement how much her bonus would be, and he responds it will be between five and ten thousand dollars. McMillan is disrupting the idea that women are not aggressive enough to effect their own advancement, and in particular, that black professional women cannot perform well in careers that are male dominated.

McMillan replicates the same detailed account of the career woman's work in her representation of Gloria's beauty salon. Hair care is intrinsically woven into the fabric of black life, and McMillan helps her readership appreciate the skills needed to successfully operate such a business. Gloria structures the daily work routine to please her customers. She is astute enough to realize the different needs of her clientele, so she schedules the senior citizens in the morning and the younger patrons in the evening. Gloria seeks to please her customers. When Sister Monroe requests that the "whorish red" in her hair be allowed to stay in a little longer than usual, so she can look good on her missionary journey to Las Vegas, Gloria represses her laughter and complies. The tasks her employees perform reflect the variety of services she offers. Diseree does "weaves" despite her long acrylics; two assistants are manicurists; Philip combs "lustersilk" through Sandra's hair; and Joseph, stationed beside Cindy, applies hair rods to a man who desires "Jheri-kurl" (74).

McMillan captures the gossipy behavior that often pervades the typical salon workplace. Joseph and Phillip cannot tolerate Sister Monroe because she hypocritically poses as a Pentecostal missionary to Las Vegas, but gambles instead. Similarly, on one occasion, Joseph announces that he saw Bernadine in a distraught state at a quick food–mart after her husband left her. He describes her as still dressed in her robe "all messed-up," and how shocked he was to see Bernie so "out of it" (74). Although Gloria usually places customers' needs first, she maintains her loyalty to Bernadine by calling her immediately.

As a popular writer, McMillan concentrates on the area that generates the greatest appeal to a crossover audience. Since the divorce rate in the United States during the 1990s was about 50 percent, and since the female living alone in 1994 was 14.6 percent,[23] McMillan focuses on the private sphere of the protagonists' lives. These women face serious financial obligations and encounter discrimination in the working world on a daily basis. Janis Sanchez-Hucles explains that the "two fer" myth developed in the early

1970s whereby black women are given preferential treatment in job hiring because they are counted twice—as minority and female. To perpetuate the falsehood, black women's gains are compared with other disadvantaged groups rather than white males who dominate the most prestigious and lucrative positions. According to statistics, black women's greatest gains have been white-collar jobs traditionally designated for women, and offering fewer career advancement opportunities, lower salaries and fewer fringe benefits.[24] McMillan demonstrates how the oppressions of race, class, sex, and inordinate community service negatively impact black professional women's lives.

McMillan is subversive in criticizing racism; she presents the protagonists as being exploited in the workplace. Robin complains that her firm's white management is making her life unbearable (194). When a worker in the middle of "underwriting an account" has to leave work for personal reasons, Robin asks a rhetorical question: Who gets told to finish the project? Her supervisors could have asked other employees less busy or not pressured at the moment to complete the job. Instead, she is expected to complete the new assignment, requiring that she awake "at the crack of dawn" and arrive at work at least by 7 A.M., lest the company forfeit her account (195). The black professional woman is not consistently treated with the same courtesy as other employees. McMillan is problematizing the professional space to show that even though blatant and physically abusive racism no longer operates in corporate America, the black career woman's struggle takes on a new complexity when racist practices are subtle.

Racial oppression on the job is also present in how the rewards are distributed. Historically, black women receive the lowest remuneration although they have the same credentials and work experience as whites. Jacqueline Jones reports that as early as the 1930s, black women were forced to accept the lowest-paying jobs, and earned significantly less than white women. For instance, in the Northeast and Midwest, they received at least $12 less each week than white females, and the disparity was even greater in the South.[25] In Waiting to Exhale, Robin poses another rhetorical question: "When was the last time I got a raise?" (195). What makes the favoritism more painful is that either she will not be acknowledged for her participation, or her colleagues will misrepresent her contribution to the account. She is also exasperated with management's skepticism toward her ability, despite her continued proven dependability. Even when meeting deadlines seems impossible, she satisfies the benchmark. Her efforts require closing a ten million dollar deal at an unlikely time before Robin gets a bonus, and that she assumes is because her CEO could not renege on his public announcement. Women of other races experience similar scenarios, but McMillan shows how

America's capitalist society frequently treats black women workers as less deserving of economic parity.

Through Robin's and Savannah's working class parents, McMillan illustrates the effect of intergenerational racism on the career aspirations of these black women. Past discrimination denied their parents quality education and decent wages. Despite their hard work, they lack adequate funds during retirement, and experience different kinds of abuses. Because Savannah's mother is old and has poor vision, she checks the wrong box when filling out a form. As a result, her food stamp allowance is cut, leaving her with only twenty-seven dollars a month. The social workers are not sympathetic to her plight, showing little concern for the elderly. Sanchez-Hucles comments that older women are the recipients of low pay, part-time, and temporary employment, without health and retirement benefits, and 60 percent of these senior citizens live in poverty. Single women and the elderly experience the greatest economic difficulties, but the problem becomes compounded for the elderly since their health and finances deteriorate.[26] Savannah's mother experiences hardships, for in addition to being old, female, single, and poor, she is African American.

McMillan acknowledges other family situations that are the indirect result of racism and which have an impact on the lives of the protagonists. When downsizing begins at IBM, Savannah's brother-in-law loses his job. Young black employees lack seniority; consequently, they are often the first ones fired. McMillan also represents the issue of black male incarceration. Since Savannah's brother has just gotten out of jail, he is dependent on his mother and girlfriend. In the face of seemingly insurmountable stress, Savannah's self-confidence becomes her strength. She wills her career into being. She visualizes her success and insists that she deserves a promotion, for she has "earned" the position. She is certain that the Divine has given approval so she can assist her mother; she also ruminates on what would happen should she not receive her promotion. Savannah then expresses her appreciation for her mother who had "busted her ass" to ensure her children's well-being, and who is deserving of a comfortable life during retirement (353). McMillan demonstrates the multiple jeopardy two generations of black women experience. Savannah, the professional in her family, becomes the provider for the aging parent. Despite McMillan's claim that she does not deal with "the problem" in her novels, Savannah's family's concerns become the vehicle to interrogate socioeconomic issues as they impact women, albeit not in a polemic mode.

Waiting to Exhale shows racism frustrating the black professional woman's aspirations in yet another way—the desire for black men to have white female partners. The text does not deny genuine affection between people of different races; it does interrogate how the behavior of two generations of male characters in the novel affect the protagonists.

Interracial relationships influence Bernadine Harris's life. John, Bernadine's husband, is a handsome black male who wants to live the American Dream. In fact, he has achieved all the trappings that accompany the social status the dream represents. He is an astute entrepreneur owning a lucrative software firm with diversified assets. He owns apartment buildings, two hundred acres of farmland in California, a vineyard in Arizona, a Subway franchise, and numerous insurance policies, in addition to 401K and liquid accounts. John lives in a "dream house in a picture-perfect neighborhood; the residence is filled with picture-perfect furnishings and antiques." He owns a Porsche; Bernadine has a BMW, and the children get a Jeep Cherokee to transport them to private schools. Furthermore, he has the seemingly ideal nuclear family: a beautiful, intelligent wife and two children. He even has a dog worth $1,200.

John's world appears perfect, but from his perspective it is not. As a black man, he does not receive the requisite approval that a white male with the same level of attainment does. To achieve the same social acceptance, John feels he needs a white wife. She will be his symbolic representation of achieved whiteness. With her, he will share the white domain, since he has fulfilled all the tangible prerequisites. Feminist critic Francis Beale contributes to our understanding of the factors influencing John's behavior. First, she argues America has designated specific gender roles for males and females. Manhood is characterized by having certain materialistic icons: a good paying job, a substantial amount of money, and luxury cars. Clearly, by this definition, John has attained manhood.

Beale shows another often unarticulated part of the equation necessary to attain manhood. To be a man, John must keep a wife who is a trophy, not a wife who is a potential competitor. The ideal trophy spouse is put on a pedestal, lacks autonomy, and does no meaningful work. Her life is spent beautifying her body, keeping up with the Joneses, and being a dutiful wife. She adds that black professional women reject these arbitrary roles.[27] Since Bernadine consistently aspires to entrepreneurship by owning a catering business, she threatens John's sense of manhood. John repeatedly questions the validity of her goals.

John prefers Bernadine to be a housewife who will maintain a perfect house, raise the children, and satisfy his sexual needs. He tabulates that during their eleven-year-old marriage, they have had sex 732 times. Sex in this relationship has deteriorated from an activity whereby husband and wife share affection to a business transaction. John's recordkeeping allows him to determine how much his property has devalued with repeated usage.

Because Bernadine has already satisfied his sexual desires for eleven years, John exchanges her for a new lover. John's respect for his new wife is questionable as well. Since she is pregnant before the marriage vows, his calculator has already begun the tabulations of their sexual engagements. McMillan demonstrates that both the rejected and newly embraced wife are objectified as property; hence, racism and sexism intersect in this episode.

McMillan is careful to ascribe to her protagonists love of themselves as black women and respect for their African American heritage. The women function as a foil to John's ethnic self-hatred. He objects to his daughter's African hairstyles, and he certainly dislikes her name, Onika. He warns Bernadine that if she cuts her long, permed hair, he will leave her. He insists that she use a premium sun block to avoid any trace of tanning. John has what Michele Wallace calls "white fever," a preference for Euro-American physical characteristics. Wallace encapsulates an important aspect of the relationship between black women and black men, and it explains why John's rejection of Bernadine is so painful.

During slavery, black women supported black men. Sojourner Truth is a good example of the numerous women who risked their lives for men. Having achieved her freedom, she returns to the South nineteen times and escorts hundreds of men and women via the Underground Railroad to the North. During Reconstruction, women such as Ida Wells Barnett risked being captured or killed to expose the economic competition that motivated the lynching of black men. Wells Barnett's journalistic efforts further generated international attention to the wanton destruction of black men (and even some women) under the false pretense of rape charges. During the 1960s, black women did not immediately join the women's movement. In addition to rejecting the racism inherent in the organization, they refrained lest a feminist stance pose a threat to the supposedly fragile manhood of their companions. Wallace evaluates the outcome:

> When she stood by silently as he became a "man," she assumed that he would subsequently grant her long overdue "womanhood" just as the white man had done for the white woman. But he did not. He refused her. His involvement with white women was only the most dramatic form that refusal took. He refused her across the board.... Little did they [black women] know that one day their activities would be used as proof that the black woman has never known her place and has mightily battled the black man for his male prerogative as head of the household.[28]

Wallace is interrogating the perception of the black woman as valuable only when serviceable to others. In *Waiting to Exhale*, John internalizes both the capitalistic and patriarchal norms of the culture, but Bernadine rejects them.

As soon as the couple separates, Bernadine symbolically chops off the straight hair, and resumes wearing it naturally curly.

The interest in interracial dating is evidenced in the second generation of black males in the text, and negatively impacts Gloria. Her sixteen-year-old son, Tarik, seeks only white or fair-skinned girls as dates, though he himself is not fair-skinned. Gloria tries to elicit a response from him about his relationships, but he circumvents the issue by saying she is invading his private life. He adds that black girls are fat and he loves "this one," which is a white girl two doors away. Since his mother is black and fat, "sixty pounds overweight" (60), Tarik pities as well as rejects her. He once questioned how she intends to ever find him a father and herself a husband since she is obese. At sixteen, Tarik has learned the mainstream media's aesthetic of a beautiful woman as found on numerous magazine covers and television advertisements; a body that is white skinned, tall, very slender, and young embodies a beautiful woman. Gloria is pained to realize that the media have more influence on her son's choices than she does.

After his mother cautions him about being found sexually engaged in the white girl's house by her parents, he then brings the white girl home where Gloria discovers them having coitus. Tarik's behavior causes Gloria so much anguish, not only because his actions may result in unfavorable consequences for his lover and himself, but because his choice of partner may be a rejection of his ethnic self and of Gloria as a black woman. Gloria lives the absence of available black professional men. Her concerns for Tarik, for her business, and her weight problem eventually lead to a heart attack. Emotionally charged issues that are disruptive to a career woman's private life extend to and impede her professional progress. These sexist attitudes towards black women are based on capitalistic notions of what is valuable on the market. Intra-ethnic racism still operates on some level within the black community.

Some readers question McMillan's treatment of white women characters in *Waiting to Exhale*, and raise the charge of racism. Heather Greenwood confirms: "Others have complained about a strong anti-white-woman sentiment in *Exhale*.[29] It is important to determine what racism is: "Racism is a set of beliefs, ideologies, and social processes that discriminate against others on the basis of their supposed membership in a so-called racial group [and gives] the descriptions of practices and attitudes that produce racial DISCRIMINATION and disadvantage."[30] To further discuss this difficult term, the *Encyclopedia of Modern American Social Issues* explains that prejudice and racism are mistakenly used interchangeably:

> Prejudice is an individual, psychological phenomenon, whereas racism is a social, political, and economic phenomenon. Simply put,

it has been said that prejudice turns into racism when it begins to have significant consequences outside the minds and feelings of specific individuals, that is, when it leads to significant discrimination, or oppression of one or more racial or ethnic groups.

The text asks whether minorities can be racist. It explains that when racism is related to economics, minorities cannot be said to be racist. This statement confuses and angers Euro-Americans who argue that minorities are given special privilege that is denied them. A discussion further helps to make the distinction between the two terms:

> Those who assert that minorities cannot be racist do not argue that minority individuals cannot be prejudiced, or even that it is morally acceptable for them to be prejudiced. Rather, they assert that the prejudices of minorities cannot rise to the level of racism because minorities lack the power to oppress or repress the white majority. White prejudice, on the other hand, is racist because whites hold most of the economic and political power in the United States. White prejudices tend to be translated into economic discrimination, even enforced by political and police authorities.[31]

In light of these definitions, the charge that McMillan is racist is invalid.

The question whether she is prejudiced in her representation of white characters engenders debate. Francis Stead Sellers comments that McMillan's characters "believe in black solidarity [and] to act like white is an act of betrayal." She also notes: "'White folks' hover disconcertingly on the novel's margins."[32] All three white women characters are represented somewhat negatively. Kathleen, John's former bookkeeper-mistress and later wife, contributes to the demise of Bernadine's nuclear family. Once Bernadine becomes so enraged, she slaps Kathleen for intruding in her marriage and being present when she wants to talk privately to her now-separated spouse. Not once in the text is Kathleen given a voice. Tarik's girlfriend is presented only in terms of two young teens' sexual exploration. His mother discovers her engaged in oral sex with Tarik, and orders her out of her house. She has no name and never speaks. James Wheeler is a black civil rights lawyer whose wife, a white woman, is dying of cancer when he meets Bernadine. He appears to have respected his marriage vows, for Bernadine reports him saying he has not had sex in six months (suggesting he has not been unfaithful to his spouse until then), even though the relationship had deteriorated before she was diagnosed as terminally ill. The wife is not named, nor does she speak.

McMillan's treatment of white women in the novel (and film) elicits varied responses. Joan Walsh interprets the issue as not relating to the white female characters per se, but to a larger concern: male bashing. She argues it is the black men's problematic social and psychological needs that impel some of them to want interracial marriages. She is dismayed at the simplistic treatment given the romantic relationships in the movie and novel. The biracial relationships are presented as either good or bad, and there is no sense that they could be otherwise, except that they are improper or are vindictive acts against black women. She acknowledges the pain Bernadine feels, and thinks some bashing is appropriate after such a wrenching break-up. However, she cautions that excessive male bashing is destructive because it releases women from taking responsibility for the improper choices they make. She finds an unsettling "psychological subtext—the only good white woman is a dead white woman."[33] Walsh's critique raises some concerns of how women *write* women, especially since McMillan herself reports, "Everything I write is about empowerment, regardless of what kind it is."[34] Although the three white women are not presented as mere sex objects, it would be an oversight not to note that their primary roles have a strong sexual component.

In the novel, the white female character who died is not disrespected. A divorce was pending due to a conflict in wanting children. The second white female marries the black man with the most money and prestige in the novel, even though she has a confrontation with the rejected wife. The teenage white girl is simply exploring her sexuality when she faces a shocked and angry mother. These three episodes bring with them strong emotional responses because of the historical implications surrounding the black-white sexual taboo in the United States. McMillan, in Greenwood's discussion, addresses the criticism from an artistic perspective: "'I can't be sitting around thinking what white people are gonna think. Or what black men are gonna think. I don't write to offend, but if that's the case....' her voice trailing off."[35]

McMillan's novel concentrates primarily on the lives of four black women, so the protagonists are the only fully developed characters. The novelist is interested in the other characters as a means of commenting on the central issues influencing the lives of the women. The critique that McMillan is prejudiced in her portrayals of white women is important to note, but the charge may have greater credibility if leveled against her harsh representation of black men, since they are more visible but get hardly more developed than the white women characters. Although Kathleen participates in the breaking up of Bernadine and John's marriage, she is not the one the reader remembers as being vilified. Instead, it is the black male characters.

Severe criticism has been leveled against McMillan for her negative portrayal of black men in *Waiting to Exhale*. Paulette Richards comments that

McMillan's name is "synonymous with male bashing"[36] All four protagonists participate in harshly criticizing most of their lovers or husbands for their unsavory behaviors. Only two men escape the diatribe: Marvin, Gloria's new "friend," and James Wheeler, Bernadine's new lover, possibly because they are introduced late in the narrative, and because McMillan must provide some balance or be castigated for stereotyping all black men. McMillan counters that the angry black males are not upset about the media coverage of them involved with drugs or living in poor housing projects, so why should they be so angry about images reflecting their "sexual prowess"? McMillan explains that she writes about the bad choices the women make. These men are not the ones girls should bring home to meet their parents. "That's the reason why they weren't three-dimensional. They were kind of an aside, almost."[37] A critic could take McMillan to task since many black males are disturbed about the negative media coverage of them. Furthermore, McMillan's linking of drugs, poverty, and black male sexuality comes dangerously close to stereotyping. Two other reasons are posited here.

The minimal treatment of white women characters may be understood in terms of what one writer/respondent said earlier. Black women writers need more time to better understand their Euro-American counterparts in order to represent them as the well-rounded characters and as autonomous professional women. Furthermore, the writer has choices, and in this particular case, the novelist chooses to focus on four black career women. It must also be remembered that while writing this novel, McMillan attempted to expand her range of characters by creating a biracial character, but deleted that section, for she needed to better understand the culture to imagine a genuine slice of the protagonist's world. Maybe the absence of African American women dating Euro-American men can be accounted for in the same way: a need for greater familiarity with the subject. It will be interesting to see how McMillan treats women characters of other ethnic groups in subsequent narratives. Other representations will allow for fuller analysis of her responses to non–African American women. That the novel appealed to millions of consumers across racial lines is testament that the subject of women's relationships with women, as well as with men, resonated deeply with the readership.

Class oppression receives less attention than racism in *Waiting to Exhale* because the protagonists are middle or upper class women who suffer less class discrimination in the mid–1990s than their peers did in the 1970s. However, the women are segregated in their predominately white neighborhoods. They do not have any social interaction with white people, though John, Tarik, and James have intimate relations with white women.

Nevertheless, they purchase homes in expensive neighborhoods because they can afford them. Their children go to either public or private schools depending on their parents' wishes. The extreme forms of class oppression have abated between blacks and whites in the social arena within the text.

In the novel, class discrimination is subtly practiced in the work force. Even though many women experience sexism in employment, white women are more privileged than black women. This unfair treatment is demonstrated at Robin Stokes' firm where a white female employee's domestic concerns are honored. Marva is the mother of a healthy infant just a few months old. Whenever the child experiences any discomfort (as babies will, since their immune systems are not fully developed), the mother panics and leaves her work. She receives no penalty; in fact, her work is assigned to Robin.

It is possible that in the minds of her supervisors, Marva represents a modern version of the Cult of True Womanhood that was earlier only operational for aristocratic white women. Here race and class discrimination intersect. Marva is allowed some of the privileges of the more affluent stay-at-home mother while accruing advantages to climb the economic ladder. At the end of the novel, Robin is pregnant and a single mother. It is expected that she will not be so supported. Robin will find it necessary to arrange for adequate childcare. Black women in corporate America, whether in fiction or real life experience, are like the fictionalized Robin, not privileged. One finds it necessary to question the frequency any employee could be allowed to be absent from work for parental responsibilities. Be that as it may, one black female subject in Edmondson Bell and Nkomo's study was told by her CEO when she became pregnant that at his corporation, she could not be successful as mother and as executive.[38] Although Marva is here given preferential treatment, writer-scholar Stephanie Golden suggests that even employees as privileged as Marva are often the victims of craftily disguised discriminatory practices, for they are denied meaningful exposure to travel, or not assigned important projects because they are understood to have the "global" responsibility of child care.[39]

Marva's privilege, to be released from her job, must be accounted for since time is money in corporate America. It is a black professional woman's skills that are exploited to ensure that the insurance company does not lose financially. Robin is doubly victimized. She is overworked and she will not be remunerated for her efforts. The economic exploitation seen in fiction becomes a reality in the 1992 report by Sanchez-Hucles. Despite equal education and occupational status, black women ten years ago earned significantly less than either white men or women.[40] Marva began economically ahead of Robin, and now Robin works to maintain Marva's move further up the financial ladder, while as a result, Robin falls substantially further behind. Robin, as a black employee, is expected to advance the career and interests of her white counterpart, just as Aunt Jemima was expected to care for the white household at the expense of her own interests. McMillan disrupts this contemporary version of the Mammy stereotype; Robin complains about the class differentiation rather than suffer in silence.

McMillan wants the patriarchal society to acknowledge that women—as mothers or otherwise—have a right to be professionals. Adequate child care facilities with qualified staff are necessary to allow working mothers more time to concentrate on their careers the way most men do. That Marva appears haggard looking at thirty-nine years (as if she were fifty) suggests that her responsibilities as a mother and full-time employee are difficult. McMillan particularizes the problem for the black professional woman. Robin cannot perform at an optimum level if her time and cultural capital are spent advancing her white associate. There needs to be clearer specifications as to what her responsibilities are, and an end to classism in this company.

McMillan is aware that classism operates in both the white and black communities to frustrate the professional growth of black career women. At the annual meeting of Black Women on the Move, the distance materially among the upper, middle, and lower class blacks is acknowledged. It is to McMillan's credit that she does not problematize economic success by making the groups engage in destructive conflict. While the four protagonists enjoy comfortable living, Bernadine is the only one who qualifies for upper-class status, since her family has multimillion dollar assets. When the issue is raised to recruit more professional blacks to support programs for the disadvantaged, Dotty distances herself from the affluent in "Scottsdale." She naively suggests that their only anxiety is "their BMW's, their landscaping, and their annual trip to Hawaii" (247).

Intraclass struggle exists within the Black Women on the Move. Ironically enough, Bernadine is not "siddity" (snobbish), and it is through her that the reader gets a glimpse of the minor class conflicts in the group. Having forgotten the scheduled time for a luncheon, she is gratified the meeting had by then adjourned. The occasional pettiness and competition over consumptive items annoy her because they detract from the professionalism and friendliness Bernadine desires. Bernadine knows the extremes to which such rivalry can lead. Her ex-husband, John, had become consumptive. He had to have fancy cars (antique included), a large closet full of expensive clothes, and aged wine, and other items ad infinitum. Bernadine prefers meaningful discussions conducive to intellectual and professional development in a relaxed, pleasurable environment. She remains in the organization because it runs efficiently and class rivalry is discouraged.

She enthusiastically supports the organization. From her million-dollar divorce settlement, she intends to donate funds to several charities, including her own organization.

Waiting to Exhale illustrates that the oppression black women and white women experience in the job market is not the same. White women encounter sexism and some may encounter classism. Black women experience racism, sexism, and classism in the workplace, and even among themselves, class issues arise in a minor key. These black professional women cannot exercise the agency they wish because of the interlocking factors of discrimination.

In the novel, the black community is presented as less oppressive than that of *The Salt Eaters*, possibly for two reasons. First, McMillan does not want to detail the destructive socioeconomic forces that operate within it, nor does she want to portray victims. Second, McMillan is representing successful black professional women with a certain degree of agency. They have the power to reject the societal concept of black women taking on the suffering for everyone else, and they are pleasure loving.

The potential disruptions of a black community's homophobic behavior do not materialize. At Gloria's establishment, an employee named Phillip tests positive for HIV. The situation is potentially explosive and can ruin her business, for Sister Monroe, the Christian, gossips about Phillip. Gloria's customers have cause to fear this rumor, for Evelyn Hammond writes that HIV claimed the life of a black person every two hours in 1990, and it was even more rampant by 1992.[41] Before Phillip's test result, all the customers knew that the two best hair stylists were gay. Because they were so proficient and pleasant, the customers accepted them. Gloria refuses to pander to their prejudices or fears. With great finesse, she minimizes the problem by treating Phillip with dignity. She tells her customers that he is on leave and is still in her employ. Privately, she worries for him and sends him a gift of four hundred dollars since he has been denied health insurance. When Bernadine gets her divorce settlement and asks the ailing Gloria if she needs financial assistance, Gloria directs the generous offer to Phillip. Rather than emphasize the black homophobic community, McMillan has Gloria deal diplomatically with the issue both on a personal and professional level. The proprietor thus mitigates a potentially devastating situation, and maintains her successful enterprise.

McMillan further disrupts the traditional expectation of the black community in terms of the amount of service rendered by black professional women with their time, skills, and finances. Mary Church Terrell quotes the motto, "lifting as we climb," of the African American Black Club women, and speaks of the many exceptionally qualified women who have sacrificed their lives and submitted to extreme hardships for race uplift, even though poor recordkeeping did not allow for adequate confirmation of their varied activities.[42] However, serving the black community in diverse areas and for prolonged time periods sidetracks many black professional women from pursuing their own career goals of advanced degrees or upward mobility. McMillan's intervention in the debate allows her to fracture this vicious cycle for the protagonists in *Waiting to Exhale.*

McMillan's rejection of the overextended woman takes dramatic form at a Black Women on the Move meeting. The president gives a report on what has been accomplished, a critique of the past year's performance, and a list of services to be rendered on behalf of the poor such as a "permanent senior citizens program, our own Big Brother/Big Sister Program, a day care" (249). Gloria, who has been excessively overworking herself serving others (and is poised for a heart attack soon), wants the agenda extended to include other pressing concerns within the black community, such as combating drugs and school gangs. She fails to appreciate that the budget of this small organization is less than $30,000. Furthermore, the membership consists of women who must concentrate much of their energies on their executive positions. The president of the organization does not present the topic for discussion, but directly addresses the issue: *"Well, we can't do it all, but we can do our part"* [emphasis mine] (247). The statement implies that men will now have to shoulder their full share of the responsibilities.

It is important to point out that this perspective of moral responsibility is not reminiscent of all of McMillan's characters. The character Mama, in *A Day Late and a Dollar Short,* for instance, appears to have sacrificed her life to facilitate the adulterous remarried spouse and his new wife (despite her disclaimer in the letter read at Thanksgiving)[43] and possibly even her children. McMillan could be showing that women whose sense of selfhood is still in the developing stage, and who lack empowerment in their lives, do take on the role of sacrificers. Mama is not a professional woman as are the four protagonists in *Waiting to Exhale,* and she lacks empowerment in her life. This comment does not assume, however, that only professional women exhibit a strong sense of selfhood.

McMillan is concerned about the quality of life for black women in *Waiting to Exhale.* The overextendedness of an important historical figure will illustrate why this tradition of overworked black women is cause for concern. In 1899 at the Hampton Negro Conference, Lucy Craft Laney echoed that the "educated colored woman has a burden" of providing cultural and educational uplift for the race. She adds: "The educated colored woman can and will do her part in lifting this burden."[44] The long list of the women's work, though noble, reflects the maternal woman doing more than their share. Their public work included activities such as teaching from kindergarten to the college level, and lecturing publicly to the whole community on matters of marriage, thrift, hygiene in the home, and religion. Her own success is evidenced in the building of the Haines Normal and Industrial Institute, which by 1931 had "twenty-seven teachers, three hundred high school students, four hundred thirteen elementary school students, and an income of twenty-five thousand dollars." However, editor Patricia Liggins Hill notes that "Laney's zeal for her school led to her own declining health" due to nephritis and hypertension.[45] McMillan, as spokesperson for contemporary professional women, and specifically African American women volunteers, insists that they deserve a pleasurable and fulfilled life.

In the discussion on service at the Black Women on the Move meeting, McMillan demonstrates the leadership skills of black professional women. Critics could argue that Etta Mae Jenkins is autocratic, nevertheless she exercises agency by decisively handling a behavior that is detrimental to these already overworked black career women. She presents an alternative means to solve the problem: increased membership. She then graciously reminds Gloria, "Everybody's busy, got jobs and families" (248). Stephanie Golden points out "the burden of sacrifice is unequally distributed."[46] McMillan is arguing that women should not carry a disproportionate burden of the race. They, like their male counterparts, are professionals. Her response to how the needs of the black community are to be met is a radical departure from the norm, and it echoes some of the female characters' concerns in The Salt Eaters.

The final source of oppression in the lives of the four protagonists is gender. The question arises whether McMillan colluded with certain aspects of mainstream culture in her representation of black women as promiscuous beings. It is important to reemphasize that popular culture seeks to fracture the status quo. Despite the profusion of sex in the media, sexuality is still not openly discussed in conservative circles. When it is discussed, the physical aspects are glossed over. Writer Barbara Kingslover believes the scarcity of novels that frankly discuss coitus is due to cultural mores. She contends that women who discuss sex openly and intelligently are perceived as deviant. For respectable, genteel folks, sex is performed in private. She is quick to point out the irony that exists in this prohibition of reading novels that treat sex unashamedly—the activity does occur privately, within the mind. Writing about sex becomes problematic for religious and corporate belief systems, for it forces them to acknowledge that all people are similarly bound, like the animal kingdom, to procreative biological laws. She feels writers must challenge the hypocrisy, and must insist that in the overall scheme of life, sex is preeminently the important topic.[47] More contemporary writers are beginning to brave the stormy waters by presenting sexual acts.

For McMillan, the openness of her protagonists' sexual behaviors offers the women a certain amount of power over their own sexuality. Traditionally, in the Judeo-Christian philosophy, woman was made for man, and not only must he rule over her, but her desire must be directed toward his fulfillment. The novelist offers a searing oppositional gaze to this patriarchal center of power. No one can have a sense of empowerment if she is controlled by another. As professional women who have satisfied their basic needs, the four protagonists devote much of their time seeking emotional fulfillment.

One aspect that must not be overlooked in assessing whether McMillan's protagonists are promiscuous is the recognition that sex sells in America. Many readers view the characters as being sexually irresponsible, but the sexual portrayal serves a definite reason. The novelist shows the women *enjoying* the erotic in some scenes. Golden discusses the ancient myth of the mermaid whose tail represents women's sexuality. She is the equivalent of a devouring nymphomaniac who seduces men to the bottom of the ocean where they die from overindulgent sexual pleasure. Golden argues that Hans Christian Andersen changed the myth to make *The Little Mermaid* serviceable. Here the mermaid is transformed through "the amputation of her raw energy, as embodied in her tail" into a sacrificing girl who dooms herself to excruciating pain and death, but who eventually is "rewarded" as a spirit of sacrificial service. The story suggests that little mermaids (women) who dare to explore outside the circumscribed environs are harmed in the process. What the story does not emphasize is that women who continually allow others' wants to be more imperative than their own will not enjoy full autonomy and self-fulfillment. Golden feels this tale is partly responsible for many women becoming self-sacrificing fools. In interviews with about thirty grown children, she discovers that the respondents defined sacrifice anecdotally as their mother; not one identified the father as sacrificial: "Watching my mother was how I learned the word *sacrifice*."[48]

Women who do not ascribe to sacrificing themselves and who would rather gratify their erotic desires are seen as selfish and evil. Symbolically, McMillan transforms the mermaid's tale to its original intent; her four protagonists retain their "tails," which ironically become one site of their abuse. McMillan's four black professional "mermaids" encounter double jeopardy, for their princes want them to have both the sensuous tail and the blindingly painful sacrificial feet, feet interpreted here as careers. The sexual oppression of the four protagonists occurs in the private relationships of the women and the black men in their lives. None of the characters experiences overt gender discrimination in the workplace as Velma Henry endures in *The Salt Eaters*. Sexism in the workplace is practiced under the guise of work-related issues.

The inordinate amount of time the four protagonists spend "looking for a man" overshadow every facet of their lives. It consumes their time, energies, and funds that could be better used to advance their professional status, or provide other forms of pleasure. Although it is tempting to blame the women for the repeated sexual abuse they experience, especially since McMillan represents them as partially autonomous individuals, one has to consider whether they have models to help them resist the roles they play in the text. Critic Darryl Pinckney points out that the protagonists "recognize that black men have treated them the way they have because they, black women, have let them get away with it all these years."[49] Eventually, the women are able to break the cycle of their sexual exploitation.

The antagonism between the black women and black men in *Waiting to Exhale* can be attributed to the historical and ideological conflicts troubling the black community as a whole, and from the shortage of eligible black males. From an historic standpoint, the economic ramifications of Reconstruction to the present have created disparities in the gains of the sexes. Ideological conflicts stem from patriarchal expectations of the roles between men and women. In this novel, the socioeconomic position of the men determines how they treat the women with whom they have relationships; the women's socioeconomic position determines their expectations of the men with whom they fraternize.

The patriarchal construction of womanhood has antithetical approaches. According to Hazel Carby, during the 1800s and early 1900s, the aristocratic white woman (not the millions of sharecropping and frontier women) was the fragile beauty whose primary function was to produce children to inherit the father's property. As the beautiful housebound hostess who entertained her guests with music, art, dance, and sumptuous food, she (being sexually "pure") was understood to keep her house pure. The black woman being outside the value structure was perceived to be the direct opposite. She was not regarded as beautiful, but ugly, unbecoming; she was fit only to be the servant of whites and to perform manual labor.[50] It was she who prepared and served the food as well as provided many services that maintained the notion of Southern hospitality. She was meant to be sexually "impure," for during slavery, her body was the site of rape and in many cases forced breeding. Historian Winthrop Jordan comments: "The everyday buying and selling and deeding and trading of slaves underscored the fact that Negroes, just like horses, were walking pieces of property."[51] Black women longed to have their unique beauty recognized and appreciated, and eventually began to desire the physical traits and dress codes that their white slaveholders deemed beautiful.

From Reconstruction to the 1960s, emboldened with having earned income as servants, washerwomen, and factory hands, black women wanted to experience two spheres. Therein lies one reason for the antagonism between black women and black men, further fueled by capitalistic wealth and what it represents for black manhood. Black women desire the sphere of the beautiful (previously allocated to the white woman), as well as economic independence (previously allocated to the white males) and the freedom it affords. In other words, black women desire agency. However, according to the societal norm, the black man cannot have his full share of economic independence unless the black woman is willing to be the beautiful wife-hostess. The problem is compounded because until the 1970s, most black men could not afford to maintain the beautiful establishment (beautiful house, beautiful wife) alone. In other words, the black woman worked and allowed her husband to manage her income, so he was perceived to be economically sufficient. This situation was true in most white households as well, whether the women worked outside or inside the home. Problems arise when black women insist that they wish to be beautiful and financially secure.

In *Waiting to Exhale*, this conflict is played out in the three-day intense relationship between Savannah and Charles Turner. Both are professionals attending a conference for television personnel in Las Vegas. Savannah thinks she has found her prince, for he seems to satisfy her expectations: intelligent, sensitive, respectful, and fun loving. But the relationship is doomed to fail. First, Charles has the upper hand. Savannah seeks to be elegant for him by dressing nicely. She also denigrates her person; she shaves her "ugly crotch" of hair for his aesthetic pleasure. In the United States, it is not usually socially accepted for women to show secondary hair growth. Legs, thighs, underarms—all must be shorn to look preadolescent; and by extension, virginal. Men, however, glory in the evidence of sexual maturity that nature bestows on them. Second, when Charles comes to her room, she tidies up the place just for him. Her behavior is perfectly normal for someone who is in love; she desires to please. However, despite all the romantic words spoken earlier, once Charles steps into her room, he becomes the interrogator, the controller. Savannah thinks it is delightful foreplay, but Charles has a different agenda. He wants to know what kind of competition he has to face.

Early in the seemingly pleasant interrogation, Savannah loses her man. Among his long list of questions, Charles asks Savannah which of the following she wants most to achieve: "security, love, power, excitement, or money?" Apparently, Charles anticipates Savannah's choosing one from among the items listed. Unhesitatingly, Savannah answers: "All five." Apparently, in response to his involuntary reaction, she qualifies her answer by saying if she has to choose, it would be love; she wishes the others since they will make the totality of her feeling more poignant. Although the questions continue and they make passionate love, Charles's remark at the end of the sex act reveals that he is intimidated by Savannah. He could also be involved in other relationships.

Savannah is not inexperienced in the art of lovemaking. During the early evening hours, she feels euphoric and encourages the discussion toward sexual consummation. Immediately after the sex act, Charles says, "I wish I could *keep* [emphasis mine] you" while stroking her hair (366). Savannah replies that it may be a possibility, but Charles knows Savannah could never be a "kept" woman. Savannah's desire for "all five" indicates her level of autonomy. During the sex act, when she first tries to take some control, he tells her to let him be the one to give pleasure, and she acquiesces. However, Savannah soon takes a very active role: "He danced. I followed. I danced. He followed. Until we couldn't dance anymore" (366). As delightful as coitus has been, it does not fulfill Charles' needs. Savannah wants what Charles wants: all five; Charles cannot accept equal status with her.

What is the result of this conflict between two black professionals striving for agency and who seem to have the possibility for a good relationship? Possibly because Charles is unable to "keep" Savannah in whatever role he may have fantasized, he punishes her in a calculated, sophisticated manner as befits his professional status. He treats her as if she were invisible; he does not even acknowledge her by answering her phone calls. In pain she seeks an answer to the paradox—how could he have "acted so sincere [yet] be so insincere" (369). She weeps that he has broken her heart, and disrupted her world. She feels the whole experience was not worth the pain; in fact, she was less miserable before she met Charles.

Of course, Savannah must take responsibility for her sexual behavior and some of the consequent pain. If she chooses to become sexually involved with the stranger she casually meets such as at this conference, then she opens herself to possible abuse. As an adult, she has the right to make choices. Admittedly, her partner behaved shamefully, but she is not a naïve sixteen-year-old. As a professional woman, she must have known that a casual sexual encounter does not necessarily lead to a long-term relationships even if she wishes it. Bernadine is fortunate to find a love through such an encounter at a bar, but the stakes are high with black professional women outnumbering black career men.

Some respondents did not express any sympathy for Savannah, and referred to her as "sexually promiscuous." They note her long-term adulterous relationship with Kenneth and her affairs with other partners. One sees her rejection as "poetic justice. Did it not occur to her that he was another married Kenneth?" Another comments, "Now she knows what a wife feels to be rejected by the husband living under the same roof." One did mention that given the plight of the number of single black women, "It is understandable that Savannah would feel she has found Mr. Right since he seemed so desirable a partner."

Edmondson Bell and Nkomo found that the "resounding theme in the personal lives of the single black woman was an overwhelming frustration with the absence of a fulfilling intimate relationship with a man."[52] The reader hears Savannah's anger when Kenneth, still wanting his marriage, telephones her during her intense period of rejection to meet him so they can determine if what they felt previously was still strong. Completely controlling the conversation, she tells him some choice expletives and hangs up the phone. The language in this scene can be interpreted as male bashing at its ugliest, but she uses her present humiliation as a weapon to ward off other sexually attractive men who, like Charles, prey on single women.

Another element that complicates the problem between black men and women in McMillan's novel is the manner in which fantasy operates in a relationship. Robin Stokes, the youngest and most insecure of the four protagonists, dreams of a beautiful Hollywood wedding. She and her partner would be passionately in love and the ceremony would be featured in *Jet* magazine. They would have the perfect family, and she would be the "ideal mother." Their marriage would be so blissful that others would be jealous, and after forty years, people would marvel and ask what was the secret ingredient that had maintained their happiness and allowed them to escape being a divorce statistic.

Robin wants romance. Stephanie Golden argues that if one believes too early and strongly in romance, whether it relates to sexuality, religion, or politics, it is harmful, for romance compels the seeker to fervently pursue an ideal with an impassioned commitment. This illogical passion undermines the normally logical behavior, and allows competent women in positions of authority to gladly surrender their power to authoritative men.[53] Robin is a successful underwriter at an insurance company, but she confides to her friends she is addicted to handsome black men "with big dicks" (45).

A misguided ideology followed blindly leads to disaster, and Robin's romantic partners are leeches. When Robin meets Troy, she exclaims, "Good God Almighty. This man is past gorgeous" (231). Robin must have a handsome prince who is virile, one who fits the image of the prince in *Cinderella*. She enjoys the pleasures of life. She becomes the beautiful princess by adorning herself and thus becomes the "die hard shopaholic" (165), spending far too much money on revealing clothes and Victoria's Secret lingerie so as to be seductive. She has even "bought" breasts from a plastic surgeon and is planning to purchase some "ass." McMillan's portrayal of Robin shows that the desire for unrestrained perpetual romance blinds women to the potential manipulation involved in these forms of associations. Fortunately, Robin eventually sees her mistake: "I was that stupid for a long time" (45).

Why would an upwardly professional woman like Robin allow herself to be repeatedly seduced and exploited by uneducated rogues like Russell? Not only do Troy and Russell swindle her out of money, they have the potential to transmit STDs. Golden agrees with Jessica Benjamin that women are inclined to want the "perfect love," to which they defer and pay homage to ideal persons they cannot become. Lacking agency of their own, they seek men who appear to have power. Inevitably, they yield their wills to the men. Golden sees this behavior as masochistic.[54] What Robin lacks is self-esteem and self-discipline. Not feeling loved for herself, and not being valued in the job market, she fantasizes that a handsome prince will love her as the princess she wishes she were. It is a dangerous fantasy, for she opens herself to consistent abuse by exploitive males.

To express her disapproval of women participating in their own victimization, McMillan provides a partial foil to Robin Stokes in Savannah. Savannah wants a good relationship with a black male, and is willing to take chances. Unlike Robin, she is not completely misguided by the Cinderella farce. She soliloquizes that the men and the media have performed a superb job in making themselves and women believe that the lack of available males is cause for anxiety. Consequently, many women are ready to prostitute themselves to get a man. Since she is financially and emotionally secure, Savannah does not need to be rescued. She retains her autonomy and refuses to lower her standards of what she considers desirable in a partner. She says, "All I've got is *one* life." Although the "die-hard buppies" she dates call her bitch (12), her life is more harmonious that Robin's. She is an art collector, has a gorgeous house, is involved with Black Women on the Move and plans to visit a school for pregnant teens, talk to them, and be a role model. Above all, she is focused on her career as a black professional woman.

Through Savannah, the novel illustrates that a woman's intellectual articulation of her rational stance does not necessarily correlate with her behavior—that is, protect her from her fantasies or what she has concomitantly learned from watching her mother's or other women's behaviors. Arguably, Savannah does not usually accept men below her social class, but she is vulnerable to the power of romance. The need to be loved is natural, but in a society in which sex sells, even logical women fall for the deception that is so pervasive in the marriage market. Savannah eventually matures, and becomes sensitive, sensuous, and suave.

McMillan portrays another aspect of sexual oppression. Gloria Matthews is the single sacrificing mother who in the process of parenting neglects her own personhood. Though unable to pursue her career goals, she longs for the world of the theater. She wants to use her imagination in creating costumes and experimenting with stage cosmetics; however, Gloria's life revolves around "God, and hair, and kids" (71). To compensate for Tarik's absent father, Gloria spends an inordinate amount of time chauffeuring other families with children, as well as serving the needs of black men in hopes of finding a father for her son. However, mothering the men who want sex, freedom, and money only drives them away. Golden suggests that it is the inequality of power that fuels "self-defeating sacrifice," and that when such sacrifice begins to negatively impact the giver, the sacrifice becomes perverted and results in suffering.[55]

For Gloria Matthews, the result of this sacrificing is high blood pressure, obesity, and a heart attack in her mid-thirties. McMillan here addresses the diseases caused by stress within the black community, and especially those that afflict black women. Feminist scholar Elizabeth Higginbotham suggests that all aspects of black women's health care need to be examined in relation to poverty, racist and sexist policies, and other factors of oppression.[56] It is the two single parents in the novel, Gloria and Bernadine, who have high blood pressure. McMillan is concerned with showing that professional black women are often strong, courageous individuals, but not "superwomen," and they should not be expected to carry the responsibilities that black men and others refuse to shoulder. Gloria could exercise far more agency in her career and personal life if Tarik's father would parent his son, or if she insisted that he at least keep the youngster during the summers. But for a mother to insist that a male child live with his newly proclaimed homosexual father for any duration and frequency is tantamount, in some people's eyes, as betrayal of a sacred trust. These critics would have little or no concern, however, for the overextended mother whose burdens lead to a heart attack.

With both Gloria's and Robin's cases, and to some extent Savannah's, McMillan refuses the deception of victimhood. She expects professional black women to be responsible for themselves. Gloria sabotages her essential selfhood by her personal habit. Bernadine asks Gloria if a heart attack was necessary to convince her to get "her big ass on a diet" (391). Gloria is also the victim of abuse by her ex-husband who reneges his paternal responsibility as well as rejects her person as undesirable, for a homosexual partner. Golden confirms that people who survive abuse often leave their victimhood identity, only to take on the role of sacrificers and caretakers. They do not know how to live for themselves.[57] Philanthropic gestures are perfectly legitimate, but Gloria needs self-discipline. Gloria as a black career woman must choose to love herself enough to remain healthy, to feel she is entitled to pleasure, happiness, and prosperity.

McMillan not only presents the sexual exploitation of single women and single mothers, she depicts the oppression that occurs in marriage. Bernadine Harris, as the wife and mother, empties herself for her husband and children. Although she has a degree in business, she gives up her career goal to be the proprietor of a catering business, and instead initially works for her husband as "secretary, his office manager, his computer, his consultant, his accountant. His *bookkeeper*, his wife and his lover ... [she] did everything for him at once" (30). Her tasks are reminiscent of Velma Henry's in *The Salt Eaters*. Bernadine sacrifices her health to have two children, and surrenders her tastes and wishes for husband John's preferences. She gives up her personhood, for John wants her to look rich, that is, to enhance his self-image. She gives up her time so she could pour all her "energy into motherhood." Later, she ceases to concern herself with her husband's business; she just watches it prosper from the sidelines. She becomes the beautiful housewife without any control over her life. Golden provides a powerful analogy to Bernadine's behavior. She points out that it was the Little Mermaid's initial sacrifice of what was vital to her own well-being that thereafter rendered her unable to control the events of her life. Golding contends that such excessive sacrificing is performed by the powerless.[58] Romance and marriage have seduced a woman with potential and cultural capital to fail to fulfill her career dreams.

The novelist shows Bernadine later reclaiming herself. She gains power over her body when she refuses to have a third child, over her career when she goes to work to get money for her own business, over her social life when she joins Black Women on the Move and develops a close group of friends outside her husband's circle, and over her sexuality when she appropriates a lover for herself. McMillan represents these black professional women making serious mistakes that jeopardize their happiness and self-actualization, but she does not leave them victims.

Racism, sexism, classism, and the incessant demands expected of black professional women function as interlocking forces of oppression that hinder the protagonists from exercising an adequate amount of agency in their careers. Yet both novelists represent the characters as having some level of autonomy, though McMillan's characters evidence more than Velma Henry does in Bambara's *The Salt Eaters*. In each text reflects the historic moment of the writer, that is, how societal forces operate to limit the amount of agency the protagonists exhibit in the narratives. McMillan presents her characters as relatively successful in their jobs, as having freedom to express their sexuality, and having the ability to escape one of the interlocking forces of oppression—the incessant demands of the black community. The protagonists in both novels, however, are restricted in the workplace and in their private lives.

~ Six ~

Reader Response:
Findings and Applications

This text examines why so few novels represent the black professional woman with agency in both her professional and private life, what factors contribute to the dearth of such representation, what levels of agency the protagonists evidence in the narratives *The Salt Eaters* and *Waiting to Exhale,* and to what extent the readers are satisfied with the novels. This chapter presents the findings of a sociological and ethnographic component that validates the theoretical research. A survey was sent to 175 black professional women; 119 questionnaires were returned—a 68 percent response rate. The questions were designed to identify the women respondents as professionals, to determine their knowledge of contemporary black women's fiction, and to assess the degree to which the novels satisfied the desires of the readers.

This chapter partially replicates Janice Radway's and Jacqueline Bobo's ethnographic methodologies in their respective texts: *Reading the Romance: Women, Patriarchy, and Popular Literature* (1991) and *Black Women As Cultural Readers: Film and Culture* (1995). Radway agrees with other critics, such as Charlotte Brundson, that problems arise when there is "an over-reliance on audience responses at the expense of textual analysis because ... the critic can disavow any responsibility to simply suspending judgment on the text. The suspension allows the critic to ignore the ideology of the text and so deal solely with what audiences get out of it."[1] Radway adds, the critic must be careful to get a varied sample of potential respondents in the group, lest the results be flawed by too many participants having identical characteristics such as age, socioeconomic background, or even the same immediate geographic location. Bobo agrees with Radway, but emphasizes the need for careful reading of the texts. She insists that too often the critique or opinions of viewers and readers themselves are rendered invisible, thus their valuable responses are neither recorded nor analyzed.[2] The survey used for this book followed these principles.

To insure a varied, anonymous pool of professional women subjects, I chose a random distribution of the surveys at university/medical campuses in New York City, Farmington, Connecticut, and Richmond; a "Go On Girl Book Club" convention; a fine arts festival; professional offices, churches, and professional conventions in New Haven, Charlottesville, Fort Lauderdale, and Virginia Beach. Furthermore, two chapters of the book rely on textual analysis of two novels: *The Salt Eaters* and *Waiting to Exhale*. The informal discussions held with women at several gatherings proved valuable, allowing these participants to disagree, confirm, or elaborate on areas that would not have been possible from the written surveys alone.

The questionnaire confirmed most of the assumptions borne out in the academic discussion herein. It also provided some surprises, especially regarding the specific character traits the women preferred in novels, and who or what they perceived to be responsible for the paucity of autonomous black professional protagonists.

The survey contained three sets of questions totaling eleven queries. The first set, with three questions, identified the respondents' professional status: their age, their career choice, and the number of hours per week they read. The second set, with seven questions, determined whether the women were satisfied with the novels, which aspects of the texts they preferred, and specifically, what characteristics they would have liked the protagonist to have had. The third set, with one question, asks: What reasons can you suggest why there are so few books about the black professional woman having a strong sense of empowerment in the workplace? It also has an open-ended statement: Please add any comments you would like to make." This invitation allows the participants to freely discuss whatever aspects of the novels interested them that were not covered in the questionnaire.

The first component deals with demographics. Question One asks the age of the respondents, tabulated in five categories from 18–25 years to 61–72 years. The largest percentage of the respondents fell in the 46–60 bracket. Although the number of subjects in this survey is not parallel to that used by the U.S. Department of Labor, the findings are consistent in terms of percentages.[3] Statistics are analogous for black women in the workforce in 1996 except for the youngest age range. Chart 1 (see Appendix C) compares the U.S. Department of Labor statistics [4] with the following findings of this project:

Ages 18–25 = 06.7%   Ages 46–60 = 34.5%
Ages 26–35 = 23.5%   Ages 61–72 = 10.1%
Ages 36–45 = 25.2%

The age group 18–25 (though different from the national norm) validates
the findings of the survey since the majority of these young women would
still be in graduate or medical programs in preparation for their professional
careers. Although the age groups differ by one to three years in each range,
the two findings are remarkably close.

Question Two identifies the career choices of the respondents (Chart
2). Fifteen careers were recorded, arranged here from the largest to the
smallest numerical representation: professors/teachers, social workers,
sales/marketing/merchandising personnel, education administrators, physi-
cians/nurses, artists, government workers, computer technologists, administrative assistants, writers, attorneys, religious professionals, beauticians,
CEO/presidents, engineers. The percentages corroborated with the U.S.
Department of Labor's research, which in 1996 reported the five leading
occupations for black professional women as "registered nurses, elementary
school teachers, social workers, accountants, and auditors." For this work,
black women in the "occupational groups, managerial and professional spe-
cialty—technical, sales, and administrative support" were the next highest
ranked. Among the least represented was the career of engineering,[5] perhaps because no surveys were distributed at an engineering firm. The large
representation of doctors (six), compared to two nurses, is possibly the result
of surveys being left at the university campus within the medical building
rather than directly in the hospital setting.

The third question examines the number of hours the respondents
spent reading (see Chart 3). Reading hours fall into six groupings, with the
legal profession spending the most hours per week reading, 65–70 hours.
Only one lawyer reports she reads 70 hours. Since the hours exceed all the
others in the group with the highest hours (60–65), the question was whether
to drop that one high number. But because there were only four respondents from the legal field, I decided to retain the statistic, for even if it reflects
only that lawyer preparing for *one* particular case, it illustrates how much
work successful black legal professionals must perform to maintain a high
level of success in the market place. Physicians ranked next with a response
of 60–65 hours per week. Granted, four of the respondents were residents
or interns, but two were certified physicians.

The third group, college and university professors, spends 40–45 hours
per week reading for research, classroom preparation, and pleasure. The
adage in academia "publish or perish" is a reality, and for some professors,

primarily in the arts and sciences division, reading novels is a necessity. The next group—writers, administrators (including politicians), social workers, engineers, and religious personnel—spends 25–30 hours per week reading. The group consists of government administrators, administrative assistants, computer technologists, retail personnel, and marketing employees whose reading hours range between 10 and 20 hours per week. The final group includes the women in the beauty care industry. They read an average of 4–5 hours per week. Most of the respondents report that they rarely read novels; their reading is focused on their professional fields.

Although the 119 women participants is not a large enough sample to disprove the prevailing myth that guided the practices of many publishers for many years that blacks do not read, the responses of the survey participants act as an important comment on the behaviors of these career women. The implication inherent in such a presumption is significant. Writer Garvin Jones contends that there is a "prevailing belief [that a] direct correlation" exists between language (reading included) and mental "ability."[6] These women's reading practices refute the stereotype of African Americans as lacking intelligence. Demographically speaking, the results of this survey are valid because they reflect the opinions and attitudes of a representative sample of black professional women.

The next two components (sets two and three) chart the respondents' answers to the survey questions.

The second component—dealing with satisfaction of content, includes questions four through ten. Question No. Four asks: Why do you think black professional women want novels that portray the protagonists who are black career women? (see Chart 4). The answers given to this segment of the questionnaire were discussed in Chapter One. Except for two respondents, most of the women readers want novels with the protagonist represented as self-empowered professional on a regular basis. The other two contend that any request for a particular kind of book is a form of coercion, and under these conditions, writers cannot produce the best art.

In Question Five, the participants identified the realistic novels they had read in which the protagonist is a black professional with agency. Toni Morrison, Terry McMillan, Alice Walker, Maya Angelou, Julie Dash, Bebe Moore Campbell, and Paule Marshall received the most responses, in that order. Books mentioned included *Tar Baby, Waiting to Exhale, How Stella Got Her Groove Back, The Color Purple*, and *Daughters of the Dust*. The list at first may cause one to pause, but fortunately, the respondents provide a rationale for their choices. One research subject explains that she chose *The Color Purple* because Celie became a professional seamstress at the end of the narrative. Another thinks *Daughters of the Dust* qualifies because the two young women—Elizabeth and Amelia—were professionals in their day despite their ages.[7] One subject remarks on her new insight: "I do not know why I never noticed the absence of the professional protagonist before. I guess I was just happy to read anything about black women that was delightful or available. But, yes, there is a lack."

Question Six requires an evaluative response of either a "Yes" or "No" answer. It assessed the degree of satisfaction the women had with the novels they had mentioned. The question reads: Are you basically satisfied with the way the protagonists are portrayed? The results are as follows. Seventy-six percent answered "No." The "Yes" responses had to be subdivided into two groups. Twenty-two percent qualified their affirmation; two percent reported "Happy as is," that is, they were fully satisfied. Only one participant gave a response close to a blanket rejection of all the novels as inadequate in their representation of the career black woman. The large percentage of negative responses and the qualifications that followed the "Yes" responses came as a surprise, since so many black women readers buy these narratives. One could argue that for many readers there is no causal relationship between purchasing and enjoying a novel. Many people purchase narratives without having seen a review. This behavior is not typical of career women readers. Jacqueline Bobo confirms that the black middle-class professional women in her study did background checks in various ways, such as asking their friends' opinions of the novels, attending a reading, or sharing texts and reviews.[8]

Many readers are definitive about their displeasure with aspects of the books, although they are more receptive to the very recent ones. Some of the comments are generalized as they refer to the narratives as a group. For instance, one respondent writes: "It is difficult for me to visualize black professional women who rarely talk about what they actually do among themselves or with their male colleagues. What concerns do anchor women have about their jobs? Do real estate agents still find it difficult to house black clients in some predominantly white residential neighborhoods? How do they solve these difficulties; how do they celebrate their successes? A lack of real professionalism pervades the texts." Other comments are specific and address the actual professional choices of the protagonists, and how they are positioned in the workspace. One respondent records, "One *Waiting to Exhale* is enough. Now we want some Stellas—Congresswoman or a judge or a scientist or a university president actually doing their work proficiently." Another asks, "Are these writers aware of the many career fields that exist? Not one novel so far has a protagonist working in international relations though writers hear of the U.N. regularly. No character works in Silicon Valley although a black man invented the cell phone; no character works at the Federal Reserve, or Capitol Hill—not even a sharp university professor which all these novelists must have had, and some of them are."

Some respondents are primarily satisfied with the novels, but indicate their weaknesses. One statement reads:

> I am happy for the Morrisons, the Walkers, and the Goldens, but I want more narratives that are well written, so professors will use more of them in their classrooms. No matter how popular they are in the black community, we need the cross-over audience so our scholarship is not "marginalized" in academia. Some of these novels are too amateurish.

Other participants are pleased with the novels, for they are "up-beat" and are all about "us." One survey subject writes, "I can even get romance fiction written just for black folks. We are making progress by expanding our range of offerings." Another comments: "A few of the latest novels are showing that the women characters understand that in corporate America, team work pays off. We see this in *Big Girls Don't Cry* where the women, white and black and an male, work to further their own success and profit." The comments evidence that the cultural consumer market is critically evaluating the novels.

In Questions Seven and Eight, the research subjects participate in character analysis. If they report in Question Six that they were basically satisfied with the protagonists as they are represented, then they are requested to list the characteristics they feel the novelist used to captured the central character successfully. Some responses were as follows. The characters have immediacy for "many aspects of their thought processes are written out"; "the protagonists have day-to-day problems like the average person, so they are believable," and "they always grow and have some measure of success in the end." One subject thinks "the friendships women have in the novels offer a positive correction to the fairy tales we grew up on, where women are enemies to each other." Three respondents are glad to read about "beautiful black women."

Question Eight allows the participants who registered dissatisfaction in Question Six to enumerate the problems they find with the portrayal of the main character. The concerns fall into six categories: lack of adequate professional behavior; too much emphasis on sex life; lack of long term or meaningful relationships; characters not working long enough to gain credibility; too few characters in executive positions or too many in service positions; and characters overburdened with problems and so unable to enjoy life.

The first two areas, lack of professional behavior and overemphasis on sex life, received the greatest number of responses. According to one respondent, "The majority of the protagonists tarnish our image." These subjects disassociated themselves from such protagonists, either because of unprofessional behavior, or because of the low level of emotional balance the characters maintain. Respondents emphasize that emotionally stable people function as whole beings in their public and private lives: "There must be some consistency in the protagonist's behavior." One participants comments, "Terry McMillan's four protagonists in *Waiting to Exhale* are too undisciplined to succeed anywhere in the competitive corporate sector. If we jeopardized our lives as they do in *Caught Up in the Rapture*, we would literally have already been caught up in the rapture." For these women, the characters are not believable as "successful professionals."

The debate of the language as reflective of professional behavior was addressed by 96 percent of the respondents. The language did not offend some informants. Responding to *Waiting to Exhale*, one beautician reports, "I get the feeling Terry had a lot of fun writing this stuff down." Several of the subjects treat the urban vernacular as amusement. One says, "The behavior reminds me of when I was a teen; we used to belt it out for it made us feel grown-up, cool. Of course, the novel represents adult professionals, but novels are supposed to provide humor." Another critiqued the disapproval aimed at *Waiting to Exhale*. She observes that many people when angry use expletives to vent their frustrations. Although the behavior is excessive in the text, "we all need not pretend we have never been a Bernadine." By a large margin, the survey subjects are not amused; in fact, some are "literally repulsed" by the consistent use of the expletives. One respondent echoes the voice of the many, "When there is so much anger, the characters need to find a way to resolve it on a daily basis, but in another way. Racism and sexism are not easy to deal with, but our health must not suffer because of it. Yes, the language in some of the novels is unacceptable."

The private lives of the protagonists also came under scrutiny. One respondent writes, "I couldn't finish reading *Waiting to Exhale*; some areas were so distasteful. The irresponsible sexual encounters reinforce sexual stereotypes. The falsehood projects the seeming inability of black people to have meaningful relationships. Some of us have been married for forty years." Another informant reports that she tries to understand *Waiting to Exhale* and other texts in the most sympathetic way she can: "To a certain extent, the writers are presenting to us our reality, though highly exaggerated. In this way, they call our attention to areas we may want to examine and change, or keep." Some survey subjects are careful to note that not all the novels are "saturated with expletives."

Respondents expressed concerns with the lack of self-control some protagonists exhibited. They wanted to see more fiscal responsibility, and more thorough financial planning and investment. To them, the books are sending the wrong message of consumerism to readers who have no financial security. They agree everyone should live comfortably since they work hard for pleasurable commodities, but they emphasize that black women professionals are still the least paid in the corporate arena. Another saw the destruction of company data in Marshall's *Daughters* as unacceptable. In addition, the respondents feel the protagonists put themselves under undue stress. They allow themselves to be ill-used by their bosses, their men, and their civic organizations. One informant concludes, "Self-discipline is the ability to regulate your life so that you do not become incapacitated. Self-discipline is survival of the fittest."

Several comment on the inadequate development of workplace scenes in the novels. They argue that it is not necessary for most of the novels to center on work, but its presence should be a staple if we are dealing with professional women. One comments: "I spend five days a week in my office, or traveling for my firm for thirty-five years. If that time is trivialized or made to seem unimportant, then the novels suggest my working years are not meaningful."

Another area offended some readers. Many complained of the absence of enough after-work activities that provide pleasure. One respondent writes:

> It seems so many of the characters lack any form of spirituality. Too few of them are seen enjoying quiet moments when they can reflect on their lives, their families, or the world around them. Even in slavery, our ancestors created the Negro spirituals, other slave songs, stories and poems. Especially the young protagonists are made to seem vacuous. Many of us still honor the Life-Force and its creation.

The next question allowed the respondents to provide the preferred characteristics of the professional protagonists. This section presents one of the biggest surprises of the survey (see Chart 7); it recorded 68 characteristics. The responses fall into five areas: professional traits, family characteristics, humanitarian traits, becoming female traits, and no special characteristics expected. Desired professional characteristics receive 60.3 percent of the comments. The women argue that these traits are necessary for success in the corporate work force. Individual traits listed were: having power, being success oriented, being self-determined, making realistic assessments and responses to situations, using common sense practices, having financial acumen, exercising intelligence, demonstrating a cooperative spirit, exhibiting efficiency, being goal oriented, and having executive decision-making ability. Readers associated a few of these traits with all the novels, but they did not see enough of them to make the protagonists self-empowered, except at the ends of a couple of texts such as *Big Girls Don't Cry*. Neither of the two novels used in this book, *The Salt Eaters* or *Waiting to Exhale*, was identified as having protagonists with adequate agency.

It is remarkable that this area, professional traits, should so overwhelmingly get the black professional readers' approval. Some justification is necessary to account for this large preference. Evidently, the list of characteristics complements the concepts of "self-actualization" and "self-efficacy" that reflect the lives of the respondents whose physical and emotional needs have been satisfied. Furthermore, the list also correlates the respondents' unhappiness with the some aspects of most of the novels. I questioned whether the title of the survey, which includes the words "black professional woman," cued the respondents as to how they should answer the question. However, since these participants *are* career women, many with very high visibility and success in their fields, the findings may be better interpreted as their understanding of themselves. Quite possibly, it is from this list that we find their true desires.

The next aspect preferred is "Supportive Family Relationships." It rated 16.2 percent. The consensus is to see the family as viable. The participants want home to be represented more frequently as an environment in which there are harmonious relationships. The novels may dramatize members engaging in solving problems, showing kindness and respect to each individual, participating in fun and humor, and supporting one another's goals. Home also constitutes a willingness to verbalize apology and appreciation during the daily routine, express anger without verbal or physical abuse, deal with finances realistically, and exchange good communication among family members.[9] These desirable traits become particularly meaningful considering the high rate of single families in the black community.

The third characteristic desired is "Humanitarian Traits" averaging 11.8 percent. Some itemized characteristics are: interest in improving one's surroundings, helping others when possible, being fair, identifying mistakes in a kindly manner, recognizing different cultural backgrounds, helping others own their work, insisting on your ownership for inventive projects, and *being kind to the self*.[10] The last item indicates that the "Mammy" figure is not operative in their worldview.

The desire to help others is consistent with the portrait of the "self-actualized." Abraham Maslow finds that they "combine the two functions of being compassionate and understanding, and being capable of righteous indignation [more] than the average person."[11] Maslow's insight clarifies the behavior of many black professional women. They participate in charitable causes, are angered at the exploitation of the less advantaged, and resist being exploited.

The fourth area, "Elegance/Poise," received 8.8 percent of the responses. For some, "work and becomingness" are linked. The subjects see the outward adornment of the body as a reflection of their inner being. They also believe they are "worthy and deserving" of the items they own and enjoy. Several discuss deportment and carriage. One respondent observes, "Too many of us are overweight. Corporate America prefers and encourages the well-toned figure. Black women who want to climb the corporate ladder will have to keep their bodies healthy and trim." Professor Sybil Lassiter offers an even more sobering view that obesity is one of the health hazards of African Americans since it is a contributing factor to hypertension, coronary heart disease, and diabetes.[12] Another respondent writes, "One gets a thrill when she is happy about her person. Femininity when it means being beautiful for the self first, and for others after, is acceptable to me."

The last area, "No Special Traits Necessary," rates 2.9 percent. These respondents are pleased to read anything the black women's creative abilities will produce. One informant writes, "If parents want role models for their children, then they must provide it through their own behavior." The issue of the artist wanting to write as she pleases, yet needing the visibility and remuneration from her cultural production, is a delicate balance black women writers must maintain.

Another component of the survey is: What features of the novels do the respondents prefer (see Chart 5A). Three categories with the greatest responses are: Male/female/family relationships, with 62 responses (with much emendation), plot/characterization, with 41 responses, and style, which received 32. The choice of male/female relationships, given the sexist behaviors of many male characters in the novels, is surprising at first glance. Furthermore, that the respondents would add "family relationships" to the aspects they enjoy the most, despite the many conflicts the women writers present in the texts, suggests that this area is very important to the women polled. The answer may lie in the explanation of one subject: "It's what we wish for and seek to maintain."

The representation of black male/female relationship is often conflictive in many of the novels, including the two chosen for study in this book. Sexism is presented as one of the powerful interlocking forces that hinder black professional women from achieving agency in the workplace and in their private lives. The respondents themselves acknowledge abuse in many black families, and they critique the arrogance and cruelty women such as Robin in *Waiting to Exhale* encounter from male characters. They express their displeasure that husbands such as Primus (Paule Marshall's *Daughters)* and John (*Waiting to Exhale*) feel it is their right to have affairs, but cannot envision their wives entitled to the same privilege.

Remarkably, the subjects could turn from the acknowledged wrongs found in some novels to those narratives that represent the family more positively. They enumerated much more detailed comments about the positive male/female/family relationships that were more wholesome, and for the novels they perceived to have fairly healthy relationships, they elaborated over the positive episodes of the works.

What actually seems to please the informants is the way the women writers sensitively present the black family in crisis. The most often quoted texts were *Daughters of the Dust* (1997),[13] *Redemption Song* (2000) and *Big Girls Don't Cry* (1996). Several of the respondents imagine the Peazant family as a prototype of their Southern great-grandparents, except that this family experienced greater freedom to continue their family traditions for generations. One subject comments that the groups of families, despite conflicts, separation, sexual orientation, and tragedies, maintained itself and its culture. Another collaborates: "The Peazants had something valuable to pass on from one generation to the next, whether it was herbal medicine, or letters, or stories, or property on which they live. Where have we gone wrong so that so many of our youngsters no longer think they have a heritage?" Another writes, "Julie Dash has shown us that even rape of a loved one does not have to destroy the family, as difficult as it is to deal with." However, two responses were critical of how the male focused his rage of the sexual violation as it affected him, rather than on how the violence affected his wife. Some also observed that the Peazants had the advantage of isolation from mainstream thinking. Although they were not immune to its influences, "during the formative years, the children grasped the value of family."

The notion of family needs further discussion. Although the women appreciated kinship, the majority of their perceptions do not necessarily include the patriarchal construction of husband and father as "head." Paul Gilroy is keenly aware that the "family is the approved, natural site where ethnicity and racial culture are reproduced." However, "family" can become an ideological construct for the subordination of black women as seen in some black cultures, and it is here that "the question of the family begins to bite." The operational household, then, begins to look like a "disaster" for black feminists because it demands from black women too many obligations, stereotypical roles, and duties to extended kindred members.[14] Career women aspiring to reach the administrative tiers in corporations often resist these expectations.

In the black community, theoretically for some, the communal family is still operative. In practice, however, our contemporary residential housing does not allow many middle-class black professionals to have much contact with less successful African Americans, and so they do not provide sustained models for the youth. Many young people feel alienated from mainstream society and even from certain patriarchal enclaves within the black community; hence Gilroy's perception that for some, the "boys and girls are from the 'hood'—not from the race, and certainly not from the nation."[15] The need for belongingness and harmony as well as the lack of mentoring for these youngsters is cause for concern.

The second aspect of the novels the respondents liked included plot and characterization. Except for what one respondent labeled "anti-social behavior," the subjects enjoyed the various plots when they were "unpredictable, stimulating, and unique." Most like some romance in texts such as *How Stella Got Her Groove Back*, but they insist, "The career protagonists must be plausible." One woman appreciated the portrayal of the vendors from one of the most economically depressed areas of Triunion in Marshall's *Daughters* who precariously carried on their heads loads of produce to sell. Marshall writes, they "are willing to spend the day haggling to death over a penny difference in price.... Pure theater .... Every one of them should be on Broadway.... They love to put on a show, but we need them more on Wall Street. [But] they were born the wrong color, the wrong sex, the wrong class."[16] Several subjects noted the lack of professional characteristics the protagonists often display. One respondent observes, "Professional women must read extensively to remain competitive. When was the last time you read a novel in with a black professional woman goes regularly to the library for a few hours to conduct research, or does it on-line?" For many of these respondents, the protagonists need not be rich, but they must be seen behaving on a consistent basis as if they are "intelligent, love themselves, and at least some aspects of their work." Viney Daniels of *Daughters* is identified as self-empowered.

The informants also comment on the style of the novels. They particularly like narratives that have some humor in them, "but they are few and far between," writes one subject. The participants critique the way sex is handled in some texts. Romance and sex as an important aspect of the plot is desired, but they want sex presented in good taste. One respondent writes, "Sex is a physical act. It is not easy to describe for with the orgasm come pleasurable moans and grunts and giggles, and seconds of total self-absorption. But a description of coitus does not have to be violent or crude." Another subject points out that sometimes the urban dialect is particularly good at expressing strong emotions. For instance, in *The Salt Eaters*, Ruby is very angry at how poorly the Spring Festival was being organized. In frustration she says to Jan, "Too much confusion down there. No. I don't have a booth.... And everybody handing out flyers about this rally and that meeting. Scattered, fragmented, uncoordinated mess. I am sick of leaflets and T-shirts and moufy causes and nothing changing" (201). The theme of strong family relationships and the elements of plot, characterization, and style offered the informants much room for discussion.

The third component seeks reasons for the paucity of novels with the black professional protagonist exercising agency in her job and private life. This section of the survey produced some startling findings (see Chart 5B). The responses can be grouped into four areas. According to the respondents, publishers receive 38 percent of the blame, black women writers 34 percent, the American public 20 percent, and black women readers 8 percent. How is one to understand that almost as many of the professional women readers hold the women writers as accountable as the publishers for the lack of books about black career women on the market, given the marginalization of black women by the publishing industry? Equally surprising is, some of the readers blame themselves for the scarcity of these novels.

The participants clearly articulate that discrimination operates in publishing. Some believe the international conglomerates make it more difficult for black women to publish, especially new writers. One informant believes that "until more women hold management positions in the publishing industry, black women writers cultural production will be restricted." Her comment is insightful and possibly prophetic. Already we have noted one incident with Marshall's *Brown Girl, Brownstones* being reprinted by the Feminist Press when it had gone out of circulation. The greater presence of women in publishing is beginning to impact how books are packaged as well. The newly designed cover (within the year 2002) for the tenth anniversary edition of Alice Walker's *The Color Purple* by Harcourt is tastefully done. It accentuates the beautiful female character, poised and contemplative, with an elbow leaning on a chest of drawers. A fabric background is cut away to reveal the image. The character is surrounded with several colorful artistic symbols. The women and men at Harcourt received high praise from one observer for the delightful rendering of the portrait. Eye-catching jackets are also important to book sellers and consumers.

Another related problem mentioned is publishing houses operating primarily for profit. One informant comments: "They have no long-term commitment to black women writers' philosophy or interests per se. Hence, they will publish only what will sell." *Jet* magazine seems to agree with the opinion of this informant. Its position is that for the dissipation of culture, the publishing houses are the most powerful institution. But because it is "dominated by people who aren't necessarily sensitive to the needs and language of many of the readers, some Americans get left out. Certain needs aren't met." *Jet* bases its judgment on the fact that although in 1996, blacks bought 160 million books, only "3.4 percent of publishing industry professionals is African Americans."[17] One subject argues, "Readers and writers will have to demonstrate that there is a market for novels with the black female protagonist as autonomous, before the industry will invest enough money to change the formula for black women's books." Still another reports that some publishers are still skeptical about black women's concerns and their ability, even though Toni Morrison won the Nobel Prize. These companies are still privileging stereotypical images by packaging the books to look nonprofessional. For this respondent, "The problem is not just a matter of economics; its chauvinism." Despite the negative comments, one novelist/interviewee counseled, "We are making gains in publishing. My novel has been favorably received."

The subjects present publishing practices as another level of concern. One observes, "Many publishers want new writers facilitated through an agent. An agent costs, considering the percentage first writers receive from sales. Furthermore, agents can only handle a certain load. Publishing a text is easier for a 'house' if it works through agents, but it eliminates the chances of many new black writers getting published." A writer points out that it becomes difficult for the new writer to market her books since some publishers will not finance the publicity of the narratives. She notes, "The current publicist fee for three months is about nine thousand dollars plus expenses." This observation is corroborated with Terry McMillan's own experience with her first book, *Mama*. According to Wendy Smith, McMillan had to do her own publicizing. McMillan refused to accept "scattered reviews, zero publicity, and minimal sales ... [So] I wrote 3,000 letters ... to chains and independent book sellers, universities, colleges. It took me all summer long."[18]

Within the last ten years, more publishers are actively promoting novels by black women writers. Connie Briscoe's *Big Girls Don't Cry* and Sheneska Jackson's *Caught Up in the Rapture* together have sold in the hundreds of thousands. In spite of the more positive attitude publishers now have towards black women cultural producers, one respondent thinks there is only one real solution: "What is needed is for black writers and readers to create their own presses and support them." As admirable as the suggestion is, another participant counters that it is extremely difficult to be a writer and publisher simultaneously: "Alice Walker is the only famous contemporary writer I know who has attempted such a task. She is to be congratulated for managing Wild Tree Press. But it would have been extremely difficult for her to perform both careers at optimum level indefinitely, since both require an inordinate amount of time." Another participant concludes the discussion: "There is new respect and desire for novels about black women written by black women. Let's plan long term, but let's also appreciate the sensitivity the publishers are now showing our work, for we have earned it."

The informants make it quite clear that they hold the novelists partly responsible for the dearth of books about the black professional woman protagonist who is self-actualized. The first area reviewed is the competitive market. Surprisingly, some respondents position novelists as one segment of the entertainment industry. One CEO/President argues that the writers "must compete with techno-entertainment such as DVDs. All other industries do market research. Black women writers must function just as the publishers do, and supply the demand." A computer analyst reiterates that idea: "Black women writers don't seem to recognize that they are arriving on the publishing scene when print mode is becoming less appealing to many of the younger generation. The Internet is eclipsing the use of many books and hard copy journals. Novelists have to compete for people's attention."

Black novelists are also blamed for their lack of vision. One subject writes: "It seems every writer is concerned about how many books she will publish in the next five years. Unlike most business enterprises, black novelists have no long range planning strategies." Then she makes a suggestion. Each black woman writer (and the men too) could donate twenty of her books to the poorer members of the black community each year. Lending libraries could be set up in the more needy neighborhoods to give the less advantaged easy access to these books so they spend less time watching television. She envisions that as the mothers read, the youngsters will eventually value reading. They in turn would be more likely to purchase more books. In this way, everybody is served: the women would get books to read; novelists are assured an ongoing, in-built readership, and they can use their gift as a tax write-off. She concludes: "Black women writers are in competition for our money and our minds. Cyberspace is winning, or has already won."

Black women writers are partially held responsible for not producing more novels about black career women with autonomy. One respondent argues, "Black women novelists are the ones who create the images, even if they too are unconsciously responding to the media. It is they who are largely responsible for the books that still represent us as *un-professional*." Another respondent writes:

> Black women's books that are unique and interesting are in demand. Even publishing houses are studying black readership behaviors. So, black women writers, if they so choose, can produce *more* novels with the black career woman having self-empowerment. Today there are book clubs that [are] primarily made up of middle-class black professional women. Book clubs support black women writers. Black novelists can no longer use the excuse that no one will purchase their books.

The American public is also partly blamed for the lack of novels about the black professional women. One respondent writes, "The general public is so used to hearing from the media that black women are welfare queens and maids, that they conjure up a negative image in their minds. Consequently, they are satisfied with stereotypical images." Another subject suggests, "The issue concerns the positioning of the subject." She then explains that in at least 90 percent of the movies, black women are given more negative roles than white women. Even in advertising, the black woman is dressed in colors that suggest "lack of purity" if she is with white women; the black woman is either to the side or below the white characters in a scene, or somebody's hand is resting on top of hers. Sometimes, the black woman is the one being shown how to do something, or being talked to; her head is tilted or raised to look up at the speaker, often a Euro-American male. These scenes suggest "exclusion of parity in the midst of inclusion." The black professional woman with agency violates these perceptions, and some readers may not be willing to negotiate the adjustment necessary to accept the new image. One survey subject remembers hearing a colleague remark that a particular novel is "only for black women." Despite a discussion that ensued which confirmed the wide crossover appeal of that particular text, the respondent reports, "She insisted on marginalizing the narrative."

Some subjects blame themselves also. Their argument has this tenor. Up until the last thirty years, blacks could find very few books that represented them sensitively, accurately, and creatively. Today, however, there are more books on the market that represent the black professional woman, but black career women do not sufficiently articulate their desires. One informant thinks:

> Although middle-class women readers are looking for more books that represent them, most of them will purchase *any* book that is unique in plot and style, and does a good job with *any* area the black women writers choose. This is a good gesture, but the readership should be able to get what it *prefers* on a more regular basis.

The final section of the survey asks the respondents to make any comments they wish. Some of the longer comments in this chapter and Chapter Two come from this section of the questionnaire; the others are gleaned from direct statements respondents made at brief informal sessions. The women were very generous with their time and observations. A sociology professor comments:

> It is good to be alive and to be a part of this discussion. I remember when all the textbooks we used, were written by mainstream

authors. We had no input into what subjects were written, or how the writers or editors represented us. We hardly had any choice of the texts we bought for entertainment. What a wonderful opportunity for me to be able to tell black women writers some of my wishes. I hope they listen to us, as we listen to them.

This survey did not directly ask the subjects to comment on the two novels chosen for work. The rationale was to see whether the respondents would mention the texts, and what their responses would be. Some important observations were made. First, when the poled women were asked to respond to "Question 5"—to record which books they had read with a black woman professional protagonist—the results were as follows. Of the samples returned, 113 recorded having read *Waiting to Exhale* and 26 had read *The Salt Eaters*. The result is understandable since Terry McMillan is a popular writer and has millions of novels in circulation internationally. Toni Cade Bambara's *The Salt Eaters* is so experimental that many readers have difficulty understanding it fully on the first reading due to its stylistic devices. Furthermore, Bambara is deceased. The more recent writers have direct contact with cultural consumers through informal readings, interviews, and screenplays. Finally, throughout the text, we discover Velma Henry's professional status through her interior monologues and what others say of her rather than through the direct dialogue we encounter with McMillan's four protagonists.

The survey and small discussion groups clarified some of the features that were preferred in the two novels. In one informal discussion, both Bambara's and McMillan's texts were highlighted. Part of the discussion centers around Velma Henry's ability to function in many capacities simultaneously: computer analyst, social worker, administrator, wife, and mother. One subject comments, "Velma is Bambara's portrait re-imagined, for Bambara was equally involved in the Civil Rights Movement, the Black Power Movement, community outreach, her own career as writer and international activist. Furthermore, she was a parent." Another identified with Velma not being able to say "no" to urgent requests from the black community for help, especially in the 1960s and 1970s when there were so many needs. A younger participant interjects: "To survive, we must first take care of ourselves, and that was one of Velma's biggest problems." The older adult rejoined that "taking care of the community then meant taking care of the *self*—there was no other community to which the self could belong."

The subjects also discussed as admirable Bambara's attempt to confirm several of the women characters as professionals who are actually doing their work in the text. They mention the "Mom and Pop" stores, artists working with pottery ornamentations, and Velma Henry and the traveling troupe presented as entrepreneurs. Bambara having the dramatists represent several cultures reflects the novelist's interest in global issues.

Some participants enjoyed Minnie Ransom, the faith healer. Her flamboyant dress, her low-keyed approach to working with the high-profiled Velma, and her youthful behavior although she "was pushing 100 years" proved delightful. In a group discussion, one highlight was the sexual relationships between older women and younger men. One subject mentioned: "Minnie had her eye on the young doctor." Another commented that McMillan probably got her idea from Bambara for Bernadine to have a "tenderoni." Another broadened the discussion by noting: "McMillan herself is an extension of Minnie." The group erupted when a fourth said, "We are not sure if Minnie got her man for tea and for the afterwards. Knowing her powers, she did. But we *do* know that McMillan got hers."

A group of young career women in their early twenties critiqued *Waiting to Exhale*. The first to speak said, "Let's face it, this is a bad book even if it is popular." They acknowledged that the four protagonists did succeed in their jobs in the text, but they were somewhat embarrassed by the novel. One said, "It is as if their whole lives revolve around men. Where are their brains?" Another notes, "Do they ever attend cultural events other than their own little club? At least one went to a convention. The novel is not realistic. Professional development is a 'big thing' if you want to move up the ladder." The consensus is, it takes too long—the whole novel—for the protagonists to "get their act together." They prefer *How Stella Got Her Groove Back* since they "hope to earn six digit figure incomes," but they echoed a familiar complaint, "Too much of the same—men and sex and kids."

The results of the ethnographic component corroborated nicely with the theoretical findings. Many of the respondents denied that most of the characters functioned as professionals usually do, and emphasized that the protagonists did not mirror their lived lives. The research subjects helped to clarify what the black women readers enjoy in novels that represent the black career woman, and why they feel there is a dearth of them. It provided support of the theory that the protagonists in *The Salt Eaters* and *Waiting to Exhale* did not evidence the level of agency that one would have expected given the characters' intelligence, training, and job experience. Yet, it must be reiterated that two respondents liked the novels "as is."

Because the sample of women respondents in this first study was small despite the 68 percent return rate, in the future, a larger entity may be sought from a cross section representing all women readers through surveys, group discussions, and personal interviews. Furthermore, such a study would prove invaluable since all groups of autonomous professional women share the reality of underrepresentation in fiction. Publishers could be approached to determine to what extent their present policies have changed to accommodate novels with the black female protagonist as autonomous and successful, the ever-growing presence of black women writers, the large black female readership, and other female cultural consumers.

My research did not find a contested readership (that is, readers who unequivocally rejected the novels under discussion) or a preferred readership (those who willingly accepted the writer's agenda). Instead, I encountered an interpretive readership that engaged the novels and offered critiques. Thus, they sifted through the various aspects of the texts in order to identify with those areas that resonated with their lives. The results deny a monolithic black professional woman readership, but the majority of the respondents agree that the works by Bambara and McMillan analyzed in this text, and even many that were published after *The Salt Eaters* and *Waiting to Exhale*, do not exhibit adequate agency.

Conclusion

Today middle-class black professional women articulate their need for novels that represent them as having a high level of agency. Unfortunately, very few narratives written by black women writers position the protagonist in the work force as self-empowered, for internal and external factors impinge on the writing of these texts. In addition, the interlocking forces of racism, sexism, classism, and the overextendedness of the characters on behalf of the black community impede the autonomy of the protagonists. The quest for representing black women in fictive texts with a high level of agency, which began in the 1980s with Bambara's *The Salt Eaters*, is still in progress.

Three important factors provided a rationale for the new paradigm that occurred in the 1980s with respect to the representation of the fictive black woman. First, a demographic shift began with black women moving from blue-collar jobs to white-collar employment. The entrance of large numbers of black career women in the workplace acted as a catalyst in the literary consciousness to change how the black professional woman was to be perceived. This new professional class provided models from which the writers could create professional protagonists.

The second contributing factor is the Black Arts Movement of the 1960s. This literary philosophy proposed that black artists "meet the spiritual and cultural needs of black people [using their] own aesthetic."[1] Thus, its principles provided a philosophic framework that allowed a few novelists to begin envisioning more positive images of black women, especially the profile of the black professional woman. These innovative women writers, having achieved high levels of autonomy themselves, sought to convey novelistic representation of their own experience. However, the profiles were imperfect given the protagonists' limited agency. Since the characters were new to corporate America, and since many of the writers themselves had recently entered the professional ranks, the artists could only write from that historic moment. This statement is not meant to be derogatory but celebratory, for these remarkable novelists were creating from a position of absence. It was a profound moment in black literary scholarship when Toni Cade Bambara conceived the black professional woman as autonomous and performing her job within the text even though we hear of her achievements from others.

During the early 1990s, a new novelist, Terry McMillan, arrived on the scene breaking free of the academic mode of writing, and successfully introducing the black community to popular culture. Her *Waiting to Exhale* and subsequent novels (some with filmic renditions) created excitement throughout the publishing industry with their phenomenal sales. Critic Laura Randolph presents McMillan's response to the popularity of her work:

> I just think there has been a real strong identification with the sentiment that these women have.... There is [*sic*] a lot of women out there who are having a difficult time finding a satisfying partner, which is why some of the stuff is so funny to them.[2]

This quotation is important, for McMillan identifies her readership reacting to one of the characteristics of the novels the respondents in the survey preferred: meaningful relationships with males who appreciate their professional achievement and the high level of agency they have attained.

The rationale for the response of black women writers and readers to the negative portrayals of themselves and other black women in the media may be understood in terms of self-actualization and self-efficacy. Since large numbers of black women have become professionals, they are financially able to concentrate on developing their careers and creative abilities. Middle-class career women demonstrate efficacy by purchasing, reading, and analyzing the novels.

Although black career women purchase novels in the millions each year, the majority of the respondents acknowledge that the protagonists—including those in *The Salt Eaters* and *Waiting to Exhale*—do not reflect their daily lives. The enthusiasm with which they purchased *Waiting to Exhale*, for instance, evidences the pleasure these cultural consumers experience when the writers choose black professional women as subjects. The readers want to support the literary outpouring that is taking place within the black community.

This work is not isolated in its questioning the agency black middle-class professionals receive in artistic renditions. Other media are exploring similar issues. The movie, *The Best Man* (1999), attempts to project black men as professionals with some level of agency in their lives. Reviewer Lonnae O'Neal Parker comments:

> This smart debut ... centers around a group of old friends who unite
> in New York for a wedding. Tapping into the Zeitgeist of young
> black professionals starving to see themselves in film, it hits all the
> right cultural touchstones.... Although the film is produced by Spike
> Lee, don't expect racial politics.... In a world of popular Hollywood
> cinema, black characters rarely seem to be more than cardboard
> cutouts: the requisite hoodlum, ghetto goddess, or chief security.
> Not so in *The Best Man*.[3]

Although the critique is of the filmic representation of black men as opposed
to the fictive critique offered in this text, it reinforces the argument that black
professionals are seeking accurate and positive representation. Black middle-
class professional women readers in particular want adequate portrayals.

Black novelists have yet to create narratives that regularly show black
women professionals as autonomous. It could be that they prefer other character portrayals, or though self-actualized themselves, they have difficulty
transforming that agency into the lives of their fictional characters frequently. Furthermore, Maslow's findings show that self-actualization is a
fluid state, and that "peak" experiences are not a constant.[4] Writers create
characters they believe to be plausible and meaningful.

A hypothetical case suggested by Maslow may offer comment on the
dearth of novels representing black professional women. Maslow speaks of
a kind of fear that is a corollary of growth with its antecedent discomfort,
anxiety of potential dangers, and the insecurity of novel paths. It often
accompanies the increased challenge and difficulty of a higher level of actualization. Often human beings resist fulfilling their highest possibilities, that
is, they "struggle against their own greatness, the fear of *hubris*.... It is precisely the god-like in ourselves that we are ambivalent about, fascinated by
and fearful of, motivated to and defensive against."[5] Black women writers
themselves will not find the portrait of the fully actualized protagonist unsettling. It is perhaps that these writers prefer to avoid such portrayals in order
to lessen the discomfort of others whose level of consciousness does not
parallel theirs. A writer, for instance, may temper what she wants to communicate, if she perceives the representation will not be satisfying or useful, artistically or thematically, to her audience.

What would the black professional protagonist be like if she were represented as embracing her hubris, her full "humanness"? Maslow offers that
certain dangers come with Being-cognition. Some self-actualized individuals
exhibit little tolerance for others who have not attained their level of enlightenment; others feel they cannot achieve complete fulfillment without others experiencing similar heightened awareness. Still others can maintain a
delicate balance between their "homeostatic Being."[6] Could black women

novelists envision their protagonists in positions such as a successful chair-person of the Securities and Exchange Commission, a cardinal of the church, a president of the United States? These new characters may exhibit a com-bination of primary traits found in previously delineated personae. The pro-tagonist could reflect the wisdom and precision of Etta Mae Johnson in *Waiting to Exhale,* who with one sentence breaks a cycle of overextendedness for the women of her organization. She could exhibit the independence of Sula Peace (*Sula,* 1974),[7] whose autonomy allows her to disregard the estab-lished sexual mores of her community (even though her particular choice is questionable and need not be replicated). She could maintain the financial acumen and compassion of Naomi in *Big Girls Don't Cry,* who builds a finan-cial empire and nurtures her alienated and angry nephew.

Since self-actualized characters have the ability to see a clearer view of reality than their peers; they are very complex persons. Their behaviors could reflect kindness matched with self-reliance, empathy with account-ability, and service with individualism. Such an executive would possibly ini-tiate significant changes in government and corporate policies that would, for instance, allow more and varied citizens opportunities in training, jobs, and potential for advancement. She would encourage risk-taking, and reward meaningful, innovative ideas. Fair evaluative policies and equal distribution of rewards for comparable work would continue to restructure the work-place, and special arrangements would be implemented to accommodate handicapped persons or those who experience legitimate obstacles. The trained employees would be held accountable for their performance and their own fate. As such, the Sula / Etta Mae / Naomi combination would not be a replica of the paradoxical so-called bourgeois phallic-woman that some people fear powerful feminists have become. Neither is such a character a superwoman; she is merely tapping into her own genius. She is self-affirming and altruistic.

In her private life, this protagonist's behavior would be consistent with her professional persona. Maslow argues that the self-actualizing individual has an integrated personality. She would be less inclined to tolerate rela-tionships that have little potential for significant growth, and so abruptly ter-minate them.[8] For such a protagonist to function effectively, the writers would have to minimize the excessive turbulence incorporated in the lives of characters such as Velma Henry or the four protagonists of *Waiting to Exhale.* The new protagonist would also be fun-loving, cherish family and friendships that are not destructive, love the arts, read, make mistakes, and have moments of serenity and harmony to restore the self. She would rep-resent the fully vibrant individual.

One may question if our society is ready to embrace the fully actualized woman, and particularly, the black career protagonist. Our culture has certain expectations of women, and even more limiting ones for black women. Maslow remarks that self-actualized individuals are allowed to come into "Being" because society or at least individuals "permit it or help it" just as universities allow professors sabbaticals to achieve their creative potential. He also adds that individuals can accept "dangerous" knowledge if they are given encouragement and support from their communities or environment.[9] The term "dangerous" borrowed here is not literal, but interpreted to mean the representation of the autonomous black professional woman who is fully human and evidences periods of mastery over her life. The creation would affirm black and white women readers who are self-actualized, and as the respondents suggest, provide inspiration for others to imagine agency and so reconstruct their worldview.

A related question is whether a crossover readership is ready to purchase books whose characters exhibit a high level of agency. Novels of Toni Morrison such as *Beloved* and *Sula* offer startling portrayals of working-class women performing the near unthinkable. The novels sold in the millions. It is possible for black women writers to replicate the pattern of black middle-class women characters who fulfill high-profiled and demanding roles. Already models of black and white women are functioning in such capacities. Shirley Chisholm, who was the first black woman to serve in Congress and who was a member of the House of Representatives from 1969 to 1983, ran for presidency in 1972. Dr. Condoleezza Rice, a black woman, has been the national security advisor to President George Bush Affairs since 2001. Many black women officiate in the priesthood. Barbara Clementine Harris was ordained suffragan bishop in 1988, and Leontine Kelly was the first black woman bishop of the Methodist Episcopal Church in 1988. Two white women have already served on the five-person commission of the Securities and Exchange Commission. In 2000, Laura Unger was acting chairperson, and in 2002 Cynthia A. Glassman served as one of the commissioners. The time is ready for such representation, for black female professionalism *is* already a part of the fabric of black life and the national arena. Women as high profiled careerists are an international reality.

Today black women cultural consumers as well as a crossover audience appear ready to support such texts. The issue for some writers could be the wisdom of the creation, for as Maslow suggests, the fear of confronting one's own greatness is also predicated on one's willingness to challenge the "gods," since such behavior often incurs their displeasure evidenced in Oedipus, and Prometheus. The "gods" with regard to cultural production could be critics and certain enclaves of readers.

Despite the possible constraints that surround the creation of the highly self-actualized black professional woman, Maslow suggests that there are rewards for such an attempt:

> We are again and again rewarded for good Becoming by transient states of absolute Being, by peak-experiences. Achieving basic-needs Gratification gives us many peak experiences, each of which is absolute delights, perfect in themselves, and needing no more than themselves to validate life.[10]

Many artists, including some black women writers, have captured remarkably well the totality of those epiphanies.

This discussion is not presented as a formula for writing the career protagonist, but rather an inquiry of new possibilities. It is a given that writers approach their craft individually. This argument allows that character portrayal of the black career protagonist embracing her genius is yet to be fully imagined.

A quarter century ago, Toni Cade Bambara envisioned the first black career woman with some measure of agency and performing her job within the text. Subsequent novelists, such as Terry McMillan, elaborated on Bambara's conception of the professional and presented the protagonists as more self-empowered. The future is pregnant with hope for novels representing the black professional woman as fully self-actualized. Alice Walker affirms that among the gifts bequeathed to her by her mother are the "respect for possibilities—and the will to grasp them."[11] Black women writers as they confront their own genius, and build on the heritage bequeathed by their predecessors, will continue to transform the literary landscape as they represent the fully self-actualized professional female protagonist.

Occupational Distributions of Black and White Women: 1940, 1960, and 1980*

	1940 Black	1940 White	1960 Black	1960 White	1980 Black	1980 White
Professional and technical workers	4.6	18.8	7.7	15.8	16.2	20.1
Doctors, lawyers, engineers, etc.	0.0	0.4	0.1	0.3	0.4	0.7
Teachers	3.6	8.9	4.4	7.1	6.3	7.2
Nurses	0.4	5.1	1.5	3.6	2.6	3.6
Librarians, social workers, religious workers	0.2	1.4	0.5	1.0	1.6	1.2
Other	0.4	3.0	1.3	3.8	5.2	7.4
Managers	0.9	4.9	1.1	4.3	2.5	6.4
Manufacturing	0.0	0.3	0.0	0.3	0.2	0.7
Wholesale	0.0	0.1	0.0	0.1	0.1	0.4
Financial, insurance, real estate	0.1	0.6	0.1	0.4	0.4	1.0
Retail, personal service, entertainment, recreation	0.7	3.1	0.7	2.2	0.9	2.8
Other	0.0	0.8	0.2	1.2	0.8	1.3
Clerical workers	1.3	24.2	8.0	34.1	29.0	36.5
Secretaries, typists, stenographers	0.4	10.1	2.3	11.7	7.5	13.0
Other	0.9	14.1	5.7	22.4	21.5	23.5
Sales workers	0.7	7.8	1.5	8.7	2.8	6.9
Financial, insurance, real estate	0.0	0.5	0.1	0.8	0.4	1.7
Other	0.6	7.3	1.3	8.0	2.4	5.2

*The United States Commission on Civil Rights, The Economic Status of Black Women: An Exploratory Investigation (Washington, D.C., Oct., 1990) 45.

APPENDIX B

Family Assets of Black and White Women by Employment Status*

This partial table may be helpful to readers to see how race and class intersect. These figures are for 1960–1980.

	Employed	
	Black	White
A. *Percent with Asset Type*		
Home	45.8	61.1
Business	2.5	12.5
Vehicles	67.0	82.5
Other Savings and Investments	61.0	80.8
Stocks and Mutual funds	4.9	19.2
Interest-earning money in banks	47.3	69.7
Interest earning money not in banks	1.8	8.2
Other assets, inc'l. checking acc't	41.1	64.1
Other real estate	6.4	17.4
IRA and KEOGH accounts	6.0	26.1
B. *Average Value Assets, if possible*		
Home	32,973	49,662
Business	10,657	56,124
Vehicles	3,822	6,126
Other Savings and Investments	5,381	27,552
Stocks and mutual funds	2,438	13,822
Interest-earning money in bank	2,429	9,162
Interest-earning money not in bank	2,692	13,371

*The United States Commission on Civil Rights, The Economic Status of Black Women: An Exploratory Investigation (Washington, D.C., Oct., 1990) 103.

	Employed	
	Black	*White*
Other assets inc.; l. checking can't	956	4,805
Other real estate	39,378	48,460
IRA or KEOGH	3,713	7,225
C. Average Household wealth, debt, and net worth		
Household wealth	26,999	77,132
Debt	13,765	32,854
Secured	11,181	29,203
Unsecured	2,585	3,651
Household net worth	24,412	72,894

APPENDIX C

Respondent Information and Questionnaire Results

Chart 1

175 questionnaires were sent. 119 responses were received, for a response rate of 68%.

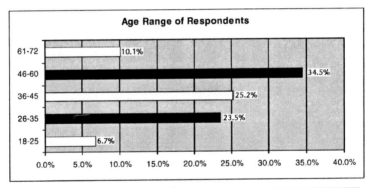

Age Range of Respondents

Age Range	Percentage
61-72	10.1%
46-60	34.5%
36-45	25.2%
26-35	23.5%
18-25	6.7%

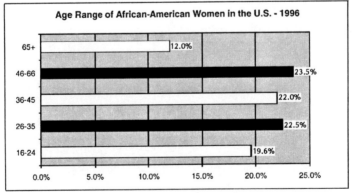

Age Range of African-American Women in the U.S. - 1996

Age Range	Percentage
65+	12.0%
46-66	23.5%
36-45	22.0%
26-35	22.5%
16-24	19.6%

Chart 2

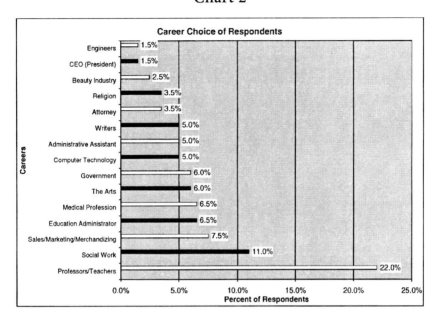

Career Choice of Respondents

Chart 3

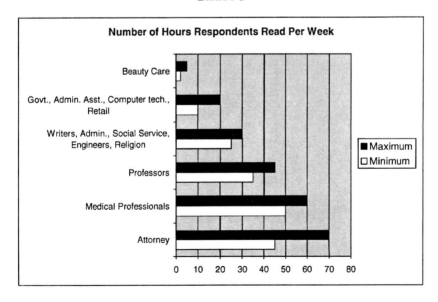

Number of Hours Respondents Read Per Week

Appendix C

Chart 4

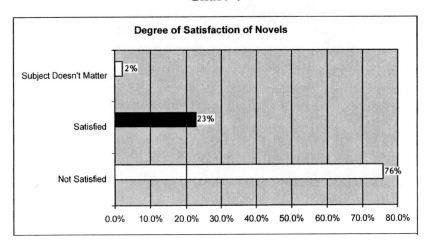

Chart 5A

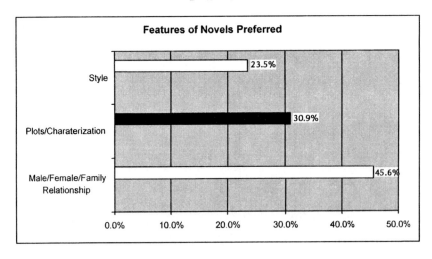

Chart 5B

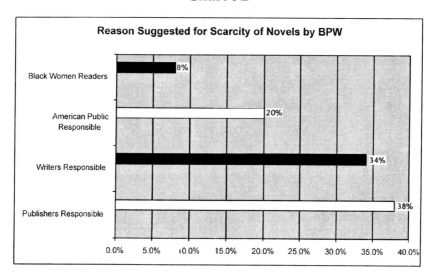

Chart 6

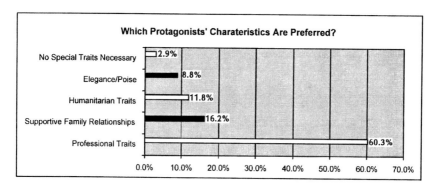

Chart 7

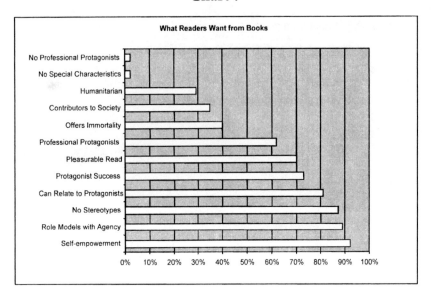

Notes

1. Edmondson Bell, Ella L.J. and Stella M. Nkomo. *Our Separate Ways: Black and White Women and the Struggle for Personal Identity*. Boston: Harvard Business School, 2001. 11.

Introduction

1. U.S. Department of Labor, Bureau of Labor Statistics. "Employed Persons by Occupation, Race, and Sex." http://stats.bls.gov/cps/cpsaat10.pdf. Of the 8,143,000 black women employed in 2001, 26 percent or 2,117,180 were employed in managerial and professional specialties.

2. Briscoe, Connie. "Author's Success Better Than Fiction." Interview by Toni Marshall. *The Washington Times* 2 B1. 1996.

3. Neal, Larry. "The Black Arts Movement." 62–78.

4. Ife, Zadia. "The African Diasporan Ritual Mode." 31.

5. Washington, Mary Helen. "Teaching Black-Eyed Susans: An Approach to the Study of Black Women Writers." 212. Washington points out that though the schema is an oversimplification, it nevertheless shows the progress black women characters have made in fiction and a correspondence to the lived lives of black women.

6. McMillan, Terry. *Breaking Ice: An Anthology of Contemporary African American Fiction.* xx.

7. Ford, Jesse Hill. "The Making of Fables." 200. Ford believes that the South's topography and enclaves do influence people's writings as everywhere else. However, he denies that there is anything special about the South that makes for better writers, or that does not allow Northern editors to understand Southern writers.

8. Maslow, Abraham. *Toward a Psychology of Being.* 26–49. This text is revolutionary in its argument that human beings are intrinsically good—a definite break from the predominantly Western philosophy that man is inherently evil, or at best aggressive and selfish. Maslow argues that if people have their physical and emotional needs satisfied, then they have the urge to become self-actualized beings.

9. Riley, Denise. *"Am I That Name": Feminism and the Category of "Women" in History.* 5–7.

10. Edmondson Bell, Ella L.J. and Stella M. Nkomo. *Our Separate Ways: Black and White Women and the Struggle for Professional Identity.* 229.

11. Lowery, Rodney. "Foreword." *Toward a Psychology of Being* by Abraham H. Maslow. viii. This discussion incorporates the ideas of both Maslow's earlier text, *Motivation and Personality* (1954) and his later revised version, *Toward a Psychology of Being.*

12. Ibid. viii.

13. Ibid. viii–ix.

14. Ibid. viii–xxxiii.

15. Maslow, Abraham H. 167. Maslow discovers a wonderful principle of human higher values in the experiment of the chickens and their choices of food. The better choosers chose food that was healthier for them, while the others chose the unhealthy diet. However, when the poorer choosers were fed the better diet, they too became healthy but not to the extent as the first set of better choosers. Maslow finds a correlation between the better choosers of chickens and self-empowered human beings.

16. Ibid. 169.

17. Lowery, Richard. xxvi–xxvii.

18. Collins, Patricia Hill. "The Meaning of Motherhood in the Black Culture and the Black Mother-Daughter Relationships." 51.

19. Grant, Jacquelyn. "Black Theology and the Black Woman." 326–33.

20. Gregory, Sheila T. Black Women in the Academy: The Secrets of Success. 8. Gregory gives a comprehensive coverage of the status of black woman in the academy—what have been the perennial problems, and some possible solutions. She argues that women internationally have a secondary place in universities.

21. Jones, Jacqueline. Labor of Love, Labor of Sorrow: Black Women, Work, and the Family from Slavery to the Present. 257–318. Jones gives a comprehensive history of black woman's work from slavery to 1980. She sees black women as overburdened with community activities.

22. Ashe, Arthur. Days of Grace. 110–115, 131, 262–264.

23. Graham, Lawrence Otis. Our Kind of People: Inside America's Black Upper-Middle Class. 88.

24. Jones, Jacqueline. 318.

25. Golden, Stephanie. Slaying the Mermaid: Women and the Culture of Sacrifice. 229–230, 119, 243.

26. Gregory, Sheila. 20–27, 94.

27. Ibid. "Foreword." xi.

28. Ibid. 24–28, 88.

29. Harris, Trudier. Saints, Sinners, Saviors: Strong Black Women in African American Literature. 12.

30. Ibid. 17.

31. Bambara, Toni Cade. "What It Is I Think I'm Doing Anyhow." The Writer on Her Work. 157, 168.

32. McMillan, Terry. Breaking Ice: An Anthology of Contemporary African American Fiction. xxiv.

33. Bambara, Toni. The Salt Eaters. New York: Vintage, 1992. 1. (All subsequent references will be to this edition.)

34. McMillan, Terry. Waiting to Exhale. New York: Pocket, 1992. 1. (All subsequent references will be to this edition.)

35. Campbell, Bebe Moore. Brothers and Sisters. 1.

36. Decker, Jeffrey Louis. Made in America: Self-Styled Success from Horatio Alger to Oprah Winfrey. 117.

37. George, Lynell. "Full Exposure: A Boom in Fiction by Black Women Writers Has Bought a Wealth of Voices Telling Tales That Defy Stereotypes." Los Angeles Times 7 July 1996, Home Ed., E-1.

38. Bambara, Toni Cade. "Toni Cade Bambara." With Claudia Tate. Black Women Writers at Work. 14.

39. Bambara, Toni Cade. "What It Is I Think I'm Doing Anyhow." The Writer on Her Work. 153–168.

40. Ibid. 153–168

41. Bell, Ella L. Bicultural Life Structures and Stress Among Black Women. 1–25.

42. George, Lynell. E-1.

43. Fiske, John. Understanding Popular Culture. 4–5, 19–38.

44. Griffin, Ada Guy. "Seizing the Moving Image: Reflections of a Black Independent Producer." 228–33.

45. McMillan, Terry. Breaking Ice: An Anthology. xx.

46. Fiske, John. 56.

47. McMillan, Terry. Breaking Ice: An Anthology xx.

48. Fiske, John. 50.

49. McMillan, Terry. Breaking Ice: An Anthology. xx.

50. Fiske, John. 25.

51. White, Jack E. "Heavy Breathing: Forget About Sisterhood and No-Good Guys. Waiting to Exhale Is About the Bottom Line." 73.

52. Bobo, Jacqueline. Black Women as Cultural Readers: Film and Culture. 21, 17.

53. Said, Edward. Culture AND Imperialism. xviii.

54. Ibid. 3.

55. Radway, Janice. Reading the Romance: Women, Patriarchy, and Popular Literature. 18.

56. Booker, Keith. *Practical Introduction to Literary Theory and Criticism.* 47–51. This text offers a usable definition and accessible discussion of what reader response entails. It removes the focus from the writer and text to the reader, especially in terms of how readers and texts communicate, and how readers take meaning from the writing to empower their lives.

57. Bobo, Jacqueline. 11.

58. Ibid. 38.

Chapter One

1. The "Go On Girl Book Club" is a nationally represented book club of black women readers that buys, reads, and critiques books written by black women. It has become a powerful force in negotiating with publishers about books written by black professional women.

2. Rogers, Carl. *The Carl Rogers Reader.* 244–245. In addition to the theories and therapeutic information, it adds some of the lived experiences of Rogers, such as his response to his wife dying, and his interest in extrasensory experiences.

3. Nye, Robert D. *Three Psychologies: Perspectives from Freud, Skinner, and Rogers.* 94. This text provides a synopsis of the theories of psychoanalysis by Rogers, Skinner, and Freud.

4. Rogers, Carl. *The Carl Rogers Reader.* 245.

5. Bandura, Albert. "Albert Bandura and Social Cognitive Theory." *Psychology.* 449–451. Social cognitive psychology does not address the unconscious or the innate hostilities and aggression Freud emphasized. Editors Hockenbury and Hockenbury comment that it works best in laboratory situations.

6. Beale, Francis. "Double Jeopardy: To Be Black and Female." 146–155.

7. "The Other Half: Blacks in America." *The Economist (U.S.)* 337. 7939 (Nov. 4, 1995): 35.

8. U.S. Department of Labor: Women's Bureau. "Black Women in the Labor Force." *Facts On Women Working.* No. 97-1. Washington, D.C. (March 1997.) The text provides information on the gains of black women, but the disparities between blacks and the mainstream population are so glaring that the gains seem minuscule.

9. Golden, Marita. *The Edge of Heaven.* 168. Although most of the text does not focus on the protagonist's professional career, but rather on her life in prison and her heroic attempt to reclaim her life and daughter, the book gives a good yet brief representation of the black professional woman's success.

10. Eagleton, Terry. *Literary Theory: An Introduction.* 198–199. Raymond Williams. "Culture Is Ordinary." *Studying Culture: An Introductory Reader.* 5. These two works demonstrate that what is often understood to be "high culture" is the means whereby one group uses its private taste in art forms to dominate and control the production and creativity of other groups. The second text offers a wide array of discussions on what culture is, but Williams is definitive in his assessment that culture is the lifestyle of everyone; it is ordinary. Therefore, each is valuable.

11. Du Bois, W. E. Burghardt. *The Souls of Black Folk: Essays and Sketches.* 16–17. This seminal text allows for an understanding of the sense of two-ness blacks in America experience.

12. Boston Women's Health Book Collective. *Our Bodies, Ourselves for the New Century: A Book By and For Women.* 33. The text presents a holistic approach to the needs of all women internationally. What is of particular importance for this study is, it is a united project of women of different races.

13. Ross, Catherine. "Finding Without Seeking: What Readers Say About the Role of Pleasure Reading as a Source of Information." 6–12.

14. Hughes, Langston. "Harlem." 1267. Hughes imaginatively captures how the creative energy of individuals, if denied positive expression, can become nonproductive.

15. Hansberry, Lorraine. *A Raisin in the Sun.* 1217–1267. This drama is Hansberry's imaginative rendition of Langston Hughes' poem "Harlem." The full potential of the dream, here middle-class professional attainment, is deferred in the drama, though the potential lingers on.

16. Dennison, Dorothy L. "Early Fiction by Paule Marshall." 35–36, 40–41.

17. *Writers [on Writing]: Collected Essays from the* New York Times. The text gives the direct responses of writers to their craft.

18. Said, Edward W. *Culture AND Imperialism*. 13. This work is a seminal critique of literature and the arts as a vehicle for creating and maintaining colonialism even after the conquerors have been forced to leave their conquered territories. Said demonstrates that literature, by degrading the native populations and making the violence of the conqueror seem natural while blaming the conquered, helped to create a feeling of normalcy for invasion. It allowed for the rightness of the imperialists to brutalize the conquered and appropriate their property, bodies, and culture.

19. Walker, Alice. "In Search of Our Mothers' Gardens." 2380–2387. Walker "specifies" on Virginia Woolf's *A Room of One's Own*, which suggests that all people have the creative spark within them. The Shakespeare Sister(s) who was denied artistic expression could not even imagine the horror black creative slave women endured, yet both groups of women kept the creative imagination alive for their posterity.

20. Harris, Trudier. *Saints, Sinners, Saviors: Strong Black Women in African American Literature*. 13, 16–17.

21. Ashe, Arthur and Arnold Rampersad. *Days of Grace: A Memoir*. 153, 301.

22. Ibid. 111.

23. Foote, Shelby. "It's Worth a Grown Man's Time." 7, 19.

24. Sicherman, Barbara. "Reading and Ambition: M. Carey Thomas and Female Heroism." 73, 75, 77, 90. The writer, using reader response criticism, shows how Minnie Carey Thomas's diaries and papers evidence her "positioning" herself into the texts she read, thereby defying the Victorian conventions that hampered women from becoming highly successful professionals. The writer acknowledges that it is easier for privileged women to "read in self-authorizing ways" than for women of the working class, who primarily read works such as the romances for pleasure.

25. Sabine, Gordon and Patricia Sabine. *Books That Made the Difference: What People Told Us*. Using reader response criticism, the writers interviewed, analyzed, and reported the comments of the readers. The readers report the diverse ways books have changed the course of their lives.

26. Ibid. 3.

27. Bobo, Jacqueline. *Black Women as Cultural Readers: Film and Culture*. 6. Bobo finds a symbiotic relationship between readers and writers. Black women's texts "nourish and sustain their readers, while readers are indispensable for interpreting the works."

28. Whitman, Walt. "Song of Myself." In *Leaves of Grass*. 28. Whitman is the most democratic American writer. He writes that when he celebrates the self, he celebrates all humankind, since he and they are one.

29. Wallace, Michele. *Invisibility Blues: From Pop to Theory*. 1990. 7–8.

30. De Bottom, Alain. "The Sorrows of Young Alain." 1. The notion here is that literature connects to the human condition for the need to be loved.

Chapter Two

1. McMillan, Terry. "Everything I Write Is About Empowerment." Interview with Anne Bowling. 1–9. In this interview McMillan discusses her craft as a fiction writer.

2. Johnson, Diane. "Pesky Themes Will Emerge When You're Not Looking." 113. This selection of essays by writers discusses how the craft of writing is actually accomplished.

3. Brown, Roseleen. "Character's Weaknesses Build Fiction's Strength." *Writers [on Writing]: Collected Essays from the* New York Times. 34.

4. Howard, Maureen. "The Enduring Commitment of a Faithful Storyteller." *Writers [on Writing]: Collected Essays from the* New York Times. 99.

5. Busch, Frederick. "Preface." *Why People Publish: Essays on Writers and Writing*. xix. The book explores many aspects of writing and the writers' responses to their craft.

6. Chappell, Fred. "Dealing with the Grotesque." Interview by John Sopko and John Carr. 229. Chappell believes the

South as location and history has influenced his writing.

7. Busch, Frederick. 71. 45–50. This study gives an in-depth look at how the writers' experiences informed the texts they write. Busch illustrates, for example, how Dickens' childhood experiences of being left alone at a boarding school when all the other children had gone home at Christmas became a "psychic investment" in his writings, and was epitomized in Scrooge, whose similar experience accounted for his unkind behavior. Dickens' pain is artistically transferred into championing the cause of abused children. Thus the novelist repeatedly "rehearsed his tragedy."

8. Marshall, Paule. "An Interview with Paule Marshall." With Daryl Cumber Dance. 1–9. In Paule Marshall's works, the absentee father or father figure is clearly delineated. In *Souls Clap Hands and Sing*, all the protagonists are emotionally wounded males, and function as exploiters of women. In *Praisesong for the Widow*, the father remains in the home, but because he works three jobs to maintain a middle-class lifestyle, he is only present with the children on Sundays. In *Brown Girl, Brownstones*, the father has abandoned the family. Finally, in *The Fisher King*, no father is present. A grandfather is father to his grandchildren after he failed to properly father his own daughter.

9. Erikson, Erik H. *Childhood and Society*. 421. Although the psychologist is speaking here from a medical perspective in terms of natural childbirth, the point is appropriate for this discussion.

10. Ibid. 412. Erikson discusses how one, particularly the child, develops a sense of identity. He thinks the process is based on "social health and cultural solidarity" after the crises of maturation which allows for the "integration of the ego stages."

11. Busch, Frederick. 156.

12. Richards, Paulette. *Terry McMillan: A Critical Companion*. 7.

13. Golden, Marita. *The Edge of Heaven*. 101.

14. Ibid. 160.

15. Ashe, Arthur. *Days of Grace: A Memoir*. 139.

16. Hockenbury, Don H. and Sandra E. Hockenbury, Eds. *Psychology*. 222–228.

17. Simmons, Ruth J. "My Mother's Daughter: Lessons My Mother Taught Me About Civility and Authenticity." 20–29.

18. "Black Women in the Labor Force." *Facts on Women Working*. U.S. Department of Labor: Women's Bureau. No. 97-1. March 1997. Washington, D.C. 1–9.

19. Erikson, Erik. 216. Although the quotation is somewhat long, it is important for the reader to see the text: "We also suspect that it is not so innocently accidental that some people make the same mistakes over and over again; that they 'coincidentally' and in utter blindness marry the same kind of impossible partner from whom they have just divorced; or that a series of analogous accidents and mishaps always must happen just to *them*. In all of these cases, so Freud concluded, the individual unconsciously arranges for variations of an original theme which he has not learned to overcome or live with: he has tried to master a situation which in its original form has been too much for him by meeting it repeatedly and of his own accord."

20. Golden, Marita. 128–129.

21. Berne, Eric. M.D. *Transactional Analysis in Psychotherapy: A Systematic Individual and Social Psychiatry*. 91–92. The text provides a useful methodology for psychotherapy, and deals with specialized concepts of the social dynamics of the roles people play during social interaction. It discusses the need of the three aspects of the individual's personality, the "adult," the "parent," and the "child" (counterparts of the id, ego, and super-ego), to function harmoniously, if all the parties in relationships (seen as a power struggles) the individual is involved with are to benefit.

22. Marshall, Paule. "Shaping the World of My Art." 97–112.

23. Edmondson Bell, Ella L.J. and Stella Nkomo. 122. The writers emphasize that while most white women had to handle gender and some class issues, black women had to deal with gender, race and class.

24. Dance, Daryl C. "Introduction." *Honey Hush! An Anthology of African American Women's Humor*. xxix.

25. The Boston Women's Health Book Collective. *Our Bodies, Ourselves for the New Century: A Book by and for Women.* 36–37. This text addresses some of the major areas that impinge on women's lives such as nutrition and weight problems, body image, sexual violence, women loving women, and cooperating with each other.

26. Shields, Cydney and Leslie Shields. *Work Sister Work: Why Black Women Can't Get Ahead and What They Can Do About It.* 118–137.

27. Ibid. 138–143. In this chapter, "The ABC's of Making It to the Top," the writer makes twenty-six such recommendations. How the injunctions are to be detailed and carried out are missing.

28. Ibid. 86–87. In later chapters, the writers do make suggestions as to how one may change one's image through dress and other recommendations. In Chapter 7, "Shaping Up Your Image," this task involves recognizing certain types of employees such as the "the corporate diamonds," "bench warmer," "the Queen B," and "The Whiner," all defined in a few lines. The reader is given an image inventory, and is told to create "the right image."

29. Edmondson Bell, Ella L.J. and Stella Nkomo. 5, 11. The writers mention texts that discuss white professional women, but they do not interrogate the issue of race.

30. Ibid. 227, 223, 145.

31. Ibid. 140–143.

32. Ibid. 153–168.

33. Ibid. 725.

34. Ibid. 152–174.

35. *Forbes.* "The World's Richest People." 3 March 2003. http://www.forbes.com/static_2003/rank.html. The list registers the wealthiest people in the world. Oprah is listed as number 427 in the world, and the first African American woman to become a billionaire.

36. *Richmond Times Dispatch.* "Australian Open—Sole Sister: Serena Williams Stands Alone at the Top After Fourth Major Crowns in a Row." January 25, 2003. C11.

37. Edmondson Bell, Ella L.J. and Stella Nkomo. 152–154. The writers also note that in their study, 90 percent of white women have access to the "buddy system" while only 59 percent of black women did.

38. Ibid. 156–158.

39. Harris, Trudier. *Saints, Sinners, Saviors: Strong Black Women in African American Literature.* 4.

40. Ibid. 13.

41. Ibid. 7–13.

42. Ibid. 19, 179.

43. Edmondson Bell, Ella L.J. and Stella Nkomo. 160–161.

44. Ibid. 160.

45. Childress, Alice. "A Cradle in the Gale Wind." *Black Women Writers (1950–1980): A Critical Evaluation.* 111–116.

46. Hull, Gloria T. and Barbara Smith. "Introduction." *All the Women Are White, All the Blacks Are Men, But Some of Us Are Brave.* xvii. This text is one of the seminal works used to launch the Black Studies Program.

47. Wall, Cheryl. Ed. "Introduction: Taking Positions and Changing Words." 1–3. The introduction celebrates the entrance of black women writers and their works as they begin to impact the national consciousness.

48. Lassiter, Sybil M. *Cultures of Color in America: A Guide to Family, Religion, and Health.* 38.

49. Morrison, Toni. "The One Out of Sequence." 207–21.

50. United States Commission on Civil Rights. *The Economic Status of Black Women: An Exploratory Investigation.* 103–104. This text examines the conditions of the black woman's work and the factors that inhibit her economic progress.

51. Brown, Elsa Barkley. "Mothers of Mind." 82.

52. Willis, Susan. "Problematizing the Individual: Toni Cade Bambara's Stories for the Revolution." *Specifying: Black Women Writing the Black Experience.* 50–51.

53. Naylor, Gloria. "An Interview with Gloria Naylor." 5. The interview provides glimpses of the changing awareness that was taking place as to what constitutes a valuable topic for black women writers, and the autonomy of the female protagonist.

54. hooks, bell. *Sisters of the Yam: Black Women's Self-Recovery.* 154.

55. Naylor, Gloria. 4.

56. Byerman, Keith. *Fingering the Jagged Grain.* 4, 6, 276.
57. Davis, Angela. *Women, Culture, and Politics.* 3, 14, 28.
58. hooks, bell. *Outlaw Culture: Resisting Representation.* 176.
59. Bambara, Toni Cade. *The Salt Eaters.* 32.
60. hooks, bell. *Outlaw Culture: Resisting Representation.* 176.
61. Pinckney, Darryl. "The Best of Everything." *New York Review of Books.* (4. Nov. 1993): 33–37.
62. Yankelovich Partners. "Survey Indicates Women Are Smart, Savvy, and Striving for Financial Prowess." 1–3.
63. Campbell, Bebe Moore. "Black Executives and Corporate Stress." 100–107. The article primarily discusses the causes, results, and some possible solutions to the high levels of stress black executives experience in the corporate arena.

Chapter Three

1. United States Commission on Civil Rights. *The Economic Status of Black Women: An Exploratory Investigation.* 10.
2. Fox, Mary Frank and Sherlene Hess-Biber. *Women at Work.* 157.
3. See Appendix A.
4. United States Commission on Civil Rights. 10, 81, 2.
5. Jones, Jacqueline. *Labor of Love, Labor of Sorrow: Black Women, Work, and the Family from Slavery to the Present.* 179.
6. Hull, Gloria T. "Researching Alice Dunbar: A Personal and Literary Perspective." 192.
7. *The Economic Status of Black Women: A Exploratory Investigation.* 34.
8. Jones, Jacqueline. *Labor of Love, Labor of Sorrow: Black Women, Work, and the Family from Slavery to the Present.* 253.
9. Ibid. 45.
10. United States Commission on Civil Rights. *The Economic Status of Black Women.* 45, 52.
11. Jones, Jacqueline. 304.
12. Carby, Hazel. "The Multicultural Wars." *Black Popular Culture.* 195.
13. United States Commission on Civil

Rights. *The Economic Status of Black Women.* 66–67, 94.
14. Crabtree, Penni. "Professional Black Women Jumping Corporate Ladder for Success in Self-employment." 1–5.
15. Dresser, Laura. "To Be Young, Black, and Female: Falling Further Behind in a Shifting Economy." 32–35.
16. Block, Fred, et al. "The Trouble with Full Employment: Expand the Social Programs." 694–698.
17. Church, George J. "A Futile Veto on Civil Rights." 26.
18. Jacobson, Carolyn J. "Women at Work: Meeting the Challenge of Job and Family." 10.
19. "Quota Fight: Re-thinking Affirmative Action." 16.
20. United States Commission on Civil Rights. *The Economic Status of Black Women.* 99, 103. See Appendix B.
21. Ibid. 96, 99, 103.
22. Morrison, Toni. *Playing in the Dark: Whiteness and the Literary Imagination.* 48.
23. O'Neale, Sondra. "Re-construction of the Composite Self: New Images of Black Women in Maya Angelou's Continuing Autobiography." *Black Women Writers (1950–1980): A Critical Evaluation.* 25–36. This article discusses how Angelou's autobiography challenges the negative stereotypes of black women that have become so pervasive in the media.
24. Cudjoe, Selwin R. "Maya Angelou and the Autobiographical Statement." *Black Women Writers (1950–1980) A Critical Evaluation.* 11.
25. McDowell, Deborah E. "Reading Family Matters." *Changing Our Own Words: Essays on Criticism, Theory, and Writing by Black Women.* 95–97.
26. Max, Daniel. "McMillan's Millions." 20, 22, 24, 26.
27. Richards, Paulette. *Terry McMillan: A Critical Companion.* 3–4. This text is important because it is a part of the emerging scholarship on Terry McMillan.
28. Harris, E. Lynn. *Invisible Life.* 207.
29. Harris, E. Lynn. *Just As I Am.* 1, 6. This book is one in a series in which Harris seeks to sensitize the reader to the concerns, pain, and joys of the homosexual male. He does give the black female professional protagonists far more respect

than most contemporary novels written by men.

30. Ibid. 1.

31. Ibid. 6.

32. Tauris, Carol. *Mis-Measure of Women: Why Women Are Not the Better Sex, the Inferior Sex, or the Opposite Sex.* 95.

33. Wallace, Michele. *Invisibility Blues: From Pop to Theory.* 213. Wallace looks at how racism limits the production of knowledge by black women.

34. Ibid. 214–215.

35. Modleski, Tania. *Feminism Without Women: Culture and Criticism in a "Post-feminist" Age.* 129–130. The writer examines feminism's approach to interrogating popular culture, especially film.

36. Hill, Patricia Liggins. *Call and Response: The Riverside Anthology of the African American Literary Tradition.* 780.

37. Marshall, Paule. "A MELUS Interview: Paule Marshall." *MELUS.* 117–130.

38. Marshall, Paule. "To Be in the World." With Angela Elam. *New Letters.* 97–105.

39. Brown, DeNeen L. "Black Women's Book Club." A-1. The article briefly discusses the evolution that is taking place in the publishing industry regarding a more positive reception to black women novelists.

40. Skow, John. "Some Groove (Author Terry McMillan)." 77–78.

41. "Toni Cade Bambara." With Claudia Tate. *Black Women Writers at Work.* 12–37.

42. George, Lynell. "Full Exposure: A Boom in Fiction by Black Women Writers Has Brought a Wealth of New Voices Telling Tales That Defy Stereotypes." Home Ed., E-1.

43. Radway, Janice. *Reading the Romance: Women, Patriarchy, and Popular Literature.* 36.

44. Angel, Karen. "Sister, Brother, Friend, Lover: A New African American Novel? Black Booksellers Debate Whether Targeted Titles Are Effective, Patronizing, Or Just Plain Old." 22–24.

45. George, Lynell. E-1

46. Weeks, Linton. "The Burgeoning Industry of Books By and For African Americans, The Sudden Spiral of Edmond Morris's *Dutch*, Poets in the District, a Longtime Fiction Guru Hangs Up His Spurs, and the President Gears Up to Write." 13.

47. Brown, DeNeen. *Washington Post.* A1.

48. Ibid.

49. Weeks, Linton. 38.

Chapter Four

1. Onesta, Li. "Us: In Memory. Toni Cade Bambara: Passing on the Story." 79–86.

2. Wall, Cheryl A. "Introduction: Taking Positions and Changing Words." *Changing Our Own Words. Essays on Criticism, Theory, and Writing by Black Women.* 2.

3. Bambara, Toni. "What It Is I Think I'm Doing Anyhow." *The Writer on Her Work.* 156–168.

4. Eagleton, Terry. *Literary Theory: An Introduction.* 68.

5. Tomkins, Jane. *Sensational Designs: The Cultural Work of American Fiction 1790–1860.* xi.

6. Kessler, Carol Farley. *Charlotte Perkins Gilman: Her Progress Toward Utopia with Selected Writings.* 7.

7. Ibid. 4.

8. Bambara, Toni Cade. "What It Is I Think I'm Doing Anyhow." *The Writer on Her Work.* 153–68.

9. Bambara, Toni Cade, "Toni Cade Bambara." With Claudia Tate. *Black Women Writers at Work.* 12–37.

10. Bambara, Toni Cade. *The Black Woman: An Anthology.* 7.

11. Ibid. 7.

12. Bambara, Toni Cade. "Toni Cade Bambara." With Claudia Tate. *Black Women Writers at Work.* 15.

13. Blackwell, James E. *Mainstreaming Outsiders: The Production of Black Professionals.* 2. This text looks at various areas of nontraditional track for African Americans such as medicine and law. It evaluates the rate of success and failure students have had, pinpoints areas of weaknesses, and suggests what may be done to remedy some of these problems.

14. Ibid. 3.

15. Geiger, Shirley M. "Employment of Black and White Women in State and Local Government." 151.

16. Edmondson Bell, Ella L.J. and Stella Nkomo. 153.

17. Rosen, Sanford Jay and Tom Nolan. "Seeking Environmental Justice for Minorities and Poor People." 50. The article discloses that the worst pollution occurs in black neighborhoods and Indian reservations. It also points out that whites are commuted into the plants to work, thus, denying the minorities the very jobs that are destroying their neighborhoods. Hence, the minorities are doubly exploited.

18. Bambara, Toni Cade. "Toni Cade Bambara." With Claudia Tate. 24.

19. Collins, Janelle. "Generating Power: Fission, Fusion, and the Postmodern Politics in Bambara's *The Salt Eaters.*" 40.

20. Stabile, Carol A. *Feminism and the Technological Fix.* 3–4.

21. Ibid. 33–34, 59.

22. Lorde, Audre. "Age, Race, Class, and Sex: Women Redefining Difference." *Words of Fire: An Anthology of African-American Feminist Thought.* 284–91.

23. Hine, Darlene Clarke. "Rape and the Inner Lives of Black Women in the Middle West: Preliminary Thoughts on the Culture of Dissemblance." *Words of Fire: An Anthology of African-American Feminist Thought.* 380–387. This article notes that black women left the South for the Midwest to escape sexual and economic oppression. It primarily concerns the secrecy with which black women guarded their private lives from inquisitive or ill-intended white writers and publishers, in order to find some psychic space, and keep some autonomy over their persons.

24. Golden, Stephanie. *Slaying the Mermaid: Women and the Culture of Sacrifice.* 124. Since the mermaid in the original version was not "rewarded" by perpetual service, and since she represents women's sexuality (which caused her downfall), Golden suggests that women slay the "mermaid of sacrifice," but maintain autonomy over their sexuality and their lives.

25. Weathers, Mary Ann. "An Argument for Black Women's Liberation As a Revolutionary Force." *Words of Fire: An Anthology of African-American Feminist Thought.* 157–161. Weathers argues that no one will liberate the black woman but herself. She notes that while the black woman works to support the black man, he oppresses her. Women of all groups are oppressed, but black women are the most oppressed. It is time for them to unite and begin the process of their own liberation.

26. Giddings, Paula. "The Last Taboo." *Words of Fire: An Anthology of African-American Feminist Thought.* 413–28. This article provides a brief discussion of the sexual politics of black and white relationships since slavery. It primarily focuses on the sexual exploitation of black women and girls by black men, which in some instances included generational incest, pornography, and sexual favors from the upwardly mobile.

27. Lips, Hilary M. "Women and Power in the Workplace." *Gender Images: Readings for Composition.* 500–511.

28. Campbell, Bebe Moore. "BLACK Executives and Corporate STRESS." *New York Times Magazine.* 12 December 1982. 37–39, 100–107.

29. Tannen, Deborah. "Sex, Lies, and Conversation: Why It Is So Hard for Men and Women to Talk to Each Other." *Gender Images: Readings for Composition.* 113–117.

30. Traylor, Eleanor. "*The Salt Eaters*: My Soul Looks Back in Wonder." *First World: An International Journal of Black Thought.* 64.

31. Mbalia, Dorothea. "Organization as Liberation in Toni Cade Bambara's *The Salt Eaters.*" *The Western Journal of Black Studies.* 6–13.

32. Rosenberg, Ruth. "You Took a Name That Made You Amiable to the Music." 179.

33. Byerman, Keith. "Healing Arts: Folklore and the Female Self in Toni Cade Bambara's *The Salt Eaters.*" *Philological Association of the Carolinas.* (1998). 37–43.

34. Kelley, Margot Anne. "Damballah Is the First Law of Thermodynamics": Modes of Access to Toni Cade Bambara's '*The Salt Eaters.*' 79–94.

35. Willis, Susan. "Problematizing the Individual: Toni Cade Bambara's Stories for the Revolution." *Specifying: Black Women Writing the American Experience.* 129–158.

36. Wallace, Michele. "Anger in Isolation:

A Black Feminist Search for Sisterhood." *Words of Fire: An Anthology of African-American Feminist Thought.* 220–230.

37. Willis, Susan. 129–158.

38. Campbell, Bebe Moore. "BLACK Executives and Corporate STRESS." 100–107.

39. Hull, Gloria T. "'What Is It I Think She's Doing Anyhow': A Reading of Toni Cade Bambara's *The Salt Eaters.*" *Conjuring: Black Women, Fiction, and Literary Tradition.* 216–32.

40. Kelley, Margot Anne. 17.

41. Stabile, Carol. 5.

42. Willis, Susan. 155.

43. Ibid. 158.

44. Traylor, Eleanor. 46.

45. Harris, Trudier. *Saints, Sinners, Saviors: Strong Black Women in African American Literature.* 80

46. Taussig, Michael T. "Reification and the Consciousness of the Patient." *Social Science Medicine. Part B, Medical Anthropology.* 3–13. He argues that the reification of people makes them simply a commodity to be bought in our capitalistic society; hence, the patient is treated not as a subject with the right to have medical care as in other cultures, but as the center of a power struggle over who controls the power to heal. Patients with the power within to heal themselves are denied the opportunity to do so fully.

47. Campbell, Bebe Moore. "BLACK Executives and Corporate STRESS." 102.

48. Dance, Daryl Cumber. "Go Eena Kumbla: A Comparison of Erna Brodber's *Jane and Louise Will Soon Come Home* and Toni Cade Bambara's *The Salt Eaters.*" *Caribbean Women Writers: Essays for the First International Conference.* 169–84.

49. Carby, Hazel V. "The Multicultural Wars." *Black Popular Culture.* 187–199.

50. Dance, Daryl Cumber. 172.

51. Fanon, Frantz. *The Wretched of the Earth.* 209, 225–227. In this text, Fanon addresses the myriad and grave problems and challenges of postcolonial nations.

52. Malveaux, Julianne. "Popular Culture and the Economics of Alienation." *Black Popular Culture.* 200–208.

53. The Boston Women's Health Book Collective. *Our Bodies, Ourselves for the New Century: A Book By and For Women.* 46. The text is quite inclusive of all women, as it seeks to eradicate racist, sexist, and classist discrimination that has for so long plagued feminism. Here, dietary recommendations are made from different pyramids.

54. Kelley, Margot Anne. 293.

55. Shipley, W. Maurice. "Review of *The Salt Eaters.*" 125–27.

56. Traylor, Eleanor. "*The Salt Eaters*: My Soul Looks Back in Wonder." 45.

57. Butler-Evans, Elliott. "Rewriting and Revising in the 1990's: *Tar Baby, The Color Purple,* and *The Salt Eaters.*" *Race, Gender, and Desire: Narrative Strategies in the Fiction of Toni Morrison, Alice Walker, and Toni Cade Bambara.* 181.

58. Harris, Trudier. *Saints, Sinners, Saviors: Strong Black Women in African American Literature.* 84.

59. Butler-Evans, Elliott. 91.

60. Hull, Gloria T. "What Is It I Think She's Doing Anyhow." 222.

61. Kelley, Margot Anne. 9–11.

62. Maslow, Abraham. H. *Toward a Psychology of Being.* 27–49. Maslow's theory of the "Hierarchy of Needs" argues that people have an innate need for self-fulfillment. This involves three sets of needs that are all equally important, but they are sequentially arranged. The most basic are the physiological and safety needs. Once these are met, then the psychological needs for love and selfhood become important. If these first two tiers of need are satisfied, then the third need, the need for self-actualization, becomes insistent. Once one has reached this level, she or he is an autonomous individual who is free to use the creative energies to her or his full potential.

63. Collins, Janelle. 180.

64. Maslow, Abraham H. 91. Maslow speaks of "peak experiences" that self-actualized individuals have. He thinks of these periods of illumination as "pure delight." Here artistic creations of the highest forms become possible.

Chapter Five

1. Sellers, Francis Stead. "Review of *Waiting to Exhale.*" *Times Literary Supplement.* 6 Nov. 1992. 2.

2. Richards, Paulette. *Terry McMillan: A Critical Companion.* 13.

3. Stein, Ruthe. "Terry McMillan Had a Big Surprise: Oakland Declared Monday Her Day." *San Francisco Chronicle.* 1 Dec. 2000. 1. The day also celebrated on the premiering of *Disappearing Acts,* the filmic adaptation of the novel.

4. Malveaux, Julianne. "Popular Culture and the Economics of Alienation." 201.

5. Sellers, Francis Stead. "Review of *Waiting to Exhale.*" 20. Sellers points out that the literary merit of *Waiting to Exhale* is mediocre despite its popularity and commercial success. It focuses too much on the bedroom scenes and is too saturated with male bashing, but Sellers adds that McMillan has really captured the urban vernacular and touched a nerve in the American public when she showed the sexual conflicts between men and women.

6. George, Lynell. "Full Exposure A Boom in Fiction by Black Women Writers Has Bought a Wealth of Voices Telling Tales That Defy Stereotypes." Home Ed., E-1.

7. Leland, John. "How Terry Got Her Groove Back." 76–79.

8. Fiske, John. *Understanding Popular Culture.* 28. The book provides an extended discussion of what popular culture is—"a living, active process [that] can be developed from within."

9. Ellerby, Janet Mason. "Deposing the Man of the House: Terry McMillan Re-writes the Family (Popular Literature and Film)." 105–18.

10. Fiske, John. 130.

11. Williams, Raymond. *Marxism and Literature.* Williams' redefinition of "culture" is one of the hallmark texts that posed a challenge to the validity of the old canon. It was influential in getting other voices that had been previously marginalized to be accepted as valid academic scholarship.

12. U.S. Department of Labor. Bureau of Labor and Statistics. http:/ferret.bls.census.gov/macro/171996/empearn/aat10.txt.

13. Lowery, Mark. "The Rise of the Black Professional Class." 40–50. Lowery shows the gains this group has achieved in different areas, but clearly underscores the gaps that still exist for blacks to have full participation in the economy. He says blacks are still hopeful for rewards equal to those of their white counterparts.

14. Sellers, Francis Stead. 1.

15. Fiske, John. 146.

16. McMillan, Terry. "Introduction." i–xxiv. *Breaking Ice: An Anthology of Contemporary African-American Fiction.* McMillan presents her theory of writing, and contrasts it with what was imposed on writers of past generations.

17. Fiske, John. 106, 115–116.

18. Richards, Paulette. 116–118. This section of the text looks at black vernacular and the ability of the writer to use a crossover technique that has proven quite successful.

19. Ibid. pp. xix–xxi.

20. McClain, Leanita. "The Middle-Class Black's Burden." *Newsweek*: 96. 15 (Oct. 1998): 21. McClain captures the psychic, social, economic, and professional burdens the earlier groups of black middle-class women carried. In addition, their representation was understood to reflect the race.

21. Leland, John. 80.

22. McMillan, Terry. 3.

23. Hockenbury, Don H. and Sandra E. Hockenbury. *Psychology.* 373–374. This text shows current statistics, and explains that at least 3 million unwed couples lived together in the 1990s. Given that these relationships tend to have less permanence than marriage, McMillan's choice of focus on the single black woman has even greater relevance.

24. Sanchez-Hucles, Janis. "Jeopardy Not Bonus Status for African American Women in the Work Force: Why Does the Myth of Advantage Persist?" 565–581.

25. Jones, Jacqueline. *Labor of Love, Labor of Sorrow: Black Women, Work, and the Family from Slavery to the Present.* 174. Jones traces the pattern of discrimination in the workplace, which, though it has abated in some institutions, is still rampant in others and subtler than before the 1970s.

26. Sanchez-Hucles, Janis. 600.

27. Beale, Francis. "Double Jeopardy: To Be Black and Female." *Words of Fire: An Anthology of African American Feminist Thought.* 146–154. Beale explains the sexual

and economic exploitation of black women. She argues that all people, including black women, must be free to excel—and that involves women not being mere homemakers or put in supportive roles.

28. Wallace, Michele. *Black Macho and the Myth of the Superwoman.* 12–14. This text candidly describes the dominant-submissive relationship black males expected from black women in the 1960s. Black men were outraged by this supposedly male bashing text, but the text disclosed many of the conflicts that have alienated the women from the men in the Black Power Movement of the 1960s and afterwards.

29. Greenwood, Heather. "Author No Longer Waiting to Exhale: Let's Fly at Men Who Complain About Hit Movie." *Toronto Star* 30 Jan. 1996: C5.

30. Jary, David and Julia Jary. *The Harper Collins Dictionary of Sociology.* 404.

31. Kronenwetter, Michael. *Encyclopedia of Modern American Social Issues.* 207–208.

32. Sellers, Francis Stead. 20.

33. McMillan, Terry. "Everything I Write Is About Empowerment." Interview by Ann Bowling. 1–9.

34. Walsh, Joan. 2.

35. Greenwood, Heather. 1. Greenwood examines both the male bashing and possible anti-white female sentiment in the text. McMillan answers these two charges by saying the novel originated in her attempt to come to terms with some of her own experiences.

36. Richards, Paulette. 111. Richards explains that because McMillan does not allow us access to the thoughts of the men, we cannot know what motivates them psychologically to behave as they do. She points out that McMillan's critics fail to recognize that the story focuses on why the women characters made such poor choices of men.

37. Greenwood, Heather. 1.

38. Edmonson Bell, Ella L.J. and Stella Nkomo. 148.

39. Golden, Stephanie. *Slaying the Mermaid: Women and the Culture of Sacrifice.* 61. Golden argues that corporations assume that women already have "global responsibilities" with childcare, that is, parenting is their primary career. Men, however,

have their careers as the primary focus, and are therefore allowed to travel and be responsible for major projects.

40. Sanchez-Hucles, Janis. 572.

41. Hammonds, Evelynn. "Missing Persons: African American Women, AIDS and the History of Disease." *Words of Fire: An Anthology of African-American Feminist Thought.* 433–49. The writer looks at why black women disproportionately contract AIDS, how the media represents black women and the role this plays in the spread of the disease and the treatment the women receive, how very young teens are infected by older men, how medical facilities treat black female patients differently from white ones, and that it is important for black feminists to intervene, for sexism is partly responsible for the rapid spread of the disease among black women.

42. Terrell, Mary Church. "The Progress of Colored Women." 64, 67–68. Terrell argues that black women's success is a miracle (of hard work and perseverance), for they are handicapped by race and sex discrimination.

43. McMillan, Terry. *A Day Late and a Dollar Short.* 209.

44. Laney, Lucy Craft. "The Burden of the Educated Colored Woman." 635–636.

45. Hill, Patricia Liggins. "Lucy Craft Laney." 634–636.

46. Golden, Stephanie. 97–98.

47. Kingslover, Barbara. "A Forbidden Territory Familiar to All." *Writers [on Writing]: Collected Essays from the* New York Times. 130–135.

48. Golden, Stephanie. 99–103, 30.

49. Pinckney, Darryl. "The Best of Everything." 33–37.

50. Carby, Hazel. *Reconstructing Womanhood: The Emergence of the African-American Woman Novelist.* 10–27.

51. Jordan, Winthrop D. *White Over Black: American Attitudes Toward the Negro, 1550–1812.* 233.

52. Edmonson Bell, Ella L.J. and Stella Nkomo. 210.

53. Golden, Stephanie. 184–185.

54. Ibid. 186.

55. Ibid. 97.

56. Higginbotham, Elizabeth. "Two Representative Issues in Contemporary

Sociological Work on Black Women." 93–98. The concern expressed here is the lack of primary research being done on black women, and even when secondary research is used, the focus is on black men, not the women on whom far less material is available.

57. Golding, Stephanie. 177–178.

58. Ibid. 130–135.

Chapter Six

1. Bobo, Jacqueline. *Black Women as Cultural Readers: Film and Culture.* 23.

2. Ibid. 2.

3. U.S. Department of Labor, Women's Bureau. "Black Women in the Labor Force." *Facts on Working Women.* 1–9.

4. Ibid. 4.

5. Ibid. 5.

6. Jones, Garvin. "'Whose Line Is It Anyway?' W.E.B. Du Bois and the Language of the Color Line." 23.

7. Other novels mentioned were *Brothers and Sisters, Big Girls Don't Cry, The Salt Eaters, Laughing in the Park, Daughters, Caught Up in the Rapture,* and *Parable of the Sower.*

8. Bobo, Jacqueline. 10.

9. The respondents also added desirable family reunions, a knowledge of African American history, and an awareness of successful contemporary blacks in fields such as science, technology and communications.

10. Other behaviors mentioned were respect for children and the handicapped, including those not in one's clique, and communicating politely and clearly.

11. Maslow, Abraham H. *Toward a Psychology of Being.* 135.

12. Lassiter, Sybil M. *Cultures of Color in America: A Guide to Family, Religion, and Health.* 42.

13. Dash, Julia. *Daughters of the Dust.* This novel is the developed form of a 1991 video that Dash wrote, produced, and directed. The video and book have the same title.

14. Gilroy, Paul. "It's a Family Affair." *Black Popular Culture.* 307.

15. Ibid. 307–308.

16. Marshall, Paule. *Daughters.* 142–143.

17. "Blacks Purchasing More Books by Black Authors: Still Few Blacks in Publishing. EEOS (Equal Employment Opportunity Survey)." *Jet* 90. 10 (22 July 1996): 36.

18. McMillan, Terry. "An Interview with Terry McMillan." With Wendy Smith. *Publishers Weekly* 239. 22 (22 May 1992): 50–51.

Conclusion

1. Neal, Larry. "The Black Arts Movement." *The Norton Anthology: African American Literature.* New York: Norton, 1997. 1960–1872.

2. McMillan, Terry. "Terry McMillan Exhales and Inhales in a Revealing Interview." With Laura Randolph. *Ebony* 48. 7 (May 1993): 23–27.

3. Parker, Lonnae O'Neal. "The Best Man: A Joyous Occasion." *The Washington Post.* 46, 54.

4. Maslow, Abraham H. 224.

5. Ibid. 71–72.

6. Ibid. 131–133.

7. Morrison, Toni. *Sula.* 1974.

8. Maslow, 131–133.

9. Ibid. 73, 131.

10. Ibid. 169.

11. Walker, Alice. "In Search of My Mother's Garden." *The Norton Anthology: African American Literature.* 2,487. Walker's conclusion suggests that Phillis Wheatley's artistic genius was probably inherited from her African mother.

Bibliography

Angel, Karen. *"Sister, Brother, Friend, Lover*: A New African American Novel? Black Book-sellers Debate Whether Targeted Titles Are Effective, Patronizing or Just Plain Old." *Publishers Weekly* 245: 8 (Feb. 23, 1998): 22–24.

Appiah, Kwame Anthony and Henry Louis Gates, Jr. Eds. "Introduction: Multiplying Identities." *Identities.* Chicago: Univ. of Chicago Press, 1995.

Ashe, Arthur and Arnold Rampersad. *Days of Grace: A Memoir.* New York: Alfred Knopf, 1993.

Bambara, Toni Cade. Ed. *The Black Woman: An Anthology.* New York: Penguin, 1970.

_____. *Gorilla, My Love.* New York: Random House, 1972.

_____. "The Lesson." *Literature and Gender: Thinking Critically Through Fiction, Poetry, Drama.* Eds. Robyn Wiegman and Elena Glassberg. New York: Longman, 1999.

_____. *The Salt Eaters.* New York: Vintage, 1992.

_____. *The Sea Birds Are Still Alive.* New York: Random House, 1977.

_____. "Toni Cade Bambara." With Claudia Tate. *Black Women Writers at Work.* Ed. Claudia Tate. New York: Continuum, 1983. 12–37.

_____. "What It Is I Think I'm Doing Anyhow." *The Writer on Her Work.* Ed. Janet Sternberg. New York: Norton, 1980. 153–68.

Bandura, Albert. "Albert Bandura and Social Cognitive Theory." *Psychology.* Eds. Hockenbury, Don H., and Sandra E. Hockenbury. New York: Worth, 2000.

Barnes, Paula C. "A Review of *Waiting to Exhale* by Terry McMillan." *Belles Lettres* 8. 1 (Fall 1992): 56–57.

Barton, Edwin J. and Glenda A. Hudson. *A Contemporary Guide to Literary Terms with Strategies for Writing Essays About Literature.* New York: Houghton Mifflin, 1997.

Beale, Francis. "Double Jeopardy: To Be Black and Female." *Words of Fire: An Anthology of African American Feminist Thought.* Ed. Beverly Guy-Sheftall. New York: New Press, 1995. 146–54.

Bell, Ella L. *Bicultural Life Structures and Stress Among Black Women.* Diss. Case Western Reserve U. Ann Arbor: UMI 1987. Western Reserve University, May 1987. 8722233.

Bella, Robert N., et al. *Habits of the Heart: Individualism and Commitment in American Life.* New York: Harper & Row, 1985.

Bem, Sandra Lipstiz. *The Lenses of Gender: Transforming the Debate on Sexual Inquiry.* New Haven, Conn.: Yale UP, 1993.

Berne, Eric. *Transactional Analysis in Psychotherapy: A Systematic Individual and Social Psychiatry.* New York: Grove, 1961.

Berry, Bertice. *Redemption Song.* New York: Doubleday, 2000.

"Blacks Purchasing More Books by Black Authors: Still Few Blacks in Publishing." *Jet* 90. 10 (22 July 1996): 36.

Blackwell, James E. *Mainstreaming Outsiders: The Production of Black Professionals.* New York: General Hall, 1987.

Block, Fred, et al. "The Trouble with Full Employment: Expand the Social Programs." *Nation* 242 (17 May 1986): 694–98.

Bobo, Jacqueline. *Black Women as Cultural Readers: Film and Culture.* New York: Columbia UP, 1995.

Bole, William. "Books Better Than Bars When It Comes to Reforming Lawbreakers." *National Catholic Reporter* 32. 36 (9 Aug. 1996.): 12.

Booker, Keith M. *Practical Introduction to Literary Theory and Criticism.* New York: Longman, 1996.

Boston Women's Health Book Collective. *Our Bodies, Ourselves for the New Century: A Book By and For Women.* New York: Simon & Schuster, 1998.

Briscoe, Connie. "Author's Success Better Than Fiction." Interview by Toni Morrison. *The Washington Times* 2 B1, 1996.

_____. *Big Girls Don't Cry.* New York: Harper Collins, 1996.

_____. *Sisters and Lovers.* New York: Harper Collins, 1994.

Brooks, Gwendolyn. *Maud Martha.* Chicago: Third World, 1995.

Brown, DeNeen L. "Readers with a 'Go-Girl!' Mission: Black Women's Book Club Lobbies Publisher for African American Stories." *Washington Post* 23 March 1999, A1.

Brown, Elsa Barkley. "Mothers of Mind." *Double Stitch: Black Women Write About Mothers & Daughters.* Eds. Patricia Bell-Scott, et al. New York: Harper, 1991.

Brown, Roseleen. "Character's Weaknesses Build Fiction's Strength." *Writers [on Writing]: Collected Essays from The New York Times.* New York: Henry Holt, 2001. 28–34.

Busch, Frederick. *When People Publish: Essays on Writers and Writing.* Iowa City: Univ. of Iowa Press, 1986.

Butler, Judith. *Gender Trouble: Feminism and the Subversion of Identity.* New York: Rutledge, 1990.

Butler, Marilyn. "Editing Women." *Studies in the Novel* 27. 3 (Fall 1995): 1–8.

Butler-Evans, Elliott. "Rewriting and Revising in the 1990s: *Tar Baby, The Color Purple,* and *The Salt Eaters.*" *Race, Gender, and Desire: Narrative Strategies in the Fiction of Toni Morrison, Alice Walker, and Toni Cade Bambara.* Philadelphia: Temple UP, 1970.

Byerman, Keith. *Fingering the Jagged Grain.* Athens: Univ. of Georgia Press, 1985.

_____. "Healing Arts: Folklore and the Female Self in Toni Cade Bambara's *The Salt Eaters.*" *Philological Association of the Carolinas* (1998). 37–43

Campbell, Bebe Moore. "BLACK Executives and Corporate STRESS." *New York Times Magazine* 12 Dec. 1982. 37–39, 100–102.

_____. *Brothers and Sisters.* New York: Berkley, 1994.

Canty, Donnella. "McMillan Arrives." *English Journal* 85. 4 (April 1996): 86–87.

Carby, Hazel V. "The Multicultural Wars." *Black Popular Culture.* Ed. Gina Dent. Seattle: Bay, 1992. 7–199.

_____. "Policing the Black Woman's Body in an Urban Context." *Identities.* Eds. Kwame Anthony Appiah and Henry Louis Gates Jr. Chicago: Univ. of Chicago Press, 1995. 115–32.

_____. *Reconstructing Womanhood: The Emergence of the African-American Woman Novelist.* New York: Oxford UP, 1987.

Carroll, Constance M. "Three's A Crowd: The Dilemma of the Black Woman in Higher Education." *All the Women Are White, All the Blacks Are Men, But Some of Us Are Brave: Black Women's Studies.* Eds. Gloria T. Hull, et al. New York: Feminist Press, 1982. 115–28.

Chappell, Fred. "Dealing with the Grotesque." With John Sopko and John Carr. *Kite-Flying and Other Irrational Acts: Conversation with Twelve Southern Writers.* Baton Rouge: Louisiana UP, 1972. 216–235.

Childress, Alice. "A Cradle in a Gale Wind." *Black Women Writers (1950–1980): A Critical Evaluation.* Ed. Marie Evans. New York: Anchor, 1984. 111–16.

Church, George J. "A Futile Veto on Civil Rights." *Time* 113. 13 (28 March 1988): 26.

Clarke, Breena. *River Cross My Heart*. New York: Little Brown, 1999.

Collins, Janelle. "Generating Power: Fission, Fusion, and Postmodern Politics in Bambara's *The Salt Eaters*." *MELUS* 21. 2 (Sum. 1996): 1–2, 37–47.

Collins, Patricia Hill. "The Meaning of Motherhood in Black Culture and the Black Mother-Daughter Relationships." *Double Stitch: Black Women Write About Mothers & Daughters*. Eds. Patricia Bell-Scott, et al. New York: Harper, 1993.

Coughlyn, Ruth. "Let's Hear It for the Girls: 'Serious' Women Writers Are Giving Readers Page Turners to Cheer About." *Detroit News* 4 April 1994, C1.

Crabtree, Penni. "Professional Black Women Jumping Corporate Ladder for Success in Self-employment." *Memphis Business Journal* 11. 34 (Jan. 1999): 1–5.

Cudjoe, Selwyn R. "Maya Angelou and the Autobiographical Statement." *Black Women Writers (1950–1980): A Critical Evaluation*. Ed. Marie Evans. New York: Anchor, 1984.

Dance, Daryl Cumber. "Go Eena Kumbla: A Comparison of Erna Brodber's *Jane and Louise Will Soon Come Home* and Toni Cade Bambara's *The Salt Eaters*." *Caribbean Women Writers: Essays for the First International Conference*. Ed. Selwyn R. Cudjo. Wellesley, Mass: Calaloux, 1990. 169–184.

_____. "Introduction." *Honey Hush! An Anthology of African American Women's Humor*. New York: Norton, 1998. xxxv.

Dash, Julia. *Daughters of the Dust*. New York: Dutton, 1997.

Davies, Carol Boyce and Ogundipe-Leslie. *Moving Beyond Boundaries: International Dimensions of Black Women's Writing*. New York: New York UP, 1995.

Davis, Angela. "Reflections on the Black Woman's Role in the Community of Slaves." *Words of Fire: An Anthology of African American Feminist Thought*. Ed. Beverly Guy-Sheftall. New York: New Press, 1995. 200–18.

_____. *Women, Culture, and Politics*. New York: Random House, 1989.

Davis, Arthur P. "Trends on Negro American Literature." *Dark Symphony: Negro Literature in America*. Eds. James A. Emanuel and Theodore L. Gross. New York: Free Press, 1968. 519–26.

De Beauvoir, Simone. *The Second Sex*. Trans. H. M. Parshley. New York: Vintage, 1989.

De Bottom, Alain. "The Sorrows of Young Alain." *New Statesman* 127. 4398 (Aug. 14, 1998): 49.

Decker, Jeffrey Louis. *Made in America: Self-Styled Success from Horatio Alger to Oprah Winfrey*. Minneapolis: Univ. of Minnesota Press, 1997.

Dennison, Dorothy L. "Early Fiction by Paule Marshall." *Callaloo* 6. 2 (Spr.-Sum. 1983): 35–36, 40–41.

Dresser, Laura. "To Be Young, Black, and Female: Falling Further Behind in the Shifting Economy." *Dollars & Sense* 99 (May-June 1995): 32–35.

Du Bois, W. E. Burghardt. *The Souls of Black Folk: Essays and Sketches*. Greenwich: Fawcett, 1961.

Eagleton, Terry. *Literary Theory: An Introduction*. 2nd ed. Great Britain: Blackwell, 1996.

Edmondson Bell, Ella L.J., and Stella M. Nkomo. *Our Separate Ways: Black and White Women and the Struggle for Professional Identity*. Boston: Harvard Business School Press, 2001.

Ellerby, Janet Mason. "Deposing the Man of the House: Terry McMillan Rewrites the Family (Popular Literature and Film)." *MELUS* 22. 2 (Sum. 1997): 105–18.

Epstein, Cynthia F. "Positive Effects of the Multiple Negative: Explaining the Success of Black Professional Women." *Changing Women in a Changing World*. Ed. Joan Huber. Chicago: Univ. of Chicago Press, 1973. 150–71.

Erikson, Erik H. *Childhood and Society*. 2nd rev. ed. New York: Norton, 1975.

Fanon, Frantz. *Black Skin, White Masks*. New York: Grove, 1967.

_____. *The Wretched of the Earth*. New York: Grove, 1963.

Fauset, Jessie Redmon. *Plum Bun: A Novel Without A Moral*. Boston: Beacon, 1929.

Fiske, John. *Understanding Popular Culture*. Boston: Unwin Hyman, 1989.

Foote, Shelby. "It's Worth a Grown Man's Time." With John Carr. *Kite-Flying and Other Irrational Acts: Conversations with Twelve Southern Writers*. Baton Rouge: Louisiana UP, 1972. 3–33.

Forbes. "The World's Richest People." 28 Mar. 2003. http://www.forbes.com/static_html/bill/2003/rank.htm.

Ford, Jesse Hill. "The Making of Fables." With James Seay. *Kite-Flying and Other Irrational Acts: Conversations with Twelve Southern Writers*. Baton Rouge: Louisiana UP, 1998.

Ford, Richard. "Goofing Off While the Muse Recharges." *Writers [on Writing]: Collected Essays from the* New York Times. New York: Henry Holt, 2001.

Fox, Mary Frank, and Sherlene Hess-Biber. *Women at Work*. California: Mayfield, 1984.

Gates, Henry Louis Jr. and Nellie Y. McKay. Eds. "Jessie Redmon Fauset." *The Norton Anthology: African American Literature*. New York: Norton, 1997.

_____. "Nella Larsen." *The Norton Anthology: African American Literature*. New York: Norton, 1997.

Geiger, Shirley M. "Employment of Black and White Women in State and Local Government 1973–1995." *NWSN Journal* 10. 13 (Fall 1998); 151.

George, Lynell. "Full Exposure: A Boom in Fiction by Black Women Writers Has Brought a Wealth of Voices Telling Tales That Defy Stereotypes." *Los Angeles Times* 7 July 1996, Home Ed., E-1.

Giddings, Paula. "The Last Taboo." *Words of Fire: An Anthology of African American Feminist Thought*. Ed. Beverly Guy-Sheftall. New York: New Press, 1995. 413–28.

Gilroy, Paul. "It's a Family Affair." *Black Popular Culture*. Ed. Gina Dent. Seattle: Bay Press, 1992. 303–316

Golden, Marita. *The Edge of Heaven*. New York: One World, 1999.

_____. *Long Distance Life*. New York: Doubleday, 1989.

Golden, Stephanie. *Slaying the Mermaid: Women and the Culture of Sacrifice*. New York: Harmony, 1983.

Graham, Lawrence Otis. *Our Kind of People: Inside America's Black Upper-Middle Class*. New York: Harper Collins, 1999.

Grant, Jacquelyn. "Black Theology and the Black Woman." *Words of Fire: An Anthology of African American Feminist Thought*. Ed. Beverly Guy-Sheftall. New York: New Press, 1995. 320–36.

Graves, Earl G. "20 Black Women of Power & Influence." *Black Enterprise* 28. 1 (Aug. 1997): 60–73.

Greenwood, Heather. "Author No Longer Waiting to Exhale: Let's Fly at Men Who Complain About Hit Movie." *Toronto Star* (30 Jan. 1996): C5.

Gregory, Sheila T. *Black Women in the Academy: The Secrets of Success*. "Foreword." Rev. ed. Lanham: Univ. Press of America, 1998.

Griffin, Ada Guy. "Seizing the Moving Image: Reflections of a Black Independent Producer." *Black Popular Culture*. Ed. Gina Dent. Seattle: Bay, 1992. 228–33.

Hall, Stuart. *Critical Dialogues in Cultural Studies*. Eds. David Morley and Huan-Hsing Chen. New York: Rutledge, 1996.

_____. "Introduction: Who Needs Identity." *Questions of Cultural Identity*. Eds. Stuart Hall and Paul Du Guy. London: Sage, 1996.

_____. "What Is This 'Black' in Black Popular Culture." *Black Popular Culture*. Ed. Gina Dent. Seattle: Bay, 1992, 21–33.

Hammonds, Evelynn. "Missing Persons: African American Women, AIDS and the History of Disease." *Words of Fire: An Anthology of African American Feminist Thought*. Ed. Beverly Guy-Sheftall. New York: New Press, 1995. 334–49.

Hansberry, Lorraine. *A Raisin in the Sun*. In *The Norton Anthology: African American Literature*. Eds. Henry Louis Gates Jr. and Nellie Y. McKay. New York: Norton, 1997. 1728–1789.

Harris, E. Lynn. *Abide with Me*. New York: Doubleday, 1990.

_____. *Invisible Life.* New York: Doubleday, 1991.
_____. *Just As I Am.* New York: Anchor, 1995.
Harris, Tina M. and Patricia S. Hill. "'Waiting to Exhale' or 'Breathing Again': A Search for Identity, Empowerment, and Love in the 1990s." *Women and Language* 21. i2 (Fall 1998) 1–17.
Harris, Trudier. *Saints, Sinners, Saviors: Strong Black Women in African American Literature.* New York: Palgrave, 2001.
Higginbotham, Elizabeth. "Two Representative Issues in Contemporary Sociological Work on Black Women." *All the Women Are White, All the Blacks Are Men, But Some of Us Are Brave: Black Women's Studies.* New York: Feminist Press, 1982.
Hill, Patricia Liggins. Ed. *Call and Response: The Riverside Anthology of the African American Literary Tradition.* Boston: Houghton Mifflin, 1998.
Hine, Darlene Clarke. "Rape and the Inner Lives of Black Women in the Middle West: Preliminary Thoughts on the Culture of Dissemblance." *Words of Fire: An Anthology of African American Feminist Thought.* Ed. Beverly Guy-Sheftall. New York: New Press, 1995. 380–87.
Hockenbury, Don, and Sandra E. Hockenbury. *Psychology.* New York: Worth, 2000.
Holan, Stacey. "The Black Book Club Boom." *Black Issues Book Review* March-April 1999, 61–62.
hooks, bell. *Feminist Theory: From Margin to Center.* Boston: South End, 1984.
_____. *Outlaw Culture: Resisting Representation.* New York: Routledge, 1994.
_____. *Sisters of the Yam: Black Women and Self-Recovery.* Boston: South End, 1993.
Howard, Maureen. "The Enduring Commitment of a Faithful Storyteller." *Writers [on Writing]: Collected Essays from The New York Times.* New York: Henry Holt, 2001.
Hughes, Langston. "Harlem." *The Norton Anthology: African American Literature.* Eds. Henry Louis Gates Jr. and Nellie Y. McKay. New York: Norton, 1997. 1267.
Hull, Gloria T. "'What Is It I Think She's Doing Anyhow': A Reading of Toni Cade Bambara's *The Salt Eaters.*" *Conjuring: Black Women, Fiction, and Literary Tradition.* Ed. Marjorie Pryse and Hortense J. Spillers. Bloomington: Indiana UP, 1985. 216–32.
Hurston, Zora Neale. *Their Eyes Were Watching God.* New York: Harper & Row, 1990.
Ife, Zadia. "The African Diasporan Ritual Mode." *The African Aesthetic: Keeper of the Traditions.* Ed. Kariamu Welsh-Asante. Westport, Conn.: Praeger, 1994. 31–51.
Jackson, Sheneska. *Caught Up in the Rapture.* New York: Simon & Schuster, 1996.
Jacobs, Harriet A. *Incidents in the Life of a Slavegirl: Written by Herself.* Ed. Jean Fagan Yellin. Cambridge, Mass.: Harvard UP, 1987.
Jacobson, Carolyn J. "Women at Work: Meeting the Challenge of Job and Family." *American Federationist* 93 (5 April 1986): 5–12.
Jacques, George. "More Than a Niche (Publishing of African American Literature) (Includes Related Information)." *Publishers Weekly* (12 Aug. 1997): 38.
Jary, Davis and Julia Jary. *The Harper Collins Dictionary of Sociology.* Ed. Eugene Ehrlich. New York: Harper Collins, 1991.
Johnson, Diane. "Pesky Themes Will Emerge When You're Not Looking." *Writers [on Writing]: Collected Essays from The New York Times.* New York: Henry Holt, 2001.
Jones, Barbara A. P. "Black Women and Labor Participants: An Analysis of Sluggish Growth Rates." *Review of Black Political Economy* 14 (Fall-Win. 1985): 11–31.
Jones, Garvin. "'Whose Line Is It Anyway?' W.E.B. Du Bois and the Language of the Color Line." *Race Consciousness: African American Studies for the New Century.* Eds. Judith Jackson Fossett, et al. New York: New York UP, 1997. 19–31.
Jones, Jacqueline. *Labor of Love, Labor of Sorrow: Black Women, Work, and the Family from Slavery to the Present.* New York: Basic, 1982.
Jones, Malcolm. "Successful Sisters: *Faux* Terry Is Better Than No Terry." *Newsweek* 199. 18 (29 April 1996): 1.
Jordan, Shirley M. "*Daughters*: The Unity That Binds Us." *American Versions* 6. 5 (Oct. 1991) 38–39.

Jordan, Winthrop D. *White Over Black: American Attitudes Toward the Negro 1550–1812*. Chapel Hill: Univ. of North Carolina Press, 1968.

Josephs, Gloria. "Black Feminist Pedagogy and Schooling in Capitalist White America." *Words of Fire: An Anthology of African American Feminist Thought*. Ed. Beverly Guy-Sheftall. New York: New Press, 1995. 461–71.

Kelley, Margot Anne. "Damballah Is the First Law of Thermodynamics": Modes of Access to Toni Cade Bambara's 'The Salt Eaters.'" *African American Review* 27. 3 (Fall 1993). 79–94.

Kessler, Carol Farley. *Charlotte Perkins Gilman: Her Progress Toward Utopia with Selected Writings*. New York: Syracuse UP, 1995.

King, Deborah. "Multiple Jeopardy; Multiple Consciousness: The Context of a Black Feminist Ideology." *Words of Fire: An Anthology of African American Feminist Thought*. Ed. Beverly Guy-Sheftall. New York: New Press, 1995. 294–317.

Kingslover, Barbara. "A Forbidden Territory Familiar to All." *Writers [on Writing]: Collected Essays from The New York Times*. New York: Henry Holt, 2001.

Kronenwetter, Michael. *Encyclopedia of Modern American Social Issues*. Santa Barbara: ABC-CLIO, 1997.

Laney, Lucy Craft. "The Burden of the Educated Colored Woman." *Call & Response: The Riverside Anthology of the African American Literary Tradition*. Ed. Patricia Liggins Hill, et al. New York: Houghton Mifflin, 1998. 634–638.

Larsen, Nella. *Quicksand; and Passing*. New Brunswick, N.J.: Rutgers UP, 1986.

Lassiter, Sybil M. *Cultures of Color in America: A Guide to Family, Religion, and Health*. Westport, Conn.: Greenwood, 1998.

Leland, John. "How Terry Got Her Groove Back." *Newsweek* 127. 18 (29 Apr. 1996): 76–79.

Lips, Hilary M. "Women and Power in the Workplace." *Gender Images: Readings for Composition*. Eds. Melita Schaum and Connie Flanagan. Boston: Houghton Mifflin, 1992. 500–511.

Locke, Alain. "The New Negro." *Dark Symphony: Negro Literature in America*. Eds. James A. Emanuel and Theodore L. Gross. New York: Free Press, 1968. 74–84.

Lorde, Audre. "Age, Race, Class and Sex: Women Redefining Difference." *Words of Fire: An Anthology of African American Feminist Thought*. Ed. Beverly Guy-Sheftall. New York: New Press, 1995. 284–91.

Lowery, Mark. "The Rise of the Black Professional Class." *Black Enterprise* 26. 1 (Aug. 1995): 43–50.

Lowery, Rodney. "Foreword." In *Toward a Psychology of Being* by Abraham H. Maslow. 3rd. ed. New York: John Wiley, 1999. v–xxxiv.

McClain, Leanita. "The Middle-Class Black's Burden." *Newsweek* 96. 15 (Oct. 1980): 21.

McDowell, Deborah. "Reading Family Matters." *Changing Our Own Words: Essays on Criticism, Theory, and Writing by Black Women*. New Brunswick, N.J.: Rutgers UP, 1989.

McMillan, Terry. *A Day Late and a Dollar Short*. New York: Penguin, 2001.

_____. "Introduction." *Breaking Ice: An Anthology of Contemporary African American Fiction*. New York: Penguin, 1990.

_____. "Eating My Heart Inside." *Why I Write*. Ed. Will Blythe. New York: Little Brown, 1998.

_____. *How Stella Got Her Groove Back*. New York: Signet, 1996.

_____. "Everything I Write Is About Empowerment." Interview with Ann Bowling. *Writers' Yearbook*. http://writersdigest.com/newsletter/mcmillan2.html.

_____. "An Interview with Terry McMillan." With Wendy Smith. *Publishers Weekly* 239. 22 (22 May 1992): 50–51.

_____. *Mama*. New York: Houghton Mifflin, 1987.

_____. "Terry McMillan Exhales and Inhales in a Revealing Interview." Interview with Laura Randolph. *Ebony* 48. 7 (May 1993): 23–27.

_____. *Waiting to Exhale*. New York: Pocket, 1992.

Malveaux, Julianne. "Popular Culture and the Economics of Alienation." *Black Popular Culture*. Ed. Gina Dent. Seattle: Bay, 1992. 200–208.

_____. "Shaping the World of My Art." *New Letters* 40. 1 (Autumn 1973).

_____. "Sisters of Science." *Black Issues of Higher Education* 15. 3 (2 April 1998): 33.

Marshall, Paule. *Daughters*. New York: Plume, 1992.

_____. "An Interview with Paule Marshall." With Daryl Dance. *Southern Review* 28. (1992): 1–9.

_____. "A *MELUS* Interview: Paule Marshall." With Joyce Pettis. *MELUS* (Winter 1991): 117–130.

_____. *Praisesong for the Widow*. New York: Putnam, 1983.

_____. "Shaping the World of My Art." *New Letters* 40. 1 (Autumn 1973): 97–112.

_____. "To Be in the World." With Angela Elam. *New Letters* 62: 4 (1996): 97–105.

Maslow, Abraham H. *Toward a Psychology of Being*. 3rd ed. New York: John Wiley, 1999.

Max, Daniel. "McMillan's Millions." *New York Times Magazine* 2 Aug. 1992. 20, 22, 24, 26.

Mbalia, Dorothea. "Organization as Liberation in Toni Cade Bambara's *The Salt Eaters*." *The Western Journal of Black Studies* 16. 1 (Spr. 1992): 6–13.

"Media Darlings." *Forbs: The Richest People in America*. 170. 6 (30 Sept. 2002): 126–142.

Modleski, Tania. *Feminism Without Women: Culture and Criticism in a "Postfeminist" Age*. New York: Rutledge, 1999.

Moi, Toril. *Sexual/Textual Politics: Feminist Literary Theory*. New York: Rutledge, 1990.

Morgan, Shirley M. "*Daughters*: The Unity That's [*sic*] Binds Us." *American Versions* 6. 5 (Oct. 1991): 38–39.

Morrison, Toni. *The Bluest Eye*. New York: Plume, 1969.

_____. "The One Out of Sequence." With Anne Keonen. *History and Tradition in African American Culture*. Ed. Gunter H. Lenz. New York: Campus Verlag, 1984. 207–21.

_____. *Paradise*. New York: Knopf, 1998.

_____. *Playing in the Dark: Whiteness and the Literary Imagination*. New York: Vintage, 1990.

_____. *Song of Solomon*. New York: Knopf, 1977.

_____. *Sula*. New York: Knopf, 1973.

_____. *Tar Baby*. New York: Knopf, 1981.

Naylor, Gloria. "An Interview with Gloria Naylor." With Charles H. Rowell. *Callaloo* 20. 1 (1997) 179–192.

Neal, Larry. "The Black Arts Movement." *Visions of a Liberated Future: Black Arts Movement Writings*. New York: Thunder's Mouth Press, 1989. 62–78.

Nye, Robert D. *Three Psychologies: Perspectives from Freud, Skinner, and Rogers*. 5th ed. New York: Brooks/Cole, 1996.

O'Neale, Sondra. "Re-construction of the Composite Self: New Images of Black Women in Maya Angelou's Continuing Autobiography." *Black Women Writers (1950–1980): A Critical Evaluation*. Ed. Marie Evans. New York: Anchor, 1984. 25–36.

Onesta, Li. "Us: In Memory. Toni Cade Bambara: Passing On the Story." *Race and Class* 28. 1 (July–Sept. 1996). 79–86.

"The Other Half: Blacks in America." *The Economist (U.S.)* 337. 7939 (4 Nov. 1995): 35.

Painter, Nell Irvin. "Hill, Thomas, and the Use of Racial Stereotype." *Race-ing Justice, En-gendering Power: Essays on Anita Hill, Clarence Thomas, and the Construction of Social Reality*. Ed. Toni Morrison. New York: Pantheon, 1992. 220–214.

Parker, Lonnae O'Neal. "The Best Man: A Joyous Occasion." *Washington Post* 22 Oct. 1999, 46, 54.

Pinckney, Darryl. "The Best of Everything." *New York Review of Books* (4 Nov. 1993): 33–37.

"Quota Fight: Re-thinking Affirmative Action." *Time* 126. (26 Aug. 1985): 16.

Radway, Janice A. *Reading the Romance: Women, Patriarchy, and Popular Literature*. Chapel Hill: Univ. of North Carolina Press, 1991.

_____. "The Wonder Woman Within." *Ebony* 54. 12 (Oct. 1999): 34.

Reed, Ishmael. *Mumbo Jumbo*. New York: Macmillan, 1972.

_____. *Reckless Eyeballing*. New York: St. Martin, 1986.

Reid, Calvin. "Another Book Club Set to Test the Waters." *Publishers Weekly* 241. 10 (7 March 1994): 13.

Richards, Paulette. *Terry McMillan: A Critical Companion.* Westport, Conn.: Greenwood, 1999.

Richmond Times Dispatch. "Australian Open—Sole Sister: Serena Williams Stands Alone at the Top After Fourth Major Crown in a Row." C 11. January 24–26, 2003.

Riley, Denise. *"Am I That Name": Feminism and the Category of "Women" in History.* Minneapolis: Univ. of Minnesota, 1988.

Robinson, Marilynne. "Fiction in Review." *The Yale Review* 80. 1–2 (April 1992): 227–235.

Rogers, Carl. *The Carl Rogers Reader.* Eds. Kirschenbaum, Howard, and Valerie Land Henderson. Boston: Houghton Mifflin, 1989.

Rosen, Sanford Jay, and Tom Nolan. "Seeking Environmental Justice for Minorities and Poor People." *Trial* 12 (Dec. 1994): 50.

Rosenberg, Ruth, "You Took a Name That Made You Amiable to the Music: Toni Cade Bambara's *The Salt Eaters,*" *Literary Onomastics* 12 (1985): 165–194.

Ross, Catherine. "Finding Without Seeking: What Readers Say About the Role of Pleasure Reading as a Source of Information." *Australasian Public Libraries and Information Services.* 13. 2 (June 2000): 72.

Sabine, Gordon, and Patricia Sabine. *Books That Made the Difference: What People Told Us.* Hamden, Conn.: Library Professional. 1983.

Said, Edward. *Culture and Imperialism.* New York: Vintage, 1993.

Samuels, Allison, and Jerry Alder. "One for the Sistas." *Newsweek* 127. 2 (Jan. 1996): 66–68.

Sanchez-Hucles, Janis. "Jeopardy Not Bonus Status for African American Women in the Work Force: Why Does the Myth of Advantage Persist?" *American Journal of Community Psychology* 25. 5 (Oct. 1997): 565–581.

Sellers, Francis Stead. "Review of *Waiting to Exhale.*" *Times Literary Supplement* (6 Nov. 1992): 20.

Sexton, Anne. "Cinderella." *Literature and Gender: Thinking Critically Through Fiction, Poetry, and Drama.* Eds. Robyn Wiegman and Elena Glasberg. New York: Longman, 1999. 26–28.

Shields, Cydney, and Leslie T. Shields. *Work Sister Work: Why Black Women Can't Get Ahead and What They Can Do About It.* New York: Birch Lane, 1993.

Shipley, W. Maurice. "Review of *The Salt Eaters.*" *CLA Journal.* Xxxvi 1 (Sept. 1982): 125–27.

Sicherman, Barbara. "Reading and Ambition: M. Carey Thomas and Female Heroism." *American Quarterly* 45: 1 (March 1993): 73–104.

Simmons, Ruth J. "My Mother's Daughter: Lessons My Mother Taught Me About Civility and Authenticity." *Texas Journal of Ideas, History and Culture* 20. 2 (Spr.-Sum. 1998): 20–29.

Skow, John. "Some Groove (Author Terry McMillan)." *Time* 147. 19 (May 6, 1996): 77–78.

Smith, Barbara. "Racism and Women's Studies." *All the Women Are White, All the Blacks Are Men, But Some of Us Are Brave: Black Women's Studies.* Ed. Gloria T. Hull, et al. New York: Feminist Press, 1982. 294–371.

_____. "Terri McMillan." *Waiting for Your Life.* Ed. Sybil Steinberg. New York: Pushcart, 1995. 139–144.

Stabile, Carol A. *Feminism and the Technological Fix.* New York: St. Martins, 1994.

Stanford, Ann Folwell. "He Speaks for Whom? Inscription and Reinscription of Women in *Invisible Man* and *The Salt Eaters.*" *MELUS* 18. 2 (Sum. 1993): 1–12.

_____. "Mechanisms of Disease: African American Women Writers: Social Pathologies, and the Limits of Medicine." *NWSA Journal* 6. 1 (Spring 1994): 28–47.

Stein, Ruthe. "Terry McMillan Had a Big Surprise: Oakland Declared Monday Her Day." *San Francisco Chronicle.* 1 Dec. 2000. 1.

Stetson, Erlene. "Studying Slavery: Some Literary and Pedagogical Considerations on the Black Female Slave." *All the Women Are White, All the Blacks Are Men, But Some of Us Are Brave: Black Women's Studies.* Ed. Gloria T. Hull, et al. New York: Feminist Press, 1982. 61–84.

Tannen, Deborah. "Sex, Lies, and Conversation: Why It Is So Hard for Men and Women to Talk to Each Other." *Gender Images: Readings for Composition*. Eds. Melita Schaum and Connie Flanagan. Boston: Houghton, 1992. 113–117.

Tauris, Carol. *The Mis-Measure of Women: Why Women Are Not the Better Sex, the Inferior Sex, or the Opposite Sex*. New York: Simon and Schuster, 1992.

Taussig, Michael T. "Reification and the Consciousness of the Patient." *Social Science Medicine. Part B, Medical Anthropology*. New York: Oxford, 1980. 3–13.

Taylor, Carol. "A Diverse Market for African-American Books Keeps Growing." *Publishers Weekly* 246. 50 (13 Dec. 1999): 37.

Terrell, Mary Church. "The Progress of Colored Women." *Words of Fire: An Anthology of African American Feminist Thought*. Ed. Beverly Guy-Sheftall. New York: New Press, 1995. 64–68.

Tomkins, Jane. *Sensational Designs: The Cultural Work of American Fiction 1790–1860*. New York: Oxford UP, 1985.

Traylor, Eleanor. "*The Salt Eaters:* My Soul Looks Back in Wonder." *First World: An International Journal of Black Thought* 2 (Spr. or Sum.): 44–47, 64.

United States Commission on Civil Rights. *The Economic Status of Black Women: An Exploratory Investigation*. Ed. Nadja Zalokar. Washington, D.C., 1990. 10.

United States Department of Education, National Center For Education Statistics, Higher Education Survey (HEGIS). "Digest of Higher Education: Post Secondary Education." Washington, D.C., 1998.

United States Department of Labor, Bureau of Labor Statistics. *Employed Persons by Occupation, Race, and Sex*. 2001. http:/stats.bls.gov/cps/cpsaat10.pdf, 157.

United States Department of Labor, Bureau of Labor Statistics. *Employed Persons by Occupation, Race, and Sex*. 1996. http://Ferret.bls.census.gov/macro/171996/empearn/att10.tex.

United States Department of Labor, Women's Bureau. "Black Women in the Labor Force." *Facts on Women Working* 97. 1. Washington, D.C., March 1997.

Walker, Alice. *The Color Purple*. New York: Pocket, 1982.

_____. "In Search of Our Mothers' Gardens." *The Norton Anthology of African American Literature*. Eds. Henry Louis Gates Jr. and Nellie Y. McKay. New York: Norton, 1997.

Wall, Cheryl A. "Introduction: Taking Positions and Changing Words." *Changing Our Own Words: Essays on Criticism, Theory, and Writing by Black Women*. New Brunswick, N.J.: Rutgers UP, 1989. 1–15.

Wallace, Michele. "Anger in Isolation: A Black Feminist Search For Sisterhood." *Words of Fire: An Anthology of African American Feminist Thought*. Ed. Beverly Guy-Sheftall. New York: New Press, 1995. 220–230.

_____. *Black Macho and the Myth of the Superwoman*. New York: Verso, 1991.

_____. *Invisibility Blues: From Pop to Theory*. New York: Verso, 1990.

Washington, Mary Helen. "Teaching Black-Eyed Susans: An Approach to the Study of Black Women Writers." *All the Women Are White, All the Blacks Are Men, But Some of Us Are Brave: Black Women's Studies*. Eds. Gloria T. Hull, et al. New York: Feminist Press, 1982. 208–217.

Weathers, Mary Ann. "An Argument for Black Women's Liberation as a Revolutionary Force." *Words of Fire: An Anthology of African American Feminist Thought*. Ed. Beverly Guy-Sheftall. New York: New Press, 1995. 157–161.

Weeks, Linton. "The Burgeoning Industry of Books By and For African Americans, The Sudden Spiral of Edmond Morris's *Dutch*, Poets in the District, A Longtime Fiction Guru Hangs Up His Spurs, and The President Gears Up to Write." *The Washington Post* 9 Jan. 2000. 13.

Welsh-Asante, Kariamu. "The Aesthetic Conceptualization of Nzuri." *The African Aesthetic: Keeper of the Traditions*. Ed. Kariamu Welsh-Asante. Westport, Conn.: Praeger, 1994. 1–20.

Whitaker, Charles. "Exhailing! Terry McMillan Hits Jack Pot in Romance and Fiction." *Ebony*. 1 April, 2001.

White, Jack E. "Heavy Breathing: Forget About Sisterhood and No-Good Guys. *Waiting to Exhale* Is About the Bottom Line." *Time* 147. 3 (15 Jan. 1996): 71.

Whitman, Walt. "Song of Myself." No. 6. *Leaves of Grass.* Eds. Bradley Sculley and Harold W. Blodgett. New York: Norton, 1973.

Williams, Raymond. *Marxism and Literature.* Oxford: Oxford UP, 1977.

Williams, Shirley Anne. "Solidarity Is Not Silent." *Belles Lettres* 7. 2 (Winter 1992): 2–3.

Willis, Susan. "Problematizing the Individual: Toni Cade Bambara's Stories For the Revolution." *Specifying: Black Women Writing the American Experience.* Madison: Univ. of Wisconsin Press, 1987. 129–158.

Wolitzer, Hilma. "Embarking Together on Solitary Journeys." *Writers [on Writing]: Collected Essays from The New York Times.* New York: Henry Holt, 2001. 263–268.

Woolf, Virginia. *A Room of One's Own.* New York: Harcourt Brace, 1990.

Yankelovich Partners. "Survey Indicates Women Are Smart, Savvy and Striving for Financial Prowess." http://www.microsoft.com/presspass. 1–3.

Index